HEALING INTO LIFE AND DEATH

Also by Stephen Levine

GRIST FOR THE MILL (with Ram Dass)

A GRADUAL AWAKENING

MEETINGS AT THE EDGE

WHO DIES?

*Cassette recordings of
Stephen Levine's guided meditations
and talks are available from:*

WARM ROCK TAPES
P.O. Box 108
Chamisal, New Mexico 87521

Healing into Life and Death

STEPHEN LEVINE

ANCHOR BOOKS
DOUBLEDAY
NEW YORK   LONDON   TORONTO   SYDNEY   AUCKLAND

AN ANCHOR BOOK
PUBLISHED BY DOUBLEDAY
a division of Bantam Doubleday Dell Publishing Group, Inc.
1540 Broadway, New York, New York 10036

ANCHOR BOOKS, DOUBLEDAY, and the portrayal
of an anchor are trademarks of Doubleday, a division of
Bantam Doubleday Dell Publishing Group, Inc.

The Anchor Books edition is the first publication
of *Healing into Life and Death*.

Grateful acknowledgment is made for permission to reprint the following:

Excerpts from *Open Secret: Versions of Rumi* copyright © 1984 by John Moyne and Coleman Barks. Reprinted with permission of Threshold Books.

Excerpts from *The Kabir Book* by Robert Bly copyright © 1971, 1977 by Robert Bly. Copyright © 1977 by The Seventies Press. Reprinted by permission of Beacon Press.

Excerpt from *A Part* by Wendell Berry copyright © 1980 by Wendell Berry. Reprinted with permission of North Point Press.

Excerpt from *Being Peace* by Thich Nhat Hanh © 1987 by Thich Nhat Hanh. Reprinted with permission of Parallax Press.

Library of Congress Cataloging-in-Publication Data
Levine, Stephen, 1937–
Healing into life and death.
    1. Spiritual Healing. 2. New age movement. I. Title.
BP605.N48L48   1987   155.9'37   11498

ISBN 0-385-26219-1

Contents

Acknowledgments

Many teachers have affected and encouraged the transmission of these words. Whatever merit might accrue from this work is returned wholly to them.

First and foremost have been the teachings received from thousands of patients as they shared a moment or two on the path of their life. Some shared the very last moments of the earthly aspect of that path. Others, though seeming to have approached that end, survived their illness and continued wholeheartedly in their bodies. This book of healing is dedicated no more to the latter than the former. In both we often noticed remarkable healings.

On our own path of healing, of awakening, we have many teachers from many traditions to thank and acknowledge. Though some we have never met, their teachings, their example, have had a profound influence on our lives.

In the Theravadan Buddhist lineage, first and foremost we bow to the teachings of the venerable Aachan Cha and to the foundation practice of Mahasi Sayadaw.

In the Advaita, nondualist tradition, we sit with the direct transmissions of Ramana Maharshi and the remarkable writings of Nisargadatta.

In Zen, a deep gasho to Suzuki Roshi and Sueng Sahn and to their teachers, and their teachers, back to the crystalline light of Hui Neng and the spacious Tao of Chuang Tzu.

In the unnameable tradition of the heart we touch the feet of Neem Karoli Baba and offer flowers to our beloved friend Ram Dass, whose heart accompanies us with each step on the path of healing.

And to the songs of Kabir and Rumi, whose lyric softens the beat of the heart and clears the eyes to see beyond the mind to the divine presence we all share.

And to this lineage of great hearts we would add the ever-patient and merciful care of Jakki Walters, who brought this manuscript into being in hundreds of hours of transcription and typing. And to Barbara Iannoli great thanks for her care and perseverance in reading early versions of this work.

Introduction

There are many ways this work can be used. It can be read like a book, not unlike passively sitting on a river bank listening to the rippling waters, or, one can go swimming in it, actively participating in it as a healing process. Indeed there is a story about an intellectual youth who felt he could learn everything from books. He read about the stars and became an astronomer, he read about history and became a historian, he read about swimming and drowned. Some things we can only learn by wading in slowly, from the direct experience of the ocean of being lapping against our body. To enter this process directly is to participate in the healing we took birth for, is to become fully alive.

> The secret of healing is
> there's no secret at all.
> Healing is an open book.
> You are now on page 13.

HEALING INTO LIFE AND DEATH

CHAPTER 1

What Is Healing?

The first time a cancer patient asked, "Should I stop trying to heal and just let myself die?", my stomach turned and my knees began to buckle. For nearly three years Robin's steady focus had been the healing of her cancer. Practicing various techniques, she had gone into remission. But after nine months the cancer returned full-blown, draining the body with multiple secondary tumors (metastases) in her spine and major organs. She was in great pain. Unable to sit or lie in any position for more than a minute or two, she had come to the end of her rope. Her question penetrated my body and froze my mind in place. I looked into her eyes, unable to respond from anything I knew or had ever experienced.

Clearly it was a question only the heart could answer. And my heart, knowing deeper, whispered, "The real question is, 'Where is healing to be found?' " It is the question life asks itself: "What is completion?" It brings into focus the no-man's-land between the heart and mind. Where is wholeness to be found in the seemingly separate? Where is the heart of healing in which all duality is resolved?

As healing became more an investigation than a preconception, Robin's pain began to diminish. The deeper she explored her process, asking, "At what level is healing to be found?", the less her original question about life as opposed to death arose. A few weeks into this process, Robin requested a healing circle. Several well-known healers came to form a circle about her and to channel into her body whatever energy might serve to heal. There was a powerful laying-on of hands. A few friends, observing from just outside the circle, said the energy was quite palpable. There was no question about the "presence of healing" in the room.

A week later Robin discovered thirty new tumors on her scalp and back, and told me, "The healing worked, my heart has never felt more open, and it seems the disease is coming to completion."

Indeed, it seemed "the healing had worked." In the weeks before she died, she spoke of experiencing a sense of wholeness she had never known.

Ondrea and I had been working with the terminally ill for several years before we began to explore the nature of healing. For much of that time we directed the Hanuman Foundation's Dying Project, maintaining, for a few of those years, a free, twenty-four-hour-a-day counseling phone service for those confronting serious illness, grief, or death.

Our experiences with the terminally ill were an integral part of our deepest healing. Encouraged by years of psychological and spiritual practices, and an increasing appreciation of meditative service we were drawn to the work. It tore our hearts open. It gave us new heart.

It was a painful grace to share in the death of children, who often reminded us of our own, or to hold the soft, well-worn hand of a dying great-grandmother, our eyes bound together in the enormous moment, audibly sharing her last breath as the light went out and away. Or to sit beside the lawnchair of a dying young man in a summer garden having asked for the last time to go outside, surrounded by his children and loved ones, taking his last sip of water. A minute later, noticing a tiny garden flea walk across his unblinking eye, we rejoiced that after years of pain and difficulty, he had breathed his last so peacefully that no one knew just when he left.

But these remarkable sharings with those who approached us were not limited to the superficiality of "Death Prep 101." With each there was an exploration. For each a unique path led to a common goal. It was a deeper seeing of life, a deeper participation. Some took to the work of deep investigation and the cultivation of such qualities as loving kindness and mercy like a lost child might, an open path through the woods—the absolute joy of at last making direct contact with the moment, with life itself. For others it was a struggle, but a very satisfying relinquishment of old fears and hold-ings—the hard-earned path-breaking of a brand-new life.

For years our work with the dying has been an encouragement to open fully to this moment in which all of life is expressed, that the optimum preparation for death is a wholehearted opening to life even in its subtlest turnings and changes. But it turned out for some that this opening to life did not pave the way to death but instead resulted in a deepening access to levels of healing beyond imagin-ing.

So it became evident that a preparation for dying, a new opening to life, allowed deeper healings to occur. For some these healings affected the body as well as the heart. Not all who came to us to die actually died. Indeed, over the years, many seemed at a certain point of opening to start to become physically well again. Sharing with those who had come to die with advanced tumors the joy of a whole new life ahead, devoid of cancer, gradually brought our attention to this process, this phenomenon, called healing.

Some who came to us, as they began to investigate and let go of the holdings of the mind, discovered the healings of the body. As they cultivated a certain heartfulness, they began to touch their pains and fears with mercy and awareness—an optimum strategy for dying or living, a profound healing in itself.

As Ondrea and I began to investigate what healing might be, the context rapidly expanded. If healing was as it seemed, the harmo-nizing of the disquieted, a balancing of energies to bring about peace where before there had been war, then healing clearly was not limited to the body, or even the visible. It includes the possibility of quieting even the deepest, unseen wounds—the discomforts which make death seem a respite.

As one therapist said after using these techniques for about a year with her patients and then beginning a daily practice for herself, "I got healed where I didn't even know I was hurting. I mean, I cer-tainly didn't have any life-threatening disease such as cancer. But I had the life-threatening dis-ease of despair, depression, anger, alco-holism, and self-hatred. Pretty, huh! But when I started to sit down with it all, instead of therapizing my way out of it—analyzing, analyz-ing, analyzing—I began to investigate it. What a relief to get inside it all instead of always bouncing off the surface. I got so much closer to myself. I stopped drinking. I got myself a puppy, the first pet I've ever allowed myself. I'm not so afraid of what's coming."

Indeed, in trying to define the work we do, the difficulty of limiting healing to any particular level became more apparent. If healing is as it seems, the integration of body and mind into the heart, then our only direction has always been healing. Healing is the growth that each person seeks. Healing is what happens when we come to our edge, to the unexplored territory of mind and body, and take a single step beyond into the unknown, the space in which all growth occurs. Healing is discovery. It goes beyond life and death. Healing occurs not in the tiny thoughts of who we think we are and what we know, but in the vast undefinable spaciousness of being—of what we essentially are—not whom we imagined we shall become.

On examining the last ten years of work with those in crises, what arises is a recognition that our intention is not to keep people alive or help them die either. Our work seems to be an encouragement to focus on the moment. To heal into the present and to allow the future to arise naturally out of that opening. If the moment holds pain, awareness is brought to pain. If the moment holds grief, then grief is the focus. If the moment holds illness, then illness is the teaching to which awareness is directed.

When we first began this work, like most of those who came to us, we thought that healing was something for the body. But after accompanying several hundred toward death and seeing the course of illness change for many we recognized that healing goes on at many levels.

What became very noticeable was that those who got well were often more well than before they became ill. This "extra wellness," I thought for some time, was a by-product of healing. But then I came to see that it was just the other way around. That the healing of the body for many was a by-product of a new balance of mind and heart. It wasn't that these people felt better than ever because they had healed, but rather that they had healed because they had come upon a place of a bit more ease and peace within. It seemed for many that their healing was a blossoming fed by deep roots extending into the dark, moist soil of the previously uninvestigated mind. By investigating the mind the heart was uncovered, and its light caused so much to come to flower.

Though each seemed to experience a greater wellness, a sense of quiet completion, not all who opened to life survived in the body. Each healed into life. Some experienced their body returning to wholeness. Others experienced the wholeness of death. There were those with whom we sat deathwatch, whose dying expressed a wholeness of being; their hearts were so open, their spirits so fully released that it was evident how well they had become during the weeks and months of their dying. How much healing had occurred! They were more healed, more whole at the moment of their dying than at any time in their life. They had healed into death, their business finished, their future wide open.

In the nine years since Robin's question and the beginnings of our exploration of what healing might be, we have accumulated a large library dealing with hundreds of different healing methods from Western medical traditions as well as alternative and Eastern healing practices: books on the Gerson method, wheat-grass therapy, fever therapy, macrobiotics, acupuncture, moxibustion, nutritional and exercise therapies, autohypnosis, Bach flower remedies, color therapy, urine therapy, radiation therapy, chemotherapy, various forms of prayer, and any number of lesser-known experimentations. All these books were left to us by patients when they died.

Over the years it became clear that there wasn't any one method that worked for everyone. Indeed, there seemed to be no method notably more useful to the body than any other. It might also be mentioned that on a parallel shelf sat dozens of books about spiritual disciplines and the healings entailed therein—Buddhism, Christianity, Sufism, Hinduism, Hebrew techniques for self-discovery, given to us by many who suggested that this was "the Best way," whose insights seemed no more remarkable than any others. The parallel between body healing and a healing into the spirit was difficult to ignore.

There seemed no bodily healing technique that worked for everyone, no one method held in common by all those who seemed healed. We did, however, see a few shining beings here and there, who had cultivated an investigation of the mystery and letting-go of the seeming solidity of the isolated personality, merged with something universal in themselves. Often without a need or even ability to define or delineate it, these beings opened wholeheartedly into something beyond their old ways of being. Clearly it was more than the healing technique that was allowing the healing in. Something within the heart met the disease with a newness that allowed harmony where imbalance had existed before.

Some suggest that the techniques we are employing lead to what they call a "spiritual healing." But I do not feel comfortable with that term because it leads one to believe that the spirit can be injured. Which it cannot. It is the uninjured, the uninjurable, the boundarilessness of being, the deathless. So what is offered here is not a spiritual healing, but rather a healing into the spirit. Just as the phrase "opening the heart" can be misleading because it implies that the heart is at times closed—when actually the heart, like the sun, is always shining, though occasionally obscured by passing phenomena. We are not so much opening the heart as clearing the way to the heart, recognizing that the hindrances to the heart are the hindrances to healing. So our path becomes a letting go of that which blocks the path. Healing is not forcing the sun to shine but letting go of the personal separatism, the self-images, the resistance to change, the fear and anger, the confusion that form the opaque armoring around the heart. This process begins with the dissolution of the dense clouds of our forgetfulness and unkindness. It opens the way to reveal the ever-healed within.

Ondrea and I noticed after a few years of working with seriously ill patients that the word "healing" gave us a shudder. We saw many who suffered greatly in the name of healing. We noticed that what was referred to as healing might be hastening death on one level or another. Many seemed, in the battle for their "healing," to be manifesting considerable self-rejection. In some cases this low self-esteem was manifested as disgust; in others, as guilt or shame; and in still others, as abject fear. All of these qualities seemed to disempower the individual. It seemed that many were actually cultivating antihealing qualities in the name of healing. Fear and dread were being sent into illness. The tension and confusion seemed to be feeding "the mind of illness," while obscuring the "heart of healing."

Originally our attention had been drawn to healing by those few patients who had come to us with fourth-stage cancer or advanced degenerative heart disease and who did not die. We saw illness being dispelled from bodies which had before seemed on the very verge of dissolution. These were the people whose doctors sheepishly pronounced them "cured," but shook their heads in bewilderment as to the actual cause.

Indeed, there is a "school of inquiry" into such remarkable remissions and cures of long-established illness. But rather than accentuate the "specialness" of patients who seem to heal the body, or even the specialness of just bodily healings, I sense something quite the opposite at work. I see that which is most common, that which is indeed universal to all, at the very foundation of our healing. Indeed, many healings seem to entail the most ubiquitous of qualities —awareness itself—focused into an area of illness. In those we saw heal from what seemed an impossible physical or mental state, we noticed something very common at work, something essential. Not wanting to make physical healing something unreachable, a luxury for the elite, creating an autocracy of the ill, we entered instead the miracle of deeply exploring that which blocks healing—a release of long-held posturing and hiding, an expanding trust in the mystery, an ever-deepening focus of mercy and awareness into the area of discomfort. Gathering as one might the diffuse light of the sun through a magnifying glass to brilliantly pinpoint and illuminate an area of mental or physical discomfort, a healing awareness is focused into the previously shadowed and darkly held.

But there is indeed a paradox here, for though what makes us remarkable, the power of awareness to heal and deepen, is nothing special, a common gift to all, when focused on the mind it reveals our uniqueness. The particular constellation of qualities which is able to find its own way through, its own path, its own genius for healing.

As we came to see that healing occurs on many levels, it became obvious that there was not something spiritually or psychologically amiss with those who did not cure their bodies. It was from observing in many who died the healings of long-pained minds into the heart of great peace that we came to notice some discomfort with the appellations of some doctors that only those who physically healed were "superstars" or "exceptional patients." Because what does that make all those whose diseases increased unto death—low-normals, second-stringers? The confused elitism that somehow those who heal their body are "better" than those who don't has a tendency to come back as a sense of failure on the death bed when the last disease inevitably comes along and displaces us naturally from the body. Death is not a failure, but rather an event during the ongoing process which one survives on the path of healing to continue toward even greater learning and growth.

Some seemed to be almost effortlessly led in the direction of their healing, while others stumbled and fell again and again, never quite trusting in their own great capacity for wholeness, never quite willing to ask "At what level is my healing to be found?" We witnessed deep healings into the spirit of some who lived as well as miraculous healings in some who died. Some who discovered this innate balance were freed of illness, while others continued toward death. Some seemed to have healed the mind in a manner which left all about them at peace, yet their body continued to decay. Clearly, healing was not what we had imagined. Clearly, healing was not limited to the body.

The question "Where might we find our healing?" expanded. It was the healing of a lifetime. The healing we each took birth for.

Among those who seemed to move toward healing, physical and psychological as well as spiritual, there seemed to be many who had a certain quality in common. They had a willingness, a kind of open relationship to the conditions they were experiencing, a certain nonresistance. It wasn't always noticeable at first glance because different temperaments manifested these qualities in such different ways. It wasn't one way, one tone, one use of language. But for each individual it seemed to be a learning to let go and meet life in a fuller way, moment to moment, the living of life a breath at a time.

We noticed that many who seemed unable to heal, instead of embracing their illness, met it with an "I'm going to beat this thing!" attitude. Most were *at* their illnesses, their tumors, with a stick—self-flagellation, self-negation, "me against me," "me against the pain." Others, we noticed, were *with* their illness rather than *at* it, touching it deeply, examining it, drawing the self-torture out of it by meeting it with tenderness and mercy—"me for me." "Me with my pain, with my illness." It was those who were against themselves, at odds with themselves, trying to "beat their illness," who seemed to have the hardest time and the slowest healing, if healing was present at all. But those who seemed to meet their illness in their heart instead of their mind appeared to have a radically different experience. Not all those who embraced their illness survived in the body, but we observed a healing which occurred beyond our previous definition or understanding. Unfinished business melted in the loving kindness with which they met the pain in their body and the confusion in their minds. Pain began to float at times. Ancient resistances and resentments seemed to come into a deeper harmony. Faith became the priority.

These were the patients who saw that illness was not a failure and that pain was not a punishment. Exploring their pain and illness with a healing awareness, examining the self-doubt, distrust, and resignation that so readily regards life as "unlivable"—a new direction seemed to arise. A new willingness to take the teaching from whatever moment illness presented; the leading edge of life to be examined and participated in. These were the people who embraced their pain and fear, and met what had always been conditioned by fear and loathing with a new openness, and at times a new wonderment at life.

One fellow was having a particularly difficult time with pain associated with his cancer. One day he told us, "When I could stay with it softly, I saw through my pain." He saw the other side of pain. He saw that pain was not a punishment. He had always thought that somehow all the pain in his body was due to previous life errors. He said, "But I see now that was just the old perverse reverse of long-stashed guilts projected onto the body." Since he was a child, he had always equated punishment with pain. When he got sick, he therefore took his pains to be punishments. "I felt like such a failure. I felt almost like I deserved it." No wonder it was so hard for him to heal! As he began to stop trying to beat his sickness and began to allow himself into it, perhaps at times even to forgive it, his body became stronger and stronger. "And my pain is not such a problem anymore. It's a miracle to have made friends with myself after all these years. I have more reason to live now than I ever have. And I probably will."

Now, two years into remission, he says that cancer showed him his fear and put him in touch with "the lost places inside me." It taught him to find himself. "Cancer began for me a healing that will never end."

We have been told by many patients in hospitals that their fatigue and illness highly sensitized them to their environment—every sound, every smell, every word penetrated through the frail and sensitive outer layers. Illness had left them raw and alert. Many said that among those who visited during the day—hospice workers, doctors, nurses, relatives, and friendly droppers-by—it was noticeable after they left that some gave energy and some took energy. With some the patient felt more whole and confident and well-grounded after the visit. When others left, the patient's body felt jangled and tense and self-protective, the mind filled with half-statements and confusion about "just what was meant by that." It may well be that the experience that these patients had was in part the difference between one's pain being touched with fear and one's pain being touched by love.

A woman in a hospital in considerable pain told us she felt there were two kinds of people who came into her room. She said she noticed one kind of person could hardly sit down next to her, and when they did, "they used to shift from cheek to cheek, they couldn't sit still at all. They would fluff my hair or put lipstick on me, or thumb through my magazines. They would go to the window and open it if it was closed or close it if it was open. But they couldn't stay long with my pain." She said they had no room in their hearts for her pain because they had no room in their hearts for their own. "But," she said, "there were others who could just come in and sit down with me. And if my pain was so intense or I was too fidgety that day and couldn't stand to even be touched, they would just sit quietly next to me. They didn't *need* to give me anything or to take anything away for themselves. They didn't need to take my pain away, and they didn't make me feel that I needed to be different when I was in pain. They had room for my pain because they had room for their own."

What this woman experienced from the group who could hardly stay with her was their pity. Pity is the experience of meeting pain with fear. It makes one want to change the givens of the moment: "I want you out of your pain because I want me out of my pain." Pity can be a very self-oriented emotional state, very dense, very uncomfortable. Pity has a quality of considerable need about it. Pity, when directed toward one's own pain, because of its "I and other" quality, creates a sense of separation—the unholy wars of the mind and body which are capable of intensifying illness. But when we touch that same pain with love, letting it be as it is, meeting it with mercy instead of fear and hatred, then that is compassion. When I can be with your pain or my pain in a gentle exploration of the moment, observing wholeheartedly any sense of urgency or distress, the despair that often arises when we find difficulty healing seems not to interfere. And even fear may be seen as just another bubble floating through a cloud temporarily passing, despair dissolving, mercy and a healing awareness arising.

If our habitual conditioning is to overcome our pain, we will have a tendency to feel overwhelmed when things don't go the way we wish. We may even feel a need to "beat" another's pain. We will find it difficult to connect with them just where they are. We won't be able to touch them with love because if we want anything from somebody, even for them to be out of pain, they will be an object in our mind rather than the subject of our heart. If we can open to our own pain and explore our resistances and long-held aversions, there arises the possibility of touching another's pain with compassion, of meeting another as we meet ourselves with a bit more clarity and tenderness. We see in such instances how the work we do on ourselves is clearly of benefit to all sentient beings. Each person who works to open their heart touches the heart of us all. When we are no longer recreating the problem, we reaffirm the solution. We discover from day to day how the healing we do for ourselves is a healing for all.

We were working with Hazel, a woman who had come into the hospital in a very contracted state. She was a very difficult patient. The nurses called her "a real bitch on wheels." Few wished to spend time with her. Hazel's physicians and attendants said that whenever she rang the bell, they were greeted with nasty comments and considerable verbal abuse. And so, of course, every time she rang the bell, it took a bit longer to be answered. All her life had been a struggle for control. Seldom had she just let life be. All that she didn't want or could not have was judged and pushed away from her heart. All that she could get was grasped at feverishly. And so she found herself dying alone in a great deal of pain. She had judged so many so often that even her grown children would not visit. She was becoming a self-fulfilling prophecy of anger and despair.

For six weeks her isolation and pain increased until one night something changed. She came to a point where she could no longer stand the suffering in her back and legs, or the pain of her unlived life. At four A.M., feeling like jumping out of her skin, she began to review her life amidst the pulsations of her pain. Never had it been so clear how her intense holding had created such intense pain, such a sense of desolation and aloneness. She saw how the considerable suffering she had caused during her lifetime had come back to her at deathtime. She had nowhere to turn. She had never felt more alone or helpless. Feeling death approach, she remembered herself as a youngster, open and hungry for the world. She saw how she had closed down over the years. With a deep sigh she let the helplessness wash over her and, exhausted, unable to fight another moment, she surrendered, she let go and "died into her life," into the moment. Letting go into the pain in her spine and legs, she began to sense, quite beyond reason, that she was somehow not alone in her suffering. She felt what she later called "the ten thousand in pain." She began to experience all the other beings who at that very moment were lying in that same bed of agony. At first there arose the experience of herself as a brown-skinned woman, breasts slack from malnutrition, lying on her side, a starving child suckling at her empty breast, spine and legs twisted in pain, the musculature contracted from starvation and disease. For an instant, she became this Ethiopian woman with this same pain in the back and legs and hips, lying on her side, dying in the mud. Then there arose the experience of an Eskimo woman lying on her side dying during childbirth, tremendous pain in her back, hips, legs and dying the same death. Then her experience became that of the body of a woman in a twisted car wreckage, her back and legs broken, slowly dying alone by the side of a deserted road.

Image after image arose of the "ten thousand in pain." She experienced herself as a youth with yellowed skin curled up on his side on a dirty mattress, dying of hepatitis in a junky flat, as an old woman with grayish skin dying of old age—each with the same pain in the lower back and legs. She saw herself as a woman, her lower back crushed by a rockfall, dying by the banks of a river alone, bereft of the touch of another human being. She saw herself dying of cholera, as an Asian mother with an ill child in a thatched hut. She was each dying beside the others. She experienced "the ten thousand suffering simultaneously."

In the hour of her greatest agony, something in her connected with the enormity of the suffering she was sharing at that moment. "The pain was beyond my bearing. I couldn't stand it any longer and something broke. Maybe it was my heart. But I saw it wasn't just *my* pain, it was *the* pain. It wasn't just my life, it was all life. It was life itself." As the days unfolded after this extraordinary experience, Hazel's heart opened more and more to all the others in pain in the hospital. She constantly asked after them. As the weeks went by, she continued to get a deeper sense of what she had participated in . She went beyond herself. And the room became a place where the nurses would come on their break because it was a room of love. Soon her children came to visit because of the warmth and surrender of her phone calls, responding to her plea for forgiveness. Her grandchildren sitting on the edge of her bed, the grandchildren she had never met, the hearts she had rejected before they were born. Her room became a place of healing, of finished business, of universal care. Some weeks later, a few days before she died, someone brought her a picture of Jesus as the Good Shepherd lovingly surrounded by children and animals. And this woman, whose life had been one of such hardness and isolation, looked at the picture and said with her voice cracking, "Oh Jesus, have mercy on them, forgive them, they are only children." Hazel's was one of the most remarkable healings we have ever seen.

For us it was an example of someone who seemed to have healed in the most profound manner, though she didn't stay in her body—a heart that opened incredibly, a deepening wisdom and a sense of participation in life which broadened with each day.

It was another teaching that healing affects the heart at least as much as the body, and that any previously held definition of healing had to be discarded so that we could discover its deeper meaning.

And we came to realize that we didn't have the slightest idea what healing was. Obviously healing was not limited to changing the nature of the body. Ondrea and I had to trust our not knowing if we were to continue to explore and perhaps discover in our own process—in the mind/body and heart we all share, what healing might be.

Hazel's teaching to us was that the deepest healing cannot be done solely in the separate. It needs to be for the whole, for the pain we all share. At the very root of healing is a sense of the universal within the separate, the personal. We saw again and again in those who seemed to heal their bodies a willingness to investigate with gentle clarity not just the pains of the moment but of a lifetime. We noticed yet a deeper healing in their hearts and minds, a deepening capacity to touch with mercy that which they had previously experienced only with fear and dread. They were learning to bring into their heart much of what had been excluded during a lifetime. Their healing seemed to be a process of letting life in. For these people, their illness, although at times extremely difficult, was more of a pilgrimage of trust and insight than a fugitive run. Illness investigated had led to a melting of the ancient prison of one's own making, the prison cell of fear and unwillingness that some part of us is perhaps willing to exchange for a hospital room.

But of course we are never speaking of someone else's fears. It is not "those people," but always some part of ourselves. There is no other but only extensions of aspects of our inner life. It is not someone else's attempt to escape. We have all tried to be model prisoners, but our pain defines our silent desperation. We are each trapped by our holding. We are a bit like the jungle monkey who is so easily captured by simply chaining a banana stalk to a tree. The monkey grabs the banana stalk fiercely, trying to wrestle it away, screaming as he hears the hunter's approach, bellowing as he is slain. Never thinking that to simply let go might lead to freedom and safety.

It seems always easier to recognize this predicament in another than in ourselves. It is difficult to acknowledge that which holds so tightly and fears pain so greatly, that which trusts the moment so little. We imagine that we must force results, must plow a path to freedom rather than discovering the ground beneath our feet. But by taking a step at a time and trusting the moment, we find that a step fully taken leads effortlessly to the next. By fully participating in this moment, the next moment takes care of itself.

Since Hazel's experience some years ago, dying in the hospital in her remarkable opening and healing, we have many times used the pain or illness in our own bodies and encouraged others to focus on theirs as a means of finding the universal in that which had always seemed so separate. In this discovery of the macrocosm in the microcosm much healing is available. Seeing it is not simply *my* pain but *the* pain, the circle of healing expands to allow the universe to enter.

For Hazel, dying and seeking mercy for all the children, there was a great healing. The condition in her body didn't change, but the condition in her heart certainly did. She learned to touch her pain with mercy instead of fear. Mercy is the opposite of judgment. It is a kindness of the mind that mirrors the spaciousness of the heart. Indeed, the term "mercy" is used here not in the context of "Oh Lord have mercy on me!", not as a begging for a removal of punishment, but as a quality of noninjury, of kindness. Mercy, like loving kindness, is a quality of the mind which emulates the nonclinging nature of the heart.

In those moments of experiencing so many others as herself, entering inseparably into their experience, her pain diminished and the space in which it floated was greatly expanded. It was not that the pain had gone away but that it had become more an experience than a problem.

She learned that pain was not simply her own but belonged to all who had ever been born. In deep surrender, in sharing her pain, her body, she went beyond her old idea of who she was as a separate being. From this experience she inherited a spaciousness which had room for life as well as death.

As we shared with such people, we began to sense the innate power at the core of such a healing. A finishing of business with oneself and all others, a participation in the unfolding moment as it is, a deep investigation of even the unpleasant with clear awareness and the slow, steady pace of one who has come upon the very heartstuff of their being. A healing that goes beyond definition or the compulsive need to fit the vastness into a tiny thought, just another insufficient label for the immeasurable.

Today, like every other day, we wake up empty
and frightened. Don't open the door to the study
and begin reading. Take down the dulcimer.

Let the beauty we love be what we do.
There are hundreds of ways to kneel and kiss the ground.

Rumi

CHAPTER 2

Developing a Healing Practice

Though grieved in mind and body and at times feeling hopeless, we are never helpless. We have ways of healing within us which have seldom been acknowledged by anyone. There are tools available, which well applied, can take us beyond even our greatest suffering.

Each of the meditations which follow is such a tool, each holds the possibility of healing. These techniques are like gardening implements. Some can be used to prepare the soil, such as the forgiveness and grief meditations. Others are nutrients which encourage germination, such as the loving kindness meditation, the soft-belly meditation, and the *ahh* breath exercise. Some are like a plow employed for ongoing cultivation, such as the mindfulness and body sweeping meditations, which are lifelong healing practices. Each creates the conditions in which grace can grow. Some of these practices are used just for moving boulders or pulling stumps, such as the heavy-state meditation, the heart-of-the-womb meditation, the discomfort meditation, or the healing meditation. They are specialized tools for the opening and removing of specific obstacles. Each is appropriate for some aspect of the preparation, planting, and harvesting of the remarkable blossoms which arise naturally in the process of our healing. These practices begin with the heart and expand into the body and mind. Each meditation has the potential of clearing another layer of obstruction between the heart and mind/body. One begins in the heart to soften the way for the mind and body to be experienced wholeheartedly without judgment or fear. As we open into the heart, certain obstacles may become evident in the pain in the mind or in the body. Specific meditations are offered to approach each with a healing wisdom and awareness which mercifully receives the moment with a new appreciation.

Indeed, it is often slow going at the beginning because concentration is still strengthening and may take a while yet to develop. But healing is a process and each step is so precious. Indeed, in the beginning, with such meditations, by oneself or even with a capable teacher, there may be difficulties. In large groups after one of these guided meditations, it is not uncommon for someone to share extraordinary openings while others sit by somewhat glumly thinking, "How come nothing happened for me? What a dud I am!" And the age-old insecurities and self-loathing which have so often blocked the heart will reassert themselves. But often it is those who said they didn't "get it" so easily who later display considerable insight into that which blocks the qualities they were attempting to cultivate. They may well have seen the nature of that which limits forgiveness or mercy or letting go or healing more clearly than one who "in a lucky moment" was able to get some depth of experience of the qualities they were examining. It is often when it "doesn't work" that the work to be done is most clearly seen.

Make these meditations your own. Experiment! Find the language and phrasing that is appropriate for you. Trust your own great genius for healing. Let the heart suggest the appropriateness of these meditations. One may be drawn to only one or two of those suggested. Work with those that "feel right," not with those you think you "should." Let the heart be the healer of the mind and body. Let these meditations become your own.

Some of these meditations are "foundation practices," lifetime practices, such as the letting-go meditation, the sweeping-the-body meditation, the mindfulness meditation. They are root practices which many employ daily for years. Other practices, such as the opening the heart of the womb meditation, the healing meditation, the discomforture meditation and the heavy state meditation, are used with special situations and to loosen specific issues or holdings. These are often "breakthrough" meditations in which long held hindrances which obstruct the deeper penetration of awareness in such root practices as mindfulness or the who am I meditation can be dissolved. Some meditations, such as forgiveness meditation, as well as the soft body practices, become ongoing adjuncts to root practices. The work with forgiveness and grief softens the way, along with lessening judgment and doubt and deepening trust in the process.

Our root practice for the last twenty years has been the mindfulness meditation (described more completely in *A Gradual Awakening*). But there have also been periods where an adjunct practice deepened our ability to apply what had been discovered in our daily meditation. The "Who am I?" and forgiveness meditation, each practiced for about two years, in addition to our daily practice, greatly deepened our healing.

As with healing techniques, there is no meditation practice that is any better than any other. There are just some practices which are more suitable to one temperament or another. Indeed, it is not the practice which does the healing but the intention, the motivation, the effort with which it is employed. Even in a practice such as mindfulness, whose basis is a development of a choiceless awareness, if it is not done heartfully, with a merciful and forgiving awareness, a subtle smugness or judgmentalness can arise which greatly slows the practice. So too, if body-sweeping practices are not done in a spirit of discovery, but instead are performed because of a "needing to overcome," there will be additional difficulty. Each practice has the potential of becoming a trap if we are trying to only become "good meditators" but not necessarily any more compassionate or any less competitive.

The more any practice is done because of a sense that it "should" be, the more self it will create. The more self, the greater the sufferer. Indeed there are practices which focus on pain, which, unskillfully done, can just create more of a holy war in the mind and body, and attempt to slay pain, which leads to just more of someone to suffer. As with the pain meditation, at times we work at the very center of discomfort but at other times we take a break and just ride the breath like a surfer on a perfect wave. Working perhaps for fifteen minutes with the healing or pain meditation, we then take a break so as not to, even subtly, reinforce the resistance which the meditation is meant to release.

It is all such a balancing act. Words such as "letting go" or "surrender" can be easily misleading, misinterpreted by old mind. Such ideas must be balanced within a sense of the appropriate. If one sees injustice, it is not appropriate to simply "let it go" and be merrily on our way. Just as when we see the cruel within our own mind, it is most skillful to approach it wholeheartedly, to investigate and explore and not too quickly allow our deepest clingings to go uninvestigated beneath the camouflage of "letting go," by which the mind really intends suppression. What to do when cruelty is observed in ourselves or in another is up to the individual. All the work one has done on oneself up until that moment will be present to bring whatever resolution the heart whispers is suitable. One need not kill the rapist in order to stop rape. Nor need one have, as the Tibetan teacher Chogyam Trungpa put it, "idiot compassion," and not restrain the rapist because you don't want to hurt anyone.

In the moment where response is called upon, there are no answers that can be carried from one moment to the next. Clear-eyed and open-hearted, we sense from moment to moment what we must do. There are no easy answers. That is why it is so important that we do the work that is to be done now, that we take on the healing that is called for.

The value of walking the path of healing with both feet, of maintaining a balance that is not easily pulled to extremes, is recognized along the healing journey when one at times experiences periods of peacefulness and begins to see the perfection of the unfolding of the process. But in its beginning glimpse of this perfection, some part of the mind impatiently begins to utter platitudes about "everything being perfect." But it is right for the wrong reasons. The perfection of the unfolding of the process is indeed awesome and wondrous to behold, but we need to balance the depths of this ocean of acceptance with concern for the drownings happening on the surface. Is cruelty perfect? Is the death of your child? Perfection is not something one can imagine, perfection is something one must participate in, appreciating the tendencies of the mind and body from the spaciousness of the heart. Just the moment to be apprehended fully so that one can respond from as deep a sense of the appropriate as possible. Which makes me think of Zen Master Suzuki Roshi's comment, "Everything is perfect, but there is always room for improvement."

So each technique needs to be done with balance and heart for the practice to take you beyond the practice itself, for one not to be a meditator but, instead, to become the meditation itself. Healing is a high-wire act, a balancing of energy with effort, of concentration with receptivity, of wisdom with compassion, of awareness with mercy, of insight with letting go, of appearances with what lies beyond appearance, of what we call birth with what we refer to as death, and of all that precedes and exceeds each.

These meditations can be read slowly to a friend or silently to oneself. Indeed many find it skillful to record them in their own voice and play them back until they know these practices "by heart". We find that we seldom offer any of these meditations the same way twice. Once committed to heart the heart whispers the appropriate guidance for the requirements of the moment.

When offering some of these practices to one who is ill, thinking they might be of some aid, it should be noted that some people who have issues around control may not appreciate guidance. We must remember when offering such fine tools that some people feel pushed even by the best intentions. Timeliness is a very important factor in the offering of these practices to another.

Introduction to
Simple Loving Kindness Meditation

As an example of the heart we all share and the healing available to each of us, we begin these healing practices with a meditation on loving kindness. It is a fundamental practice for opening healing to ourselves, to our loved ones, to this world of suffering and joy in which we live. It is a meditation which, if experimented with for ten or fifteen minutes a day for a few weeks, has the potential for softening our lives and sending healing even to those very far away. Many use it daily for years.

This simplified version of the loving kindness meditation allows one to draw the mind into the heart. As the attention gradually gathers, the words softly repeated become synchronized with each inhalation and exhalation, and begin to ride on the breath in a gentle perseverance that clears the path toward the heart.

As with all the meditations and practices which follow, the words become one's own as one takes the process within.

A Simple Loving Kindness Meditation
(To be read slowly to a friend or silently to oneself.)

Sitting comfortably, allow the attention to come gradually to the breath.

The breath coming and going all by itself deep within the body.

Take a few moments to allow the attention to gather within the even rhythm of the breath.

Turning gently within, begin to direct toward yourself feelings of loving kindness relating to yourself as though you were your only child. Silently in the heart say, "May I dwell in the heart. May I be free from suffering. May I be healed. May I be at peace."

Just feel the breath breathing into the heart space as we relate to ourselves with mercy and loving kindness.

Allow the heart silently to whisper the words of mercy that heal, that open. "May I dwell in the heart. May I be free from suffering. May I be healed. May I be at peace."

Allow a willingness to be healed to converge in your heart.

Whispering to yourself send feelings of well-being to you.

"May my heart flower. May I know the joy of my own true nature. May I be healed into this moment. May I be at peace."

Repeating gently with each in-breath into the heart, "May I dwell in the heart." With each out-breath, "May I be free from suffering."

With the next in-breath, "May I be healed."

With the following out-breath, "May I be at peace."

Repeating these words slowly and gently with each in-breath, with each out-breath. Not as a prayer but as an extending of a loving well-being to yourself.

Noticing whatever limits this love touching yourself, this mercy, this willingness to be whole, to be healed.

"May I dwell in the heart. May I be free from suffering. May I be healed. May I be at peace."

Continue with the rhythm of this breath, this deepening of merciful joy and loving kindness drawn in with each breath, expanding with each exhalation.

"May my heart flower. May I be free from suffering. May I be whole. May I be at peace."

Let the breath continue naturally as mercy for yourself, for this being within, deepens as it expresses itself.

Though at first these may only feel like words echoing from the mind, gently continuing, a feeling of warmth is drawn in with each breath, a sense of patience developing with each exhalation.

Drawing in warmth, expanding patience.

Room to live, room to heal.

"May I dwell in the heart. May I be at peace."

Each breath deepening the nurturing warmth of relating to oneself with loving kindness and compassion. Each exhalation deepening in peace, expanding into the spaciousness of being, developing the deep patience that does not wait for things to be otherwise but relates with loving kindness to things as they are.

"May my heart flower. May I be free from suffering. May I be healed. May I be at peace."

Allowing the healing in with each breath. Allowing yourself to heal into your true spacious nature.

Continuing for a few breaths more this drawing in, this opening to, loving kindness. Relating to yourself with great tenderness, sending well-being into your mind and body, embracing yourself in these gentle words of healing.

Now gently bring to mind someone for whom you have a feeling of warmth and kindness.

Picturing this loved one in your heart, with each in-breath whisper to them, "May you dwell in your heart. May you be free from suffering. May you be healed. May you be at peace."

With each breath drawing them into your heart, "May you dwell in your heart, may your heart flower."

With each out-breath filling them with your loving kindness, "May you be free from suffering."

With the next inhalation drawing their heart closer to yours, "May you be healed."

With the following out-breath extending to them a wish for their well-being, "May you be at peace."

Continuing to breathe them into your heart, whispering silently to yourself, to them, "May your heart be ever open. May you be free from suffering. May you be healed into this moment. May you be at peace."

Continue the gentle breath of connection, the gentle whisper of your wish for their happiness and wholeness.

Let the breath be breathed naturally, softly, lovingly into the heart, coordinated with your words, with your concentrated feelings of loving kindness and care.

"May you dwell in your heart. May you be freed of any suffering. May you be healed wherever healing is called for. May you know the deepest levels of peace."

Send them your love, your compassion, your care.

Breathing them in and through your heart.

"May you dwell in the open heart. May you be free from suffering. May you be healed. May you know your deepest joy, your greatest peace."

And as you sense them in your heart, sense this whole world that wishes so to be healed, to know its true nature, to be at peace.

And in your heart with each in-breath, with each out-breath, whisper, "May all beings be free of suffering. May all beings be at peace."

Let your loving kindness reach out to all beings as it did to your loved one, sensing all beings in need of healing, in need of the peace of their true nature.

"May all beings be at peace. May all beings be healed of their suffering."

"May all sentient beings, to the most recently born, be free of fear, free of pain. May all beings heal into their true nature. May all beings know the absolute joy of absolute being."

"May all beings everywhere be healed and whole. May all beings be free of suffering."

The whole world like a bubble floating in your heart embraced by your loving kindness.

Each breath drawing in the love that heals the world, that deepens the peace we all seek.

Each breath feeding the world with the mercy and compassion, the warmth and patience that quiets the mind and opens the heart.

"May all beings dwell in their heart. May all beings be free from suffering. May all beings be healed. May all beings be at peace."

Let the breath come softly. Let the breath go gently. Wishes of well-being and mercy, of care and loving kindness, extended to this world we all share.

"May all beings be free of suffering. May all beings dwell in the heart of healing. May all beings be at peace."

CHAPTER 3

Letting the Healing In

Most of the patients who came to us to prepare for death died within a year or two. While each approached the same work on themselves, some healed into death, while others, with advanced cancer or some other terminal prognosis, as they let go of the pains of the past, finishing their business with forgiveness and loving kindness, opening to death, returned to a state of considerable health. It was these "healed ones" that originally drew our attention to the investigation of what healing might be. While some seemed completely cured, others in the process of seeing their life more clearly, though their body did not become completely well, stopped the progression of disease. Also it was noticed that many, in the course of using the healing meditations, though focusing on such as cancer, healed lesser, secondary ailments and discomforts, such as kidney stones, strep throats, constipation, minor infections, burns, broken bones, etc.

Though it was the healing of the body that originally drew our attention, it was the healings, yet deeper than the body, which continued to hold our interest. We saw several preparing for death by finishing business with themselves and all else, experiencing a sense of fulfillment that touched on levels of healing previously unimagined. We saw no less of a healing balance among those who moved peacefully through death than we did among those whose bodies reestablished a certain degree of wellness. We saw so many, as they cleared their heart and resolved loose ends, discover a feeling of being "more alive than ever," sometimes with a considerable diminishment of pain and symptoms. Though their body did not reflect this extra "wellness," something had healed so deeply into life that death was no longer a problem.

It became apparent that those whose bodies healed, as well as those who completed their life before they died, had the same process in common: an openness to their illness, a receptivity, a commitment to work directly with their illness. Each seemed to enter, in their own way, and as fully as possible, the feelings, fears, and hopes, the plans and doubts, the love and forgiveness that arises in the course of healing.

This attitude toward life, this willingness to allow healing in, to investigate the nature of disease as a means of investigating life seems a basis for healing. It approaches that which limits life. One such fellow whom we lovingly referred to as "Loud Larry" had an incurable blood disease of extremely obscure origin for which there seemed no cure. Since its inception in his early teens, he had lost more and more of his physical vigor which he seemingly compensated for by louder and greater profusions of speech. By the time we met him in his late twenties one could hardly get a word in edgewise. In the midst of his second five-day conscious living/conscious dying retreat, Loud Larry fell in love. Soon thereafter he found that a different path opened up. It was a path of the heart. It was the first time Loud Larry cared for anything or anyone more than his degenerating body. When his heart reached out to his loved one, it touched his illness. As his heart and body converged during extended periods of forgiveness meditation, his body began to heal and his voice continued to soften. ("I no longer have to make more of myself than I am. I used to think the only way to survive was by making more of me. Now I find the less the better. There is so little to keep me from loving now." The doctors asked him, "How on earth did you heal?" He told them, "I took the best medicine I could find. And I was the only physician who could prepare it. I took *me*, lock, stock and barrel."

This work of opening to ourselves is taken a step at a time. It is begun with a heartful openness and investigative awareness which gently explores the physical/mental pains and holdings which become so noticeable around illness. It is an ongoing process of meeting our fear with forgiveness and a healing awareness, meeting our doubt with a new confidence which develops in each unknown step as the ground comes up to meet and support our progress. And the next step follows naturally. It is the unfolding experience of the mind/body within an accepting awareness which choicelessly observes and examines mental states, feelings, emotions, and moods as they arise and dissolve in the vastness of being.

Just as pain uncovers deep holdings within us—ancient fears, subliminal imprints, long unnoticed desires for control—so the investigation of illness begins to heal these underlying tendencies. Thus we have seen that for many working with illness in the body means working with the discomforts of the mind—a healing of one's deepest clingings and fears—which led them to the discovery of joys unimagined and a spaciousness never dreamed of. Illness causes us to confront our most assiduous doubts about the nature of the universe and the existence of God. It tears us open. It teaches us to keep our heart open in Hell.

Not all those we have known who have healed have participated in their injury or illness in the same way or at the same level. One enters oneself wherever an opening exists. Many investigated deeply the nature of their pain, releasing profound emotional energy stimulated by confusion and attending fears.

Some explored the nature of their spirit. Marty was such a person, who with years of meditative opening ended the progress of a genetic bone cancer. Letting his heart be torn open to the fears and immense questioning as to the nature of existence, his profound inquiry into "who indeed it is that resides within this diseased body" led him deeper toward his healing. Marty's sister, sharing a similar genetic inheritance (which manifested in deformation of the bones and the constant possibility of further amputations) fought the disease and fought life itself. The struggle was just too much for her. She could no longer bear the rising pressure of unexamined fears, and became afraid of all that existed around the next corner. She now resides in a state mental institution.

Marty sought healing in the heart and discovered seeking an ongoing process within. His sister, however, seeking protection in the mind, was lost in confusion.

Each seeks their healing where it is to be found. Each approaches the heart to hear the subtle whisper of the appropriate. Each uncovers whatever blocks access to the heart, to the source of healing.

A friend very ill with an advanced cancer, visited a highly respected Zen Master, hoping for some answers to her questions about healing. After explaining her circumstances, she asked, "Do I need to take on some spiritual path in order to be healed?" The Zen Master, smiling, leaned forward, pointing directly to her heart, and whispered, "You are the path!"

Recognizing that there was nowhere to go but in, that she was the path and had to tread herself wholeheartedly, her questions were answered.

Drawn by the sincerity and openness of this fine teacher, she began to attend meditation sittings each morning at the Zen Center and to participate in as many weekend intensives as she felt appropriate. She meditated for some time, investigating the nature of what she called "the visitor in the body and the egg that hatched it all." Her six-month prognosis now, six years later, seems more an initiation than a tragedy. Looking back on the meditative practices she took on, motivated by a desire to heal the body, she recently remarked, "You know, these techniques affected me in a way I never thought was possible. I saw that I could rebuild my body breath by breath, and open my mind, thought by thought."

She began a wholehearted commitment to let go of the old, to start anew each moment, a path of wonderment and discovery.

She became, as she put it, "a complete beginner." She came naked to the truth. Trusting her "new unknowing," she stepped childlike onto the wide, exciting path ahead. Willing to let go of old ways of thinking and hiding, she acknowledged "complete ignorance of life" in the face of the great quandary of disease and possible death. It was her total entrance into the process that allowed her that fulfilling sense of completeness from the very first step. She said it took about three months, but gradually a sense of ease began to emerge. She said she didn't have to have all the answers in order to solve the problem. She saw that going wholeheartedly within the problem *was* the answer. She did not lug along old concepts but learned afresh each moment, "a complete beginner," nothing absent, each moment anew. She trusted each step toward fullness, attuning to the subtle whispers of the heart, cultivating a healing awareness that received the moment in mercy, and allowed change instead of forcing it.

But just as the meditative work of the fellow with genetic bone cancer who spent so much time investigating the relationship of mind and body to the heart, is not for everyone, so our friend's way was a path she sensed was uniquely appropriate to her process. For many, the surrender, the willingness to investigate the nature of illness, comes in increments. A step at a time. The unfolding of insights and understandings deepens as one approaches the core of being.

In the beginning it may be an inner exploration of fifteen or twenty minutes every once in a while until, gradually, as the mind is drawn to the heart, yearning for spaciousness, a daily meditation practice develops. Sitting down quietly once or twice a day for a half hour to an hour, the healing extends from those quiet moments to permeate the whole day. And our healing becomes an ongoing practice of seeing the old in a brand-new way. Each moment of participating directly in the process, of seeing clearly the unfolding of mind/body in the spacious heart, each instance of insight, is a healing moment.

A healing moment is one in which the mind is not clinging to its passing show, not lost in the personal melodrama of its content, but tuned to the constant unfolding of the process in a moment of being fully alive, a moment of healing. Experiencing the vastness in which all floats for even a millisecond has the power to bring balance and harmony to the mind/body. Each moment of participating in the spaciousness of being deepens the context for healing. Each moment experienced directly releases the holding about our suffering. Insights accrue as wisdom. Mercy accrues as compassion. Healing accumulates from moment to moment when discomfort is met mindfully, openheartedly, in the present, where all that we seek is to be found.

Our old chiropractor friend Carl came to many of our conscious living/conscious dying workshops to, as he put it, "sharpen my healing practice to serve others more fully." Then Carl became ill. "I found out how real it all was when the doctor told me it was cancer. There was no bullshitting, no time to waste. It was up to me to learn about healing from the inside out." And this is just what he did. Allowing his body to be the laboratory for deeper investigations of healing, he experimented with various methods of healing. He worked with fever therapy, urine therapy, various herbs and nutritional techniques, as well as body and skeletal manipulations until it became evident that the tumor was continuing to grow. He was told by a number of physicians that his only hope was surgery, though even then the cancer might return. "At first I was fighting it. I wasn't working with the idea of surgery at all. I was struggling against the disease, and then, when the operation came along, I really closed down. I had always been so wholistic, and here I was letting them intervene in a way I had suggested to many of my patients was not such a good idea. But I was convinced by the physicians that it was a state-of-the-art surgery and that I had nothing to worry about. But the operation was not successful and the tumor did not go away. When I found out, I became really depressed, but then something broke through. I didn't know how to get 'this cure' I was looking for, but I knew I wasn't going deeply enough for my healing. So I went to this very powerful spiritual teacher whom I had heard so many good things about. I was all worn out and confused and just asked her straight out how to rid my body of cancer. And you know what she told me? 'Just love yourself.' It knocked me off my feet. I was shocked. I just didn't know what to say. She had hit the nail right on the head, and the nail was driven right through my heart. I thought she was going to give me a mantra or a visualization or something, some way to change the illness, but instead she insisted I change myself. Those were the most difficult words I have ever heard, but it was the healing that I came for. When I started to send love to myself, I discovered how much I had blocked, and it really frightened me. I saw that only by examining and letting go of that fear of loving would I ever get healthy again."

It has been nearly two and a half years now since Carl was told to "tidy up any legal loose ends." The other day he told me, "The better I like myself, the better I feel. When I look into the eyes of my fourteen-month-old son now, I realize that he was conceived at almost precisely the time they said I was going to die. Things change when you let them." As Carl walked the path of healing, spending an hour or two a day in silent contemplation, sharing with a trusted counselor and looking deeply into the mirror of his wife's heart, he was able to use his own heart as a compass toward the sometimes clouded shores of life. He discovered deeper and deeper levels of wholeness. Now he speaks of healing not as somewhere we are going, but as an ever-present process, unfolding moment to moment. The other day he said that completing our birth was the first stage of healing. He said that if we did not allow ourselves to be born, to become fully aware, to attend to our life, then we would never be able to fully live or fully die.

Recently a friend asked, "What part do karma and grace play in these spontaneous healings?" These are concepts I rarely find useful because they carry such a load of confused meaning. Nevertheless, I think it appropriate to explore these terms because they arise peripherally again and again in various discussions of healing. But grace and karma are tricky concepts to use without a full experiential understanding of their most minute subtleties. Indeed, in answer to my friend's question, I'm not sure "spontaneous" is the correct adjective. Most work very hard to open the body and clear the heart. Considerable motivation is necessary to take on the healing that is called for to complete the work of a lifetime. Although we might say that each healing moment is grace, because it brings us closer to our real nature, the remarkable outcome of such deep adventures in the spirit is not a gift from on high but the actualization of our birthright. Many take karma as punishment and grace as reward. But that is not my sense of it. Karma is a very complex, multicompartmented idea that seeks to explain an extraordinarily simple, merciful teaching process which brings to our attention again and again those qualities that block our heart and limit our experience of full being. Karma is not punishment but an opportunity offered at level after level of experience to bring us back to balance. It is the most merciful and attentive of teachers. To relegate the cause of illness to the irretrievable past as karma, or its cure to the unreachable future, as some awaited grace creates a sense of helplessness and fatalism.

I asked a group of terminally ill patients what karma might mean in the context of their illnesses. One fellow, very close to dying from a brain tumor, shakingly raised his hand and said, "Karma is a wind that is always blowing. It all depends on how you set your sails." This is as good a definition of karma as we have yet encountered. Grace is generally defined as a gift or intervention from on high, but there seems a good deal more to it than that. Grace is the experience of our true nature. Grace is the experience of the effusive peace of unbounded being. And though one cannot create grace with a snap of the fingers, it is potential in each moment. Though grace cannot be created, it can always be invited by preparing for the present. Karma is grace. Grace is karmic.

Healing, like grace, can be somewhat disorienting in its early stages. It is a breaking through of the old to reveal the ever new. Healing, like grace, always takes us toward our true nature. Indeed, healing is not somewhere we are going but a discovery of where we already are—a participation in the process unfolding moment to moment. Many of us pray for a miracle when all else has failed. We wish for grace to descend upon us. But grace comes from within. Grace arises when the work of healing is in process. A graceful healing into the spirit that goes beyond the need of definition or even words like "grace" or "karma" or "spirit." Though many of the people we worked with did not begin with a spiritual inclination, many uncovered their healing by taking on what some call spiritual practices toward the discovery of a deeper self. But we did notice that even those who had shied away from what they called "spiritual stuff," in the course of their daily confrontation with the impermanence of the body, cultivated a certain quality of heartfulness and peacefulness.

But it is not so important where or what we call our entrance into life so much as it is that we eventually begin to participate, that we eventually begin to bring our illnesses and hidden wounds into a hard-earned grace and wholeness. To at last take birth and merge within that deep inner movement toward completion and a deeper sense of healing.

Though these people might never call themselves "spiritual," theirs was the very spirit of healing. One friend, sensing the subtlety of this opening to healing, told us how she had cured an arthritic twisting of the knuckles in her right hand. "I did it by taking a little bit of apple cider and honey each morning." When I asked if that was all there was to it, she replied, "It helps if you hum a bit."

As we continued to explore the meaning of healing, we began to sense that in many ways the body is just solidified mind, and we became even more aware of how much mercy our mental and physical pain requires. We saw that healing was difficult enough without trying to force back the mind and twist the body into some imagined healing conformation. Indeed, it seemed that those whose illnesses were cured simply by strong medicine, without having their heart in it, were unusually fortunate. Obviously it is not necessary to take on these practices in order to heal. These are not the "only way" or even the "best way" toward healing. They are just a path found workable and walkable. Indeed, there are many who, without any inner conspiracy to awaken from old ways, somehow win their battle against bodily illness with one hand still tied behind their backs.

Some years ago a fellow who came to us for counseling left in a huff because our relationship to healing began in the heart. He said he had no time to waste with such nonsense, he wanted strong medicine, all this stuff about "the healing moment" was too unpredictable. Committing himself to ongoing regimens of chemotherapy and radiation, the cancer went into remission. But he was one of the "one-armed healed" who still did not feel at home in life. Within three months he called, unnecessarily apologetic, with numerous questions about how to use forgiveness as a means of letting go of unfinished business and how to apply the mindfulness meditation to some difficult issues dealing with anger.

He said he had fantasized during his cancer that if he could only get well, everything in his life would be different. But it wasn't. His life was unsatisfactory. Ironically, though his body was no longer ill, he asked to begin with the healing meditation. He said he wanted to start again on the ground floor, sending heart where fear had gone before. "Now that my body is cured, maybe I can stay alive long enough to get healed."

Which reminds me of a fellow who called one night to say that he was about to undergo radiation therapy for a cancer the next morning but felt very squeamish about it. "I just don't have my heart in it," he said. "I've eaten organic foods most of my life, and I've tried to stay pretty unpolluted. But now I am going to let them zap me with this poisonous radiation. It's all so unnatural. Something in me just rebels—how is poisoning me going to get me well? This is a hell of a way to go."

Reflecting together about these rays which make up radiation, we spoke of how they were found free-floating naturally throughout the cosmos. He began to see their naturalness. He began to discover how, although mechanically focused by a machine, they were indeed extant everywhere and certainly not created out of nothing. As he was able to sense something of the naturalness of this technique, he came across an image which he was able to use during his treatments, a visualization of these rays as a light emitting from the palm of his beloved Jesus. He found now that his heart was in it he could use a combination of techniques that were able to enormously increase the efficiency of the treatment with few or no side effects.

It should be noted that many of the techniques we are sharing here may be quite useful in combination with other techniques. None of our techniques are suggested to replace or eliminate any others. These are techniques to open the body and allow the healing in. To open the mind to its original healing nature and allow the heart its full exposure. To sense the universal within, to make contact with the very source of healing, the already healed, the ever uninjured.

One evening, after a lecture and some sharing about this new healing material, a woman approached us. She said she wanted to share her story to reaffirm for us our intuitions about healing. Loretta told us of a two-year battle with cancer that she had waged. "I fought it so hard to stay alive, but then they told me I was going to die. I was so exhausted I just didn't know what to do. I could feel death coming, so I began reading your book *Who Dies?* and started to say goodbye to all my loves and friends. But as I started to say goodbye to life, I was kind of shocked at how little I had ever lived. And even though it had seemed to me I was trying to stay alive before, it was only when I saw how much I had put on hold that I was pulled back into my life." She said that as death approached she at last saw the value of getting on with her life. She spoke of how she had been so busy trying to get well physically that she had never paid attention to the places in her that had always been so distressed, so unhappy, and perhaps forever ill. She felt very fortunate that death acted as a mirror in which she saw, "really saw," how precious life was. It was then that her body began to heal. Perhaps life felt safe to her for the very first time. Now, three years later, she is thankful that she became ill and then got well but in some ways is most thankful that something drew her out of herself. "I was so asleep that I guess it took something big as death to wake me up. But

I will never make that mistake again. I was so busy trying to get better that I never really acknowledged how bad off I was. I have never really treated myself with much kindness. I was angry at my body for punishing me, for betraying me. I was angry and frightened most of the time. But then something, as you might say, 'let go and let the healing in.' If I ever get ill again, I don't think it will be as terrible as that last time. My life was so narrow and now it is so broad. Thank God I didn't die so small."

We have worked with several who, upon approaching death, were able to acknowledge and investigate the nature of their illness and pain and were astonished to see the intensity of pain and illness start to dissolve. This seems to be because our holdings, our blockages to life, are often below the level of usual awareness. They are so "unconscious" that only upon direct investigation can they arise and dissolve in the light of a clearer awareness. It was not that pain disappeared but that the resistance melted and there was so much more room, such a greater sense of spaciousness in which these sensations could float. As they began clearing the heart, softening the armor of lifelong posturings and pretense, the distance between the mind and the heart came painfully into view. It is in such awkward moments of healing that we acknowledge the work to be done and sympathetically recognize that letting the healing in is easy in theory but often difficult in practice. And we soften the belly in order to soften the mind. And letting the mind sink into the heart, we take a deep breath and watch the terrible truth of our separation from ourselves float in a mercy and awareness that makes us feel whole at last. For the healing we all seek goes much deeper than that. It goes to the very core of what is referred to as "being." Being is awareness itself. We are not here speaking of "being" as opposed to "nonbeing," or life as opposed to death or any such dualistic concept of existence. We are speaking of the direct experience of "is-ness" of the suchness that animates all form and that goes beyond form.

Even a moment's experience of the nature of edgeless awareness can loosen the fears of death and soften the holdings which so intensify physical and mental pain. Each direct experience of the vastness of being is a healing which brings us closer to the life spark growing at the center of each cell. Each moment we enter our pain with a merciful awareness is a moment of healing. Each moment we touch suffering with love we are healed.

What a miracle to send forgiveness and love into that which we have so often met with fear and loathing. To meet our pain and illness with loving kindness instead of hatred and anger brings a new trust in life. It allows the confusion that often constellates about discomfort to release its suffocating grasp. It offers an alternative to suffering. Each time we allow a merciful awareness into our discomforts is like standing at a crossroads. Not far to the right we can see the tension of confusion. But we notice just beneath our feet something quite amazing, the state of mind that precedes this great amplifier of pain. We discover the presence of bewilderment. We recognize the state of mind that says "What do I do now?" when confronted with difficulty, the bewilderment which has for so long leaped impatiently into an insistence on an immediate answer. By not reacting to this state, but instead responding, we enter these feelings that arise when we feel we no longer have control of the situation, and we stay a moment longer to explore things as they are. We allow bewilderment in rather than compulsively running toward the confusion which turns life into an emergency. Investigating this bewilderment, as if for the first time we become "complete beginners" and notice an alternative: another road branching toward the spacious pastures and open vistas of "don't know." Toward a willingness to open to the old in a brand-new way. To take whatever teachings the moment provides in a deepening of our mercy and awareness.

The Korean Zen Master Seung Sahn often tells students to "trust that don't know." It is the space in which all wisdom arises, in which alternatives are to be discovered. "Don't know" is without all previous opinion; it does not perceive from old points of view, it is open to the many possibilities inherent in the moment. It doesn't force conclusions, it allows the healing in. If I may, I will borrow from this fine teaching to share the spaciousness inherent there. In the teachings of Zen Master Suzuki Roshi this same spaciousness is referred to as "beginner's mind," saying that when we have a beginner's mind the whole world is newly discoverable for ourselves.

The difference between confusion and "don't know" is that confusion can only see one way out and that way is blocked, while "don't know" is open to miracles and insights. Pain often calls out for immediate conclusions. The mind implodes—force closes the heart. In confusion we are so far away from our selves; in "don't know" we are right there watching, fascinated. To enter our pain with mercy and love is to change the whole world with a deepening trust even in the unknown.

To be, as our friend with advanced cancer became, a "complete beginner," is to trust this vast "don't know." To take birth each instant, open and empty, with room for it all, willing to begin again from moment to moment. The complete beginner takes nothing for granted, letting go of old mind, becoming wholly new, constantly available to healing.

Everything is burned so new
when the eyes drink
from the peace
beyond the pain—pay attention,
there is a year-end sale on suffering—
put away your credit card.

CHAPTER 4

Taking the Path of Healing

To take the path of healing is to directly participate in life, to enter the process with a light step and a merciful awareness which receives the moment as it is. To enter directly one's life means to tune to the moment-to-moment arising and disappearance of thought and feeling, of experience itself. To directly experience experience itself is to be fully alive. Much of our life is an afterthought, a dreamy mist which obscures the moment just passed. So much of our life is a reflection of what has just occurred rather than a direct participation in the unfolding moment. An example of how the path of merciful exploration heals so many levels was shared with us by Howard whose right side had been badly mutilated by a landmine in Vietnam. After spending more than a year in a Veterans Hospital, he told us he was still unable to heal completely. When we spoke of what seemed to stay his final healing, to fully restore the use of his right leg and allow the open wounds to heal, he told us of the day of his injury. He was on patrol with several close comrades. They were set upon by rocket and machine-gun fire. Running for cover, he stepped on a mine which blew him several feet across the rice paddy and left him a bloody rubble in the mud. He was bypassed by the enemy forces which eventually "wiped out my whole squad." By being injured he was the only one to survive. He felt that somehow his injury was connected with the death of the others. His profound guilt was the shame of the survivor, a condition very similar to that which we had encountered in those who survived the Nazi death camps. "How can I be walking around here when they are all six feet under?"

But the truth was that he wasn't walking around so easily. A noticeable limp and wince of pain accompanied most of his steps. His twisted limb and recognizable discomfort had become an integral part of his persona. Asking Howard about his pain one day, he laboriously unraveled a supportive elastic stocking on his leg to expose several ulcerated "weeping" sores. "They have been there for years—they never seem to heal."

We suggested that his healing might begin with the deep investigation of the shame the mind carried for having outlived his "comrades in arms." We suggested he begin to pay close attention to whatever he felt when discomfort drew his attention to the leg. To listen closely for the messages, the teachings, that his leg might offer. After a few weeks he mentioned that he noticed that each time he changed the dressing on his open sores, he could almost "smell my buddies' bodies rotting in the jungle." After attending a few conscious living/conscious dying workshops and several counseling sessions, he was drawn to working daily with the forgiveness meditation. It was an optimal beginning to acknowledge the grief in his mind/body. Sensing that cultivating forgiveness was the ideal balance for his guilt and resentment, he began to sit quietly for twenty minutes twice a day and work with the forgiveness meditation. The great difficulty he had in the beginning, touching his pain with forgiveness, defined for him the blockages to his healing. Examining his "decade of grief," he quickly began to see "how much of me was torn open in Nam." He began to see that there was more to it than just "this wrecked body." He began to notice when he was paying close attention to the pain in his leg that it seemed to connect right up through his body to the pain he had had for so long in his chest. "I've had several EKGs in the last few years, but they always tell me there is nothing wrong with my heart. But now I think I understand. How I missed this connection all these years is beyond me." The grief work and the forgiveness meditation he was so deeply committed to was making the ache in his heart all the more obvious. "It's like my leg is pulling on my heart."

Because Howard lived so far away, we could see him only occasionally, but every week or so he would call with some technical question about the forgiveness meditation: "When I am sending forgiveness into my leg and horribly bloody images arise, what should I do? Should the forgiveness be for the guys that blew me up? Will I ever be able to forgive something that causes me so much pain? Will it ever be able to forgive me?" Over the weeks one could feel that at the beginning it was the leg asking the questions, but as the process deepened, it seemed to be his heart calling out for its long-awaited healing. Within a few months his calls were less regular, and his questions yet more penetrating: "Sometimes when I go to my heart to talk to my leg, there are no words there, there is just a feeling that connects the two. When this happens there doesn't seem to be any pain in the leg—what should I focus on then?" He was working as hard as he could to stay open through it all.

At a workshop perhaps six months after the last time we had heard from him, he came walking into the room with only the slightest limp. When I asked him what had happened, he said, "The wounds stopped 'weeping' when I sent my heart into my grief, into my leg. Now I can stand on my own two feet." It was not so much that the pain had gone completely away as much as that it had changed. "It feels like my injury is forgiven and, weird as it may sound, I think it has forgiven me as well. Anyhow, it is okay that I am alive now. Now let's see what I can do with the rest of it." The work of opening to his grief was a deep healing which may continue for years, but as he says, "My body is kind of catching up now. I was closed down for so long, so afraid to feel, that I guess it took all that pain to get my attention."

This work of letting the healing in was very evident too in a therapist friend whose degenerative heart condition left him unable to climb stairs or continue his practice as a dance therapist. He told us that the work of opening "my heart to my heart" began one day sitting in front of a picture of the sacred heart of Jesus. He began to breathe that glowing heart into his "old decrepit one." He said that each breath drew in that compassion which he had so little of for himself. He drew the heart of Jesus directly into his own heart.

"I began to merge the sacred heart with my diseased heart and it really got me high." What began as a ten-minute meditation, over the months, extended to several twenty-minute periods each day. While trying to find the mercy to heal, the progress of his illness stopped. For three years there has been no further degeneration of his heart. "Now I can walk up a flight of stairs again, and once in a while my heart will take off dancing, though my body is still a bit wearied by the twirl."

For some it takes months of pain and helplessness before they look deeper for their healing. For others it seems it takes only a moment to comprehend the path on which their wholeness lies. One woman with cancer who had come to a ten-day conscious living/conscious dying retreat, came up to me on the third day and said, "I am going home to rest now—I only came to figure out what I need to do next. And I got what I came for." In the six years since that event, her brain tumor has disappeared. When I last saw her, she approached me with a broad smile and said, "No more cancer." When I asked her if it was completely gone, she replied, "I don't know, but I am more here than ever."

For some this inkling of a way through disease may come after a long period of great suffering and resistance, after feeling a failure for the difficulties illness brings until there is "just no heart left in fighting it anymore". The heart often becomes exposed when resistances fall away and, even in the midst of pain, the sense of failure dissolves into a new possibility of aliveness. As Thomas Merton said, "True love and prayer are learned in the moment when prayer has become impossible and the heart has turned to stone."

This clearly was the case with May, whose fourteen-year-old son died in her arms from what she thought was a heavy cold. She had kept assuring her son, after the visiting doctor said he had "just a little flu," that he could "just sweat it out for himself, be a man about it!" But he died. The guilt and self-doubt that ensued after his death tore her apart. "For more than a year, I went crazy till my heart just broke. I couldn't even go to the bathroom for myself. I would just lay there ruined. I was a complete wreck. I thought I would never feel okay again. I used to ask everyone I met if they ever knew anyone who did not recover from grief. I thought life was over, I had blown it. I had ruined everything. And it continued to get worse until I thought I was just going to disintegrate. After a year of contemplating suicide each day, I knew I had to "shit or get off the pot." After many therapists' encouragement, I just let the pain in. I thought it would destroy me, and maybe it did because in a way I was reborn when I let the pain, the grief, just kill me and it didn't. I saw this pain as the rest of my life, and I knew I just had to live it. From those days on I have begun to trust the pain as well as the forgiveness. And I am reunited with my family."

Most of us delay the healing that is to be done. We never ask the question "At what level is healing to be found?" until we discover cancer in our body or experience the death of a child, or the loss of a much-relied-on position in society through old age, divorce, or chronic illness.

There are many levels on which to explore the grief we hold in our aching body and painfully separate mind. Indeed, it may well be that not until a traumatic incident has occurred will we start to pay attention to life at the level where healing is to be discovered and the subtle injuries are to be released.

As I came to understand this more deeply, the way I worked with people in pain began to change. In the early years of sitting with those in great physical discomfort, I would notice at times that my heart would turn to prayer, interceding on their behalf to ask that their pain might be diminished. But as time went on, I could see that I knew too little to know what was best for that individual. And then one day, when I sat down with someone in great bodily distress, I noticed that as I turned to whatever the divine might be to ask for some surcease of their difficulties, something rose in me which disallowed that prayer. It was clearly inappropriate. Since then, I can only pray that someone might gain from their experience whatever wisdom and deep healing is available to them. I can no longer second-guess God as to the meaning, cause, or effect of illness. And I just trust "don't know" to stay open to the process and recognize how deeply we heal when we bring our attention to life and all it entails.

Our old friend Vivien awoke one morning to discover her teenage daughter had been murdered in the bedroom next to hers. She could hardly forgive herself for not coming to her daughter's aid. "How could I have not heard? How could I have not known that she needed me?!" It turned out that her daughter had not been asleep when she arrived home but had been murdered much earlier that night, yet still the rational mind boiled over with its inability to control death or protect a loved one. For the first months she said it was nearly impossible for her to believe that she slept the night through with her daughter strangled in the next bedroom. Her body began to ache, and various old physical ailments reoccurred. She said, "I am sick to death with the way things are." She said she would do anything to bring back her daughter—her body and mind showed the strain. Until one day, working with the grief meditation, she acknowledged, "Things will never be the same." She allowed the enormous pain of this enormous truth to sink into her heart and began to let the healing in. Instead of constantly struggling with the images of her strangled daughter, she let them sweep over her and cried and screamed and laughed and talked and talked and talked to her dead daughter. And finally slept. Instead of struggling against what was, she began to open to things as they were. Allowing the pain to peel levels of old holding from the heart. Burning through a lifetime of separation and fear to leave her nearly translucent in her compassion and healing. And although she says today that she recognizes that her daughter can never return, she usually adds, "But she has never been so close either."

These levels of healing and the various insights which inhabit them were never more evident than with our friend Bob, who suffered lingering pain from multiple fractures sustained during a motorcycle accident some years before. After years of working with various medical models and analgesics to quell the pain and calm the body's intense reaction to acute discomfort, he told us, "Recently I got the opportunity to realize an old dream. I was given some land and enough lumber to build my own house. But I was uncomfortable at times and thought I would just have to pass it by. But I really thought about it a lot. I asked myself how I could do it. And something in me said, 'Just remember that when you think of God your back doesn't hurt so much.' " The only way he could build the home he had always wanted back in the woods was to constantly sing to God. It did the trick. Now he lives in a temple instead of just a house. And Gods sings to him. His back still hurts every once in a while, but when it does it just reminds him to sing an octave deeper.

Perhaps when we speak of the enlightened ones, the saints, the illuminati, all we are referring to is the healed ones, those whose mind has sunk deeply into the heart, those who have discovered the One out of which the many arise, the nonfragmented, the whole. Victor Frankl, in *Man's Search for Meaning*, speaks of the few who survived the horror of the concentration camps as those who served others: the doctors, the nuns, the priests, the rabbis, the mothering and fathering care-givers. They survived because they had a reason to live: love itself, healing itself. They went beyond the illness that so often devastated the body. Even in an environment in which they lost all control, all dignity and its imagined autonomy, they saw that the gift given the gifted is love. They knew that love is the only gift worth giving. That our care for others is our care for ourselves, a deep honoring of the being we all share.

The path of healing is a process of opening our heart to the holdings of the past while maintaining a keen awareness of the present. It is a coming home, a return to the living moment. But because there is so much more to us than just mind/body, because our original nature is without boundary, its edgelessness cannot be described. It can only be participated in.

Although we speak in terms of "taking the path of healing," that is certainly not the only way to put it. The great Sioux shaman Black Elk speaks of "walking in a sacred manner." To walk in a sacred manner is to make an art of life, to attend to each moment as though it were the last, to take each step as though it were the first. To breathe love and awareness into this tiny body, entering the greater body we all share. Seeing that each step must be taken lightly, not with force, not creating more self, becoming more of a "doer," more of a separate identity, which draws suffering upon itself. To walk in a sacred manner is to let go of our suffering and allow the scintillating "thusness" of each moment to nurture and direct the next step.

When we walk in a sacred manner, nothing throws us off balance for nothing is identified with as self, as the walker, but instead all is experienced as the sacred, as process unfolding, as the divine moment provided for our healing.

In open body, in open mind, in open heart, the possibilities are endless. Healing is to be found everywhere. Each step so precious. Each step a new healing.

Are you looking for me? I am in the next seat.
 My shoulder is against yours.
You will not find me in stupas, not in Indian shrine
 rooms, nor in synagogues, nor in cathedrals:
not in masses, nor kirtans, not in legs winding
 around your own neck, nor in eating nothing but
 vegetables.
When you really look for me, you will see me
 instantly—
you will find me in the tiniest house of time.
Kabir says: Student, tell me, what is God?
It is the breath inside the breath.

Kabir

CHAPTER 5

Exploring the Unhealed

Considering how much of life is unlived and how many loose ends remain for most, it is not surprising how difficult it is for some to die. But over the years of working with the terminally ill, Ondrea and I came to recognize a rather poignant phenomenon. What struck us was how willing so many were to get out of this world, how many had become so exhausted by life, so defeated that they were ready to "just die and get it done with." Many found life unworkable. It seems natural under the circumstances in which most of us live that there might be some difficulty surrendering a lifetime's attachments at the moment of death, but this life-denying desire to escape brought our attention to how much life was left unhealed behind them.

But of course when we speak of such tendencies to escape the pains of life, we are never speaking of someone else but always of some condition that exists in each of us. Indeed, this eagerness to escape seems to block even the most superficial healing and so has to be dealt with in ourselves as well as by all who wish to heal.

Sensing the importance of exploring that which resists life and perhaps even limits our access to illness, we began to ask each new patient: If you went to the doctor today and were told that you had only six months to live and you were asked afterward to write down all the reasons why you wish to stay alive, you might have hundreds of things to put down—your interest in the world, love for your family and friends, your desire for more experience, your wish to fulfill old dreams, to resolve old nightmares, the desire to enjoy this exquisitely beautiful, often shimmering realm, to meet one's grand-children, to experience yet more learning, all the lovemakings yet to come, all the beings yet to meet, all the projects yet to complete, the sweet eyes of old friends. After you had written all these reasons in Column A, entitled "Why I Wish to Stay Alive," on the left-hand side of any number of sheets of paper, if you were then asked to go to Column B and enumerate all the reasons that somehow, beyond reason, even beyond understanding, there was some sense of relief in the terminal prognosis, what might you say? Why might the prospect of dying not be altogether unpleasant, not because of a love of God or a trust in the process but because of a resistance to life, all the places where death might be an acceptable alternative, Column B would begin to fill.

Indeed, after Column A was completed, what might you put down if you were asked why it was all right to die? What might you discover within yourself? How might it be all right to leave this world? What degree of world-weariness, of fatigue, of grief, of confusion, of fear, of pain, of unfinishedness, of feelings of unresolved abandonment, of helplessness, of hopelessness, might write themselves in the right-hand Column B, "Why It Would Be Okay To Die"?

We spend much of our energy trying to hold on to Column A, trying to reinforce the highs, trying to push away a desire to defect. We constantly find ourselves bewildered by the fact that we can't quite taste, can't quite touch, can't *quite* see, can't *quite* smell, can't *quite* feel, and are amazed when we recognize how much of what we have called life has so often been an afterthought. How much we have been thinking our lives instead of living them. How life has become a struggle and an emergency instead of an allowing and a flowing. Our struggle to stay in Column A becomes another situation leading to Column B. Perhaps our greatest pain is our lack of acceptance of pain. The storyline "And they lived happily everafter" poisons our projections and taints and abstracts our life. We are constantly looking outside ourselves for happiness, constantly depending on external circumstances for our joy, so often contracted to a sense of hopelessness and a smoldering disgust that we are constantly bargaining with, hoping for the next moment instead of living it.

For our whole life we keep feeding this left-hand column, this "Why I Want To Be Alive" quality in our lives. It is almost like writing an essay on what I did on my summer vacation, enumerating all the reasons we honor life, all the thirsts to be quenched, all the hungers to be fed, all the desires to be fulfilled. But interestingly we may notice that it is the inability to lastingly fulfill these desires or to feed our hungers and thirsts that often lead to the apathy and frustration that begins to fill Column B. In Column B there may well be a few reasons why life has become "a bit much." Indeed, these reasons may define our resistance to healing. It may even be that the attitudes of Column B somehow defend illness and find it in some way suitable.

Perhaps it is in the conflict between these qualities of eagerness and despair that such deep fatigue arises to limit our healing. In examining Column A and Column B, we can almost see the conflict between the mind and body, between whom we wish to be and what we are frightened we may become. In this no-man's-land between Column A and Column B, between the mind and body, the un-healed is defined. Into this shadowy gulf the heart is called as an intermediary, the same heart which Jung defined as "the place of the coincidence of opposites." It is here that the power of awareness and mercy to heal is so gratefully acknowledged.

We seldom explore Column B. We seldom accept all of ourselves. So many parts are pushed away. When we are feeling frightened, guilty, angry, self-loathing, do we hold ourselves in our arms and cradle ourselves? Do we treat ourselves like our only child? Or do we meet our pain with hatred, rejection, a drowsy blindness that leaves so much of ourselves unexplored and unhealed?

When we accidentally hit our thumb with a hammer while hang-ing a picture or stub our toe crossing the room, how do we meet that pain? Do we touch it with love or with aversion and disgust? Attend-ing to the reaction, we notice how often we automatically meet our pain with anger and even hatred. We see how tightly conditioned we are. Just when we are most in need of our mercy, it is often the least available. Where is that exquisite tenderness that is always a poten-tial but is so seldom encouraged? Where is it to be found? How, considering the enormity of our conditioning to escape pain, to slay the enemy within, will we ever let our healing in? How can we enter our pain with a new softness instead of that same old hardness and judgment? How do we enter with mercy that which has so often been withdrawn from with a merciless indictment, a sense of failure for even existing?

We have seen many begin to reenter their life by examining that part of themselves for which dying may somehow be preferable to living. Looking directly into the boredom and self-doubt, the confusion and intense inner judgment, we see that during these states the mind often wishes not to be. The mind's intense reaction to the unpleasant gives some insight into its relationship to discomfort in the body as well—a crushing denial, a suicidal attempt not to exist so as not to experience—the essence of Column B. Seeing the nature of mind's holding to its suffering, we begin to let go and look with mercy on a lifetime of pain so that nothing limits the resolution of ancient conflicts or blocks our natural healing.

Our healing deepens as we come to realize that we must approach these conflicts and these pains with a new gentleness, with a deeper mercy. To accept with great forgiveness that these confusions exist even though there is nothing "voluntary" in this withdrawing from life that fills Column B. It is the unexamined mind's reaction to feelings of panic and helplessness that so often arise in life and know nowhere to turn.

Indeed, there is no blame in Column B or in the conflicts we discover warring in the mind, subtly, and perhaps even below our daily awareness. They are not to be judged. They are all just to be seen. Blame is just an instance of how we meet our pain with mercilessness and anger and fear.

But how can we heal, be whole, until we can begin to bring those parts of life that we find unacceptable or even despicable, into our heart? It means to begin to investigate the mind with some lightness, mercifully observing those qualities which have blinded us to healing a thousand times before with a bit more appreciation and joy. Not being taken by surprise by the same old things, but heartfully noting the fear and the doubt with an ironic "Big Surprise!"—which, of course, means no surprise at all. By taking ourselves so deeply within, nothing in the mind takes us unawares. Not surprised by the mind's "top forty," its habituated "hits of the century," the incessant replays of the painful longings that have asserted themselves repeatedly for as long as we care to remember.

It is another case of it not being someone else's healing we are referring to but always our own. And here we all are, painfully real with nothing to blame, complete beginners taking a step at a time so that our healing will be as deep as our holdings, as deep as our pain.

Nothing has to be different for us to be whole. It is not a matter of change as much as it is of merciful acceptance. We don't even have to be less angry or less frightened or less doubtful. We don't have to be more loving, or more compassionate, or more wise. To be whole is just to take ourselves within wholeheartedly, to meet even our lovelessness, our mercilessness with a deeper "Ahhh!"

It sounds too good to be true that all we need do is mercifully acknowledge the moment. But our healing is not as far away as we imagine. In the light of clear awareness, everything becomes workable, even our pain, even our fear. In fact as we deeply investigate, awareness itself heals all that it touches. And everything begins to fall into line as it will. A deep healing, the most interesting game in town.

In the Chinese book of wisdom, the *I Ching,* in the hexagram "The Army" it says, "One cannot overcome the enemy until one has rid oneself of that which they find despicable in the other." We are constantly treating ourselves as "an other." But even here it is easy to miss the point, because we don't have to rid ourselves of anything to be whole. All we have to do is bring mercy and awareness to what already is, to allow it to unfold. Awareness heals.

To be whole is to acknowledge, not to force, change. For some it may be seen as putting faith in God; for others it may be simply trusting the process. Change comes about on its own, not as we imagine it will. It is often the urgency to be different which keeps us so much the same, unaware, feeling so incomplete, knowing so little peace. Many of the ways we have learned to be, we don't wish to be. We don't like our selfishness. We feel so hopeless and helpless. So merciless, so unreceived.

Opening to even the most personally painful content of mind gives us an opportunity to experience the essentially impersonal universality of the process in which it is all unfolding. Letting go of each thought, watching it arise and dissolve on the screen of consciousness, we begin to discern the process, the ancient momentum of experience, floating in boundaryless awareness. Even a moment's glimpse of the vastness in which it all floats changes the context. We experience the delight of the edgelessness of our being. We discover the healing that is always present when we allow ourselves in.

Letting go of our suffering is the hardest work we will ever do. It is also the most fruitful. To heal means to meet ourselves in a new way —in the newness of each moment where all is possible and nothing is limited to the old, our holdings released, our grasping seen with little surprise or judgment. The vastness of our being meeting each moment wholeheartedly whether it holds pleasure or pain. Then the healing goes deeper than we ever imagined, deeper than we ever dreamed.

This teaching of opening mindfully, heartfully, to our deepest sufferings is part of our essential healing. I vividly remember fifteen years ago coming home from a ten-day meditation retreat, so glad to be back in "the world." Sitting quietly at the kitchen table, sipping tea the next morning, watching the sun rise, all of a sudden I was overwhelmed by feelings of self-hatred. My body went from its 150 pounds to what seemed like 150 tons. I was overwhelmed and couldn't move. I was completely taken by surprise. I had never noticed, with such intensity, how profoundly I had put myself out of my heart. Fear touched the moment, and the mind thought,"Uh-oh, meditation has caused me to lose my mind." But of course that was not the case. The deepening of awareness had brought my attention to that part of the mind which had lost heart, which felt disconnected from itself and all else. Indeed, the meditation had allowed me to regain access to those parts I had closed off, to the pain that was so deep and had been pushed deeper yet with each moment of self-negation and suppression of the pain. I called the teacher in something of a panic, expecting to be consoled and told that I wasn't as bad as I thought, but instead he said, "Sit down and smell the flowers—they grew in your own shit. Don't push away this state of mind. You worked so hard to see how little heart you have offered yourself. Don't withdraw again. Enter this pain with something new, with kindness and awareness." I could see the defense mechanisms of a lifetime. And though it was exceedingly painful, it was a very precious moment. It led to a period of letting the healing sink deeper than I had previously allowed. For the next two days I sat with aspects of myself I had spent a lifetime attempting to elude. I did nothing to distract myself from the enormity of the self-loathing stored there. Whenever the sense of urgency, of fear arose, something in my heart whispered, "Don't stop now, let the healing in. Be merciful, be attentive." It was the beginning of my learning about love at a deeper level, in an area that went beyond the "me" that had demanded protection for so long and hated itself for doing so. It was what some might call a "healing crisis"—a peaking of the painful symptoms inherent in the clear seeing of the wound—a profound *clearing* of the way for life, for reentry.

As one teacher pointed out, "Meditation is just one insult after another." And as another teacher mentioned, "As long as you can be insulted, you have something to hide." For it is not *being* that can be insulted but only our addictions and illnesses, our self-images. To accept those places we don't accept in ourselves is part of the Great Healing, to become whole and really get on with it, recognizing that growth is often painful.

Indeed, if anyone reading this book should mistake the author for someone who has experienced smooth sailing rather than the waves and troughs of growth, I should call my children out from the back room so they can tell you how "off the wall" they have seen me on occasion. And though growth is at times confusing and very difficult, there seems nothing quite as satisfying. There is nothing that will give one the sense of completion and wholeness that coming into one's heart will allow.

Beginning in the separate, this investigation leads to the universal. To the source of all healing. The investigation of our experience allows us at last to fully live this moment. Eluding nothing. Participating with a clear awareness and an open heart, nothing that is touched is left unhealed. All our "business" finished in the living truth of each moment. Nothing else to be done. Nothing left injured or incomplete.

AHH BREATH EXERCISE, A BRIDGE MEDITATION

This is one of the simplest and most powerful exercises we know to give confidence that the ever-healed is never far away—to sense the heart we all share, the one mind of being. It allows levels and levels of connection to be experienced. It can take us through the mind to what lies beyond. It is an exercise in which two people can "see with soft eyes" the levels of intimacy and surrender available to an unobstructed awareness. Many we know use this exercise to deepen the connection within relationships—with lovers, children, parents, the ill, and those one wishes most to serve. It is a guide toward openness capable of giving us a glimpse of our essential spaciousness.

It is a meditation done by two people from twenty to forty-five minutes. Each time this practice is explored, the duration and experience may vary. To make the practice one's own, it is important to become thoroughly familiar with the experiences both of the giver and receiver of this technique—though at its deepest point the giver and receiver disappear into the oneness so available just beyond the separatist mind.

Do not let the simplicity of this technique cause you to underrate its potential for the two to become one.

Of such a state of boundaryless, nondualistic, awareness, Sengstan, the third Zen patriarch, says,

> For the unified mind in accord with the Way
> all self-centered striving ceases.
> Doubts and irresolutions vanish
> and life in true faith is possible.
> With a single stroke we are freed from bondage;
> nothing clings to us and we hold to nothing.
> All is empty, clear, self-illuminating,
> with no exertion of the mind's power.

Here thought, feeling, knowledge, and imagination
are of no value.
In this world of Suchness
there is neither self nor other than self.

To come directly into harmony with this reality
just simply say when doubt arises,
'Not two.'
In this 'Not two' nothing is separate,
nothing is excluded.
No matter when or where,
enlightenment means entering this truth.
And this truth is beyond extension or
diminution in time or space;
in it a single thought is ten thousand years.

In this exercise the person with whom we wish to make contact is requested to lie comfortably on a bed or on the floor as is suitable, with his (or her) body loose (belts untightened, glasses removed, arms laid gently by the side, legs uncrossed—open-bodied) and to just breathe naturally. "There is nothing you need to do but feel what is happening."

To encourage a recognition that the experience, no matter how mundane or remarkable, is totally the person's own, sit next to but do not touch the person lying on the floor. If the meditation takes this individual to the nondualistic space beyond old mind, they will not think it was due to some intervention on your part, some magic done on them, but will sense its arisal within as dependent only upon themselves.

Sitting approximate to their midsection, let your eyes focus on the rise and fall of their abdomen with the inhalation and exhalation of each breath. Encourage the person to breathe naturally, not to control the breath or to hold or shape it, but to allow themselves to be naturally comfortable. Without further communication, allow yourself to let go of your normal breath rhythm and begin to breathe as the other person breathes. As you notice the other's abdomen rising, inhale. As you notice the abdomen falling, exhale.

Completely let go of your breath and take on their respiration rate. Breathe their breath in your body.

It is important that once you tune in to another's breath, you do not "lock in" but keep the eyes steadily focused on the rising and falling abdomen of the person lying on the floor so that you can be attuned to even the subtle changes within their respiration, as different states of mind and different feelings come and go. Even if a state of great peace comes over you, do not close your eyes and disconnect from your partner. Let your attention be very closely attuned to even the subtlest changes in the rising and falling of your partner's abdomen so that your breath too can accommodate these changes.

Taking a few breaths, perhaps eight or ten, begin to breathe their breath in your own body. As you both exhale, allow yourself to make the sound AHHHH with each exhalation. AHHHH is the great sound of letting go. With each exhalation, allow this sound to drop deeper and deeper into your body until your belly breathes the AHHHH of their exhalation. It is important that the other person is able to hear your AHHHH, that it is audible and clear. Don't float off into some inaudible whispered AHHHH, which may be pleasant to you but breaks connection with your partner.

Each mutual in-breath taken silently. As your partner lying before you exhales silently, from your belly, past the heart, out of the mouth comes this great sound of letting go, the deep AHHHH of release to be heard by them as if it were their own. The person lying down need not make the AHHHH sound.

As with all these meditations, it is important to make them your own—any type of experimentation is valid. But for the first half dozen times, you do it with someone, allow your partner to maintain silence and encourage the deepest AHHHH, the deepest letting go of that profound sound within.

Maintain this breath connection, breathing your partner's breath in your body, making AHHHH on the exhale, for as long as it is comfortable. In the course of this practice, any number of states of mind may arise. Some feel a peace beyond understanding. Others moving toward this peace notice fears of intimacy, sexual energy, doubt, arising and dissolving momentarily in the breath. Just stay gently with it. But let the person lying down know that he or she is in control, and anytime your partner wishes to stop the exercise, they need only silently raise a hand and you will stop. No force here, just an allowing of the miracle of the heart to present itself as it will, and demonstrate how profoundly we share being.

This deceptively simple practice has been found to be of exceptional use to many. In hospitals we are familiar with numerous nurses and physicians who use this practice with those who are in considerable anxiety or tension. For those unable to sleep in a hospital environment, many may discover that halfway through the meditation their partner is snoring comfortably. Let it be. Don't force conclusions. Allow the meditation to be the teacher. Any preconceptions are just to be seen as another thought, another bubble floating through the overlapping vastness of a shared reality. Some speak of not being able to tell whose feeling it was that arose at any point along the process of this practice. Conversation after the exercise about what was happening during different stages often allows the connection to deepen that much further. This is an aspect of its potential to deepen relationship.

We know of many who have worked with seriously ill patients and used this exercise to help them release some of the fear in their body and mind. It even seems to work for patients in a coma. Indeed, a sign of completion noticed with several patients at the moment of their death was the deepening of the AHHHH as their breath became thinner and thinner, until at last the soft AHHHH left the body and took life with it. Many have discovered the extraordinary possibilities as another dies to share that person's death in the deep AHHH of a profound letting go, which accompanies them to the threshold and allows them to go gently beyond. It is an exercise that has many applications that each will discover for oneself as the practice deepens.

Breathing another person's breath in your body, you are paying more intimate attention to that person than perhaps ever before. We hardly listen to every syllable another speaks, much less tune in to the microscopic level of each in-breath and the space between, to each out-breath and the resulting stillness. In this deep attention we discover that one does not need to sit twenty years in a cave to get a glimpse of one's deeper nature. Many who have never before even considered meditation, after sharing this exercise, discover for themselves at three A.M., alone and unable to sleep, with restlessness or pain, that they can watch their own breath and release so much in the great AHHHH of their letting go. They discover a peace never considered possible. Indeed, this is a way of teaching a form of meditation, a deep watching of the breath, a profound release of holding that necessitates no dogma or philosophy. The truth is within the truth of it. Whatever is experienced is to be experienced fully.

CHAPTER 6

A Resistant Strain

Some years ago, during a long meditation retreat, watching thought arising and dissolving in awareness, I met myself like an ominous stranger in a dark alley. Sitting quietly one afternoon, watching feeling and thought, sensation and vision, dissolving one into the next in the unfolding process, the mind turned to itself to comment on how well it imagined it was doing. The thought passed through that I was "at last above it all," when a wave of pride swept its subtle nausea through the mind/body. Suddenly a single thought presented itself. It was the image of my six-year-old daughter lying face down in a swimming pool, drowned. Then arose the vision of my three-year-old son, his head about to be crushed beneath the massive wheel of a giant piece of earth-moving machinery. The previous moment's peace dissolving, fear arising as awareness entered the realms of mind that Hieronymous Bosch so faithfully recorded and Franz Kafka so nervously acknowledged.

The more I insisted it go away, the more painful the imagery became. My body began to burn and locked down tight. My chest turned to stone. Instantly I had gone from imagining myself above it all to a feeling of helplessness more intense than I had ever known. A primal terror I had never touched filled my body and mind; perspiration began to soak through my clothes. The imagery intensified.

Knowing there was nothing I could do about mind's content but stay with it, I attempted to sit with the moment-to-moment process. Although there were moments of seeing the thoughts as just more passing show, these moments of clarity were few and far between. The clarity was constantly being overwhelmed by a deeply conditioned resistance, a powerfully imprinted desire to protect, to change, to make things right. Indeed, toward the second hour of trying to stay with this imagery, I had to get up every ten or fifteen minutes to urinate—the visions were literally "scaring the piss out of me."

Sitting with the intensity of the negative attachment, the fear and loathing of this image, I began to see how clearly my pushing it away was causing it to continue. All the previous sense of spaciousness was lost in the density of my resistance. Awareness imploded in identification with these frightening thoughts. Toward the end of the third hour, my clothes drenched with sweat, it began to come clear that there was nothing I could do but let the pain in, to enter as fully as possible into the very center of it. The words of Rumi, the great Sufi poet, echoed in my mind, "For the person who loves God their water is fire!"

Just to stay with this for a millisecond at a time was the hardest work I had ever done—just an in breath, just the space between, just the slow release of breath breathing itself in the body. Clearly it was my pushing against that was pushing back. My resistance was my agony. The mind's contraction in fearful loathing of the contents of these thoughts was the cause of my suffering. I could not see past my fear and resistance, and it became clear that if I had any goal whatsoever, even to make these thoughts go away, that it would just create more suffering. I had to let these thoughts be and focus on the resistance itself. To find peace, I had to let go of any idea of peace, and particularly of myself as being some accomplished meditator, and enter fully the resistance that obstructed deeper healing.

Staying with the investigation of this pain and resistance—the tension in the body, the fever in the mind—just taking a breath at a time, there began to arise a little space around these images. Slowly there began to float in a choiceless awareness. As I allowed the resistance to just be there as an object of investigation, the pain began to melt in the mind, the fever broke. The resistance began to dissolve. And at last awareness had direct access to the images themselves, no longer hindered by an unexplored fearfulness and sense of helplessness within. Slowly I was able to let go of the grasping, the unwillingness and to just be in this pain.

I discovered a new tenderness, an open-hearted acceptance gravitating toward the pain in my body. I began to send love into the very images of my children dying, holding to nothing, neither fear, nor duty, nor confusion, nor grief. I let myself die into the love that so naturally approached my pain. I was learning that to let go meant simply to let be, directing a loving acceptance into the very heart of confusion.

Staying as close to the center of the holding as possible, with as much awareness as I could muster, there arose the vision of a face in whose eyes shown a light of profound compassion and mercy. It was the same light that shines in the eyes of newborn children and the most compassionate of saints. The vision, speaking in the heart's voice, told me to "keep soft eyes," to see as God sees, to see with the heart. To look on the ferocious clinging of the old mind, these frightening images, with a divine mercy and a deep human aware- ness. And though the images slowly continued, observing through soft eyes, I could see that pain did not limit love, that indeed mercy and compassion were invoked by such a nonresistant seeing of discomfort. Each object of the mind and body that we see with soft eyes is blessed. To look on the world, to look on our pains, with the eyes of loving kindness make room in our heart for our healing.

Though a bit chilled by my sweat-drenched clothing, my body began to soften once again into the spaciousness of the process, the images melting in gentle awareness. The heaviness in the mind/ body, the identification with resistance and fear, dissolved slowly into a shimmering field of light, the images flickering and igniting like a shower of sparks, illuminating the emptiness. The grasping released. The essential stillness reasserted itself. Beyond the cramped grasping of these hindrances, a sense of just being re- turned and everything including even momentary images of fear, floated softly in the vast spaciousness of the unheld mind, the open heart.

This was the first time I had experienced the power of love to dissolve pain and restore balance to the mind/body. Some days later in that retreat a sore throat developed into a strep infection. Remembering the earlier lesson, I concentrated on the sensations in my throat and sent gentle awareness into the very center of the moment-to-moment discomfort in the inflamed tissue. Within twenty minutes it felt better. Three hours later, my throat was completely healed without the least uncomfortable sensation.

I realized afterward it was one of the first times I had accepted illness lovingly enough to relate directly to it. It was perhaps the first time I had ever allowed illness to be just as it was instead of arguing with it, instead of opposing it. By softly exploring and letting go of the resistance which tightly encompasses discomforts in the mind/body, the next level is uncovered and our pain becomes yet more accessible to healing.

Over the years it has become evident how simple and natural a truth is inherent in the process of sending love and awareness into a place of mental or physical discomfort. Indeed, when injured, our hand naturally moves to touch the wound or bruise, an unconscious act which reflects the deep conscious attempt to activate healing and the relief of pain by touching with softness an area hardened in the mind or body.

This deep knowing of the body is conceptualized in the Gate Theory of pain. The observation that soft touch in an area of hard injury can confuse the pain's signal through the "neural gate," a phenomenon by which lesser sensations are able to displace the more intense by gently occupying the same message pathway to the pain receptors in the brain. This instinctual response to touch that which is in discomfort with a gentler sensation gives some indication of the fundamental healing quality of mercy and awareness.

Trusting the deeper intuition that lies just beyond mind's old conditioning to escape, we discover how entering mercifully into an area of discomfort can relieve distress. To relate to discomfort with a merciful awareness is to see with soft eyes. To see with soft eyes is to receive life with a nonjudgmental kindness and openness that makes room in the healing heart for even our most assiduous holdings. To see the mind with soft eyes is to practice forgiveness. To see the body with this same softness is to experience sympathetic joy. In soft eyes are reflected a world of peace and healing.

CHAPTER 7

Love Is the Bridge

As one teacher said, "The mind creates the abyss and the heart crosses it." Love is the bridge. It is the whisper of underlying suchness. To enter this reality, we let go of the thoughts and feelings that filter mercy and forgiveness, the resistance, the fearful doubts that seduce awareness into identification with the unhealed. We let the mind float in the heart.

To cross from the banks of "my pain" to the shores of "the pain," we must cross the river of forgetfulness, constantly remembering our true nature and the healing that ever awaits our clear entrance into the moment. The fare is love and a constant remembering, letting go of our suffering, lightening our load. Like a ship that has to jettison its heavy cargo in order to weather rough waters, we begin to cut the fetters of our attachments with mercy and awareness, to let go of all that hinders our progress.

Midway on the bridge, we meet the toll collectors in the guise of Buddha, in the guise of the Holy Mother, disguised as death, disguised as new birth, and we are asked to lay down our suffering on the collective plate and pass on such encouragement to the next in line.

When the mind is clear, we can see all the way to the heart. Recognizing how all that seems so solid—thought, feeling, the body itself—is actually in constant change, we watch the process like a complete beginner—as resistance melts and less obstructs our clear passage inward, we go beyond our suffering, crossing the chasm between the unhealed and the ever uninjured. Love is the last element of form which takes us to the formless, a quality of the mind which reflects the nature of the heart and is the essential connection between the two. When love fills the mind, it opens into the heart. It is a key to reopen the connection whose experience is a sense of fulfillment and wholeness. When a merciful awareness is sent into mental or physical discomfort, the context changes. Acceptance receives the moment like water, yielding, absorbing.

When we speak of meeting the unhealed with love instead of hatred, we cannot slip over the word "love" without some deeper examination of what is meant. Love is the natural condition of our being revealed when all else is relinquished, the shimmering awareness which receives all things with an equal openness and regard. All which is identified with as self, as mind alone, as special or separate, remains unhealed, removed from the process of being and isolated to the treadmill of becoming, more self, more suffering. Love breaks this isolation. Love brings the unhealed back into the flow in which it may dissolve, received in the depths of the healing heart.

When we speak of love, we are not speaking of the emotion called love, that ever-varying relationship of the denseness of the mind to the openness of the heart, an attitude greatly dependent on external circumstances. It is not the relationship of "I" for "other." It is the sense of the inherent connection between the two that goes beyond duality to the oneness of being. When we speak of love, we are not speaking simply of a state of mind but rather of a state of our underlying suchness. Love is not what we become but who we already are.

Many use the word "love" to define their relationship with another, the incessant trading off of favors and attention in hopes of like reward for our efforts. The emotional fragility which is only offered when it feels safe. A timid connectedness interlaced with distrust and self-interest. But ironically, and perfectly, though emotional love seems to set the stage for unfinished business, the essential love to which we refer, that experience of pure being, heals the chasm of the personal and separate. It is the love that goes beyond "love," beyond conditions, which finishes our business. For to finish our business means an end of relationships as business; it is not a totaling of accounts, not a trade-off of you "understanding me" and me "acknowledging you," but instead a letting go of that other person as separate and touching him or her with forgiveness and mercy. No longer involved in the commerce of relationships so much as committed to the process of relating. To finish business with others allows us to come to completion with ourselves, the first step and the last on the path of healing.

Love is our true nature, our birthright. To go beyond conditions and conditioning is to experience our pure, uncramped, undistorted awareness. Pure mind and pure heart are one. Undifferentiated being, the ever-connected, the deathless.

All we see is ourselves. As Krishnamurti put it, "The observed is the observer." We see only via what and how we have seen before. Even perception itself is conditioned. All thought is old, inventive at best, rarely creative. To see clearly with a healing awareness, we need to see beyond the filters and schematics of old mind, past the conditioned. We need to see anew with a profound and unlimited receptivity.

It is here that we discover the true nature of unconditional love, the love that goes beyond the mind, the love that is underlying being. It is not the personal love of "I love you," but the impersonal, though ever-connected, universal state of being which is love itself. It is a condition not between beings but within being. When I am in that place of love and you enter, then we are in love together. Then I am in love with you—I don't have love *for* you, I have love *with* you. It is the healing that transcends the individual separate suffering to merge with the universal process of unobstructed space received as the unity of being, as love itself.

Actually I am a little hesitant to use such phrases as "unconditional love" because we have already become so conditioned by the words. I have seen this concept create much confusion and suffering. In fact the phrase "unconditional love" is somewhere between a conflict of terms and a redundancy. The unconditioned *is* love. What one calls unconditional love another may refer to as cosmic consciousness or another as just pure awareness. But when I hear someone say, "I have unconditional love for that being," I sense their confusion and misunderstanding. One does not have unconditional love for another. One is unconditional love. And when one is in that place of love, one is "in love with" all that comes close. It is not sent from self to other but is the whole of which each is a part.

Unconditional love is who we are when all else is released in trust.

One does not become unconditionally loving but rather discovers at the very foundation of being the unconditioned vastness of being which embraces all with appreciation and loving kindness. Emotional love may give a varying sense of connection, but the essential love of being results in communing, a wordless sense of unity.

For too many the idea of unconditional love has kept them in their mind, in old conditioning instead of allowing them to sink freely into their heart.

Like truth, unconditional love is not something one can hold to but only something one can be in the unheld luminescence of the moment. If one uses the idea of unconditional love as a relative point of judgment, then one will forever be lost in the mind, the separate.

It is unfortunate that we have only one word, "love," to describe both the vagaries of the emotional life of the mind as well as the ever-unchanging nature of our true being. It is no wonder that so much confusion has arisen. Our personal love is there one moment and absent the next, available then obscured with the ever-changing seasons of the heart. Once again let me say that love here is not meant simply as a condition of the mind. Rather, love is a state of our being revealed when we have gone beyond the mind, beyond the conditioned to the unadulterated experience of our essential nature, beyond addiction to likes and dislikes, beyond our clinging to pleasure and pain. "Unconditional love" can be a confusing concept which for many feeds the "not-enoughness" of the mind, the self-judgment and heartlessness with which we meet so much of our life.

But of course sometimes we are closed-hearted. Indeed, many feel a bit melancholy investigating love to find themselves so often conditional and partial in their loving. Many judge themselves for not being loving enough.

But when we look on our lives and the world with a little keener awareness and deeper compassion, we see that amidst the suffering and confusion, the conflicts and attempts at escape, even a millisecond of love is a miracle. It is quite amazing that we can be loving at all. Each moment of love is indeed remarkable and great grace, considering the conditions through which it arises. We should praise ourselves greatly for each moment of such openness rather than denigrating ourselves for those moments when our heart is not open.

In fact to open our heart fully, we need to include even the times when our heart is not open. We need to accept nonacceptance so as to investigate its nature. This healing into the heart is a process of mercifully acknowledging our opening as well as our closing. Touching with forgiveness even those parts of ourselves which are unforgiving. Indeed, the more open one's heart becomes, the more pronounced will be the experience of its closing. Thus each moment of closedness seems so much more dense than ever before because each increased openness has greatened the distance it must travel to close in the natural tides of our growth. I have never met anyone whose heart was open all the time, but I know many who recognize that although at times the mind may not be clear compassion is always the appropriate response. To have mercy on our merciless-ness. To leave nothing unhealed.

So let us not use love as an idea of who we should be, another excuse to put ourselves out of our hearts, but instead as an opening to what we might really be when we have healed to the core of our being. It is a trust, a deep confidence in who we really are.

When Buddha first began roaming the countryside sharing the insights which had arisen in the course of his profound letting go of all which blocked his original nature, he is recorded as saying that one of the greatest teachings he received was not simply how we may become free, but that freedom is possible. If one learns nothing else other than to trust that completion, healing, enlightenment are possible, one will have a confidence in life that will encourage deeper participation and investigation. Buddha's great lesson was that liberation from suffering could be found in any moment.

Indeed, the answer to Robin's original question of whether to live or die is not to be found in death but in life. As Kabir said, "What is found now is found then." The question really seems to be: How can we use all that is given as a means of healing, including our fear, our doubt, our cancer, our inevitable death? It is unfortunate that many beings do not ask this question until they have found they have cancer or AIDS or some life-threatening disease, and for the first time "healing" becomes an object of awareness. Healing can't be something we call on only when we are ill. Healing becomes a way of life.

In taking the path of healing that leads to the heart, previous conflicts are seen as a rich and fertile ground for insight into that which causes suffering and that which allows us to go beyond suffering. Our investigation of the mind, of those qualities that block the heart, becomes a deeper deconditioning of old holding, a demagnetizing of our incessant and mechanical identification with all that passes through the mind/body. In watching the mind, we see who we aren't and enter the new territory of the heart. For it is in the heart that, with a deep sigh, conflict comes to peace and the illnesses and pains of a lifetime may be dispersed in the soft receptiveness of unlimited being.

Crossing the bridge, having gone beyond the blockages and armoring, the self-hatred and judgment which have for so long delayed our final healing, we sink into the heart, and the question of "life or death?" disappears. All is experienced as life, including death. All such dualities are seen as just overdefined points in a spiraling process.

Someone once asked, "What is the toll for crossing this bridge?" The toll for crossing to the other shore of wholeness is the relinquishment of our suffering. This crossing over is what is called healing; it costs each of us identification with "my pain." It may even mean that our lives will never be the same.

INTRODUCTION TO
GUIDED MEDITATION ON SHARED HEART

There is a quote in the Sufi tradition which says: "Overcome any bitterness that may have come because you were not up to the magnitude of the pain that was entrusted to you. Like the mother of the world who carries the pain of the world in her heart, each of us is part of her heart and is, therefore, endowed with a certain measure of cosmic pain. You are sharing in the totality of that pain. You are called upon to meet it in joy instead of self-pity.

"The secret: offer your heart as a vehicle to transform cosmic suffering into joy."

Discomfort uncovers deep holdings within—fear, doubt, long-unnoticed desires for control, defining the unsatisfactory in our lives. So the investigation, the participation in illness in the heart, allows the body and mind freedom to heal.

For many it was skillful to expand the mercy and heartfulness with which they touched their dis-ease. Many, drawn to healing by the resistant cries of the body, soon discover the discomforts of mind which isolate their pain. For many it was by working with illness in the body that they recognized the intense separatism and isolation of some aspects of the mind. Focusing on the separate, we discover the universal in our pain, both mental and physical.

Using the discomforts in our mind/body as a means of sensing the nature of our predicament, the thousands of bodies which share this same experience in this same moment, we tune to the shared moment. Participating wholeheartedly in our discomforts we sense the universality of our predicament. And discover that we are not alone. That we are part of a giant wave of human experience crossing the ocean of humanity.

Many found this meditation skillful to unlock their isolated identification with their pain. As one steps onto the path of healing, one begins by allowing the heart to mercifully receive the ancient fears and holdings of a lifetime. Recognizing that we are all doing the work that we took birth for, the path of healing becomes the path of life.

A MEDITATION ON GREAT HEART
THE SHARED EXPERIENCE OF ILLNESS AND HEALING

[To be read slowly to a friend or silently to oneself.]

Make yourself comfortable.

Sit or lie quietly as need be.

Let your attention settle into the body.

Just feel what sits here. Feel the body you inhabit.

Receive the body of sensation in a clear, gentle awareness.

Notice how sensations vary in type and intensity from one area to another. Some sensations are pleasant. Some sensations are unpleasant.

Let the awareness settle into the level of sensations that inhabit the body.

Notice any sense of self, of "me" or "mine," imposed around discomfort. The tension, the holding to "my suffering."

There is nothing to judge. Simply notice whatever tension or fear may hold discomfort in the body.

Does the body attempt to shut off discomfort?

Does the body close like a fist around pain?

Does anything seem to "hold on" to the discomfort?

Notice any tendency to pull the pleasant forward or push the unpleasant away.

Watch the natural aversion to the unpleasant. Focus on the resistance itself.

Examine the texture, the density, the nature, of the wall of resistance that obstructs the heart from sinking into the mind and body.

As awareness begins to meet discomfort, let the body soften, allow sensations to float. Allow the fist to open, to expose the tender sensations arising from moment to moment. Allow awareness to receive the moment-to-moment sensations arising in the body of discomfort.

Feel this body. Let awareness explore the varying sensations that compose the body.

Imagine all the other bodies elsewhere in the world experiencing this same discomfort. Not taking on their pain but healing it with your soft mercy. Sense the body of discomfort shared by so many.

Sense the ten thousand bodies experiencing this same sensation in this same moment.

Sense this discomfort not as "my pain" but as "the pain." Gently feel "the pain" in "the body."

Sense the thousands of children, women and men who, in this very moment, feel this same discomfort in this same body.

Softly allow the pain to float in the body we all share.

Letting go of the holding around pain, softening gently to allow sensation to float in the shared body, begin to gradually cradle the pain.

Take your time. There is no rush now in meeting softly that which has so often been met with hardness.

Sense the moment of the woman lying on her side in a mud hut, alone, this same pain touching this same body.

Touch the discomfort of the man, unable to rise from his sleepless bed, with a merciful awareness.

Picture the body of the child containing this same experience, gazing toward the fluorescent ceiling of his hospital room, wondering "Why me?!!"

Let their pain be healed by your mercy and awareness as it touches that same sensation in this same body.

Receive their experience in sweet mercy. Feel the shared body softening and expanding into the spaciousness of the shared heart.

Feel the joy of the connectedness, no one alone, the shared body met in the shared heart.

A vaster sense of being. Not alone in pain but at one with all those in discomfort. Meeting the moment in mercy and kindness. A new tenderness arising relating to its own pain, relating to all pain.

Let the mind float.

Let the images come and go.

Feel all those others sharing this moment, shared sensations floating in the shared body.

Nothing to create, just receiving this moment shared.

Experiencing all these bodies in our one heart in our common mercy. Let the images come. Let them be gently experienced. Let them go. Constantly sharing the healing. Touching with mercy our pain so as to free the pain of the world.

Gently receive this body as all bodies.

Allowing this comfort to float in soft flesh, in open mind, in spacious heart, healing the world by touching this moment with mercy and awareness.

Feel the single experience of the shared heart.

All one now.

Just sensation floating free in the body.

Let awareness meet all the bodies healing into the immensity of the Great Heart.

Let your heart merge with all that share the greater body.

Softening all about sensations to let them float in the shared body. To heal this moment with mercy and loving kindness.

Feel it. Let it be.

Feel it. Let it go.

Take each breath into the body we all share.

Feel this breath breathing in the greater body.

Let the breath come.

Let the breath go.

In soft body.

In shared body.

In the vast heart that merges with all.

In this moment meeting our pain in our heart, the heart opens into universal healing.

Touching with mercy and loving kindness the pain we all share, we receive the healing we each took birth for.

CHAPTER 8

Taking Heart

In ancient Chinese calligraphy, the symbol for mind and the symbol for heart are the same: hsin. For when the mind is unclouded only heart is experienced, just as when heart is exposed there are no obstacles in mind. The heart and mind only seem separate to the mind. To the heart all things are one thing.

Many, as they approach the heart, speak of the release of considerable emotion and feeling—of sadness, anger, grief, fear, and doubt. Some think of these emotions as the qualities of the heart. But actually they are the densities of mind that form the armoring through which awareness must pass to enter the spaciousness of the heart. This armoring is composed of suppressed emotions, the unfinished business of the mind. The discarded, the undealt with, the unhealed. They are feelings, states of mind, compressed over years of posturing and avoidance.

Each emotion, each state of mind, just as it displays a corresponding bodily pattern, also has a concurrent mental script. There are attending thoughts and associated images which express its inner nature. Such thoughts are in words and images, and their form is not difficult to apprehend. But the emotions and feelings which gave them their momentum are less easily noticed upon first arising. Most often we are lost in the thoughts before we can enter into the emotion itself. But in our constant remembering to be present and investigate, we begin to honor our emotions in a whole new way. No longer are they feared or hammered into some fragmented image of our imagined self, but instead they are approached directly, touched, tasted, explored.

Emotions are the variously colored lenses through which we perceive thought and reality.

For instance, the thought "rose" seen through the emotion, the lens, of joy, is: "Ahhh, a rose!" It is fragrance, it is color, it is texture. But that same thought, "rose," seen through the lens of anger is: "Damn it! A rose!" It is thorns, it is threat, it is anger itself.

Examining closely the lens, the reality just beyond is no longer distorted.

These qualities of mind that many have mistaken for qualities of the heart are explored as we pass through our armoring on the way into peace. The heart does not become lost in the separate. It sees anger but is not angry. It is ever merciful and forever loving. It is the underlying essence of mind when the separate has fallen away and only pure awareness which is pure love is experienced. It is boundaryless space, beyond definition, one's true nature, the ever uninjured and always whole.

Opening the heart to injury or illness means allowing it to be there in love. The usual colored lenses of fear, trepidation, and loathing which distort our reception of illness mindfully noted, met with the lighthearted familiarity of, "Big Surprise, fear again, anger again." The ancient reactiveness of old mind floating in a new wonderment at the possibility of freedom. One learns in time to focus a heartfelt awareness on the distorting factors.

As we develop the qualities of merciful investigation, we experience a healing connectedness with the imbalances of the mind and body. Having opened to sensations as they arise—softening, focusing, exploring—one enters the mind/body in the very instant in which life is received, in "just this much."

Not waiting for illness to overwhelm us, for the weight of old identifications to herniate us, we can employ our little pains, our everyday frustrations, our common fears, to practice healing. We use the transitory cough, the passing headache, the occasional bruise as a focus of the heart to expand the passageway within. We open to our everyday little deaths to make room for the inevitable approach of our greater deaths. In midlife, opening to the everyday aches and pains of aging does not result in our rising one morning surprised by old age. It allows more and more of our life to be lived in our heart instead of insisted upon in the body. It becomes our most interesting daily occupation.

But before we can offer such care to ourselves or anyone else, we must first explore the dictum, "Physician heal thyself!" Although we are not "healed physicians," it is the path of healing that makes life so rich and allows room for whatever holdings and fears yet remain. The preciousness of the path beneath our feet is so distinct that one hardly wishes to be elsewhere. And even these wishes, which once hardened into our greatest pains and difficulties, are met by a new softness, a willingness to be with what is, an openness to healing.

In sending love to ourselves, we send love to all. In sending healing we are healed. In letting go of that which blocks the heart, the confusions and old encrustations of the mind, we open into the heart of the world. As the sensations and thoughts and feelings that often surround illness become yet more audible, something within begins to melt in mercy for the pain we cause ourselves and the ways in which we have held so assiduously to our suffering. As the armoring melts, we experience our vastness, and the heart expands to fill the whole body with a sense of balance and wellness.

At this level of openness we begin to see the sense in what we had always resisted as "the senselessness of it all." Then love naturally gravitates toward the areas of numbness and deadness in the body, or their equal and opposite, pain and anxiety. The healing is drawn as if by osmosis to the areas where it is most needed. In the dynamics of the healer love moves from an area of greater concentration in one heart to a place of lesser concentration in another. Then it is not "healer" and "healed." There is no separation or sense of duality, but only the sense of the oneness present in all its manifestations of seeming differentiation. Letting the heart act as healer, it receives whole body, whole mind, as aspects of itself. Just as the sky is inseparable from the clouds which float through it, the blueness of sky is never so noticeable as at the edge of a dense cloud.

The cost of crossing the river of forgetfulness, moving from the unhealed to the ever healed, is "just this much." In the worlds of healing, the coin of the realm is a merciful awareness focused in this very instant of life's unfolding. "Just this much" is the millisecond in which the truth is to be found. It means opening to our whole life. It is the very moment in which existence presents itself and is received.

It is in "just this much" that our healing accumulates. All the work that is to be done is done in "just this much."

A fellow who approached us with fourth-stage terminal cancer some years ago, after hearing us speak at length about one of our most respected teachers, the venerable Buddhist meditation master Aachan Cha, resonated very strongly with his teaching of "just this much." After the lecture he took me aside to ask more about Aachan Cha's teachings and then said, "If life is just this much, then death is just this much too, yes?" His eyes filled with tears as his obviously weakened body shook with deep release. He almost swooned into my arms, saying, "I am dying, I need help." It was the beginning of a long interchange shared through levels and levels of healing.

Meeting with Bob the next day, he shared his feelings that death had always seemed so huge as to be unworkable, but that when he had heard the teaching of "just this much," he sensed the possibilities inherent in his predicament, the workability of even death. "I have always thought of death as an impenetrable wall, but now I sense that I might be able to relate to it brick by brick."

Beginning as always by exploring unfinished business, Bob began to recognize the long-held grief and sadness which had for so long accumulated around his heart and so often blocked entrance into any sense of acceptance or mercy for his predicament. So he began working with the grief meditation. Focusing his attention at the center of the chest, using his thumb to press into the grief point there on the sternum, between the nipples, just above the heart, receiving from moment to moment whatever moods, feelings, or thoughts that arose there in soft awareness. The pain of his resistance to life was never so noticeable as when he opened to his grief. Pushing the thumb with gradually increasing pressure into the center of the chest, into that mind/body sensitivity point which has correlations in so many healing systems, he experienced the resistances of a lifetime pushing back, denying entrance past the mind. Knowing there was nowhere to go but in, he began to draw each breath into the aching at the center of his chest. As level after level of holding was revealed, each previous moment of denial opened to "just this much." Rising daily to wash and have a cup of tea, he then retired to his room to sit for nearly an hour exploring the pain accumulated over a lifetime of disappointment and loss.

Over the weeks, as he allowed his feelings to arise and dissolve, he noticed more room in his heart for his sadness, for his pain, for his healing, and discovered that the grief point when opened becomes the touch point of the heart. Remembering throughout the day to breathe in and out of the grief point, he continued to expand the passageway into the heart.

No longer thinking his life but entering it directly, he discovered that in "just this much" nothing was left incomplete or unfinished. Discovering the power of forgiveness to soften the hard edges of previous loss, his work with the grief meditation lessened as the forgiveness meditation continued to quiet the mind and open the touch point of the heart. As he let go of the holdings of the past, the grief, and old resentments, he noticed a considerable softening in the body. Having cut through the resistances of anger and grief, a soft-bellied acceptance began to let the healing in. His pain diminished as resistance was resolved. His voice softened. Employing the letting-go meditation, he entered yet deeper into a sense of heartfulness. Directly participating in life—listening so deeply, seeing so clearly, tasting so appreciatively, speaking so directly, thinking so mindfully, acting so openheartedly. Entering the flow, he began deeply to trust the process of which his mind/body were so clearly a part. His healing was unmistakable.

About two months into our work together, just as he was coming to that place of feeling the extra wellness of being "more alive than ever," his physical condition took a turn for the worse. Awakening one morning to find himself aphasiac, his speech scrambled by an unsuspected brain tumor which had spread from the original site of his cancer, he was confused and dismayed, calling daily, explaining in painfully slow communication the feeling that he had somehow "lost it." We reminded him again and again to trust "just this much." It was a difficult time which caused him to return to his original grief meditations to allow release of some of the disappointment and expectation which were agitating his mind. Pushing into the grief point, his heart drew forgiveness within, and he slowly began to soften into his new condition. Gradually, instead of groaning at a mispronounced or scrambled word, he would often laugh and even use the same word playfully in another sentence as when he said, "I think this tumor in my pain is getting the best of me. Oh no, I don't mean pain, I mean brain, this brain tumor. On the other hand I never have thought too well with my pain. Or brain or whatever it is." But sometimes it was all a bit too much for him and he would lament that he couldn't "get into any of the meditations," at which time we would remind him to just breathe in and out of the heart. At other times, less overwhelmed by identification with his illness, he worked with the heavy-emotional-states meditation and was able to focus directly on the disappointment, to explore "just this much" at a time and begin to see beyond depression to the spaciousness in which it was floating. It took a lot of long hard work, but as he came through his weeks of "feeling kind of low," he displayed a new strength and groundedness. And though the aphasia would now and again present itself, each time it arose he seemed to be able to meet it that much more appreciatively in the heart instead of resistantly in the mind. Indeed, when a colleague came to visit and asked him what he was up to nowadays, he answered, "Just this much." He said his life was too big to encompass, but he had all the room in the world for his living.

Continuing to explore the mind, to investigate the nature of perception itself, to examine who it is indeed that even dies, he sometimes for long periods went beyond the separate mind of his fears and the separate body of his cancers to the shared heart of healing. He was crossing the river of forgetfulness with a constant remembering and mindfulness. In mid-river, death approached, but all the work of the past months held him in good stead, and, trusting so much in the process, he took the leap of faith, which carried him across to the shores of spacious peace.

His healing was no less than any of those we have seen who survive in the body. Though his cancer did not desist, his heart became as light as "the feather of truth." Indeed, the ancient Egyptians believed that after death the heart was placed on the scales of truth to be balanced against a feather to conclude if the life just passed was lived in healing or forgetfulness.

On the day he died, many had gathered by his bedside to wish him well, and he seemed to have time for everyone, his soft smile greeting each person like a gentle blessing. And when his wife asked what kind of frosting he would like on a cake she was baking, he said,

"Anything will do but no birthday candles. I have no breath left." He died within the hour. His death was "just this much."

As Bob cleared the heart, he recognized the mind as process. His predominant experience in those clearest moments of observing the constantly changing nature of each thought and feeling was of its essential impermanence. In opening to the ever-changing flow of impermanence, the imagined solidity of the self-image, which had gone half blind by attempting not to see for so long, was met by a healing mercy and awareness. Seeing this ongoing flow of impermanence, he saw beyond the apparent to directly participate in the unchanging nature of his underlying being. He approached directly the pain we all share and went beyond to the completion we are all capable of. Impermanence was no longer the enemy of his body, the frustrator of desires, but was instead part of a process which bred confidence. Entering each moment completely the next moment took care of itself. His trust in the process, in the continuum, in life itself, deepening with each healing moment. Entering deeply into the process, he saw that death too was impermanent. That life simply *was*—and continued.

There are many means by which we tap the resources of the heart and enter into the spaciousness of being. But all the work one does to cultivate feelings of loving kindness through exploration and service and meditation is ironically still "what to do until the doctor comes." Though our underlying nature is pure awareness, pure love, until the heart fully exhibits its true nature, it is skillful to cultivate such feelings as loving kindness in the meantime. Paradoxically, the cultivation of loving kindness through meditation and daily practice is almost like using a water drill in order to hit the water table below, the enormous rivers of compassion and mercy which lie just beneath the surface of our ever active mind. In an odd way the necessary cultivation of such qualities as loving kindness and sympathetic joy is almost a mimicry of our essential nature. The little love grows greater; the little fears disintegrate.

As we enter into the heart of the matter, the mind/body sinks into loving awareness. As the mind sinks into the heart, so the heart is allowed to enter into all matter. And we discover the heart connected with the disheartened. In this connection of the heart with the injured, a new harmonic arises, a deeper sense of being. With this connection a conduit is established between the heart and the sensations of the body through which waves and waves of loving kindness may be sent into an area of pain or illness. It is in this communion with illness that some have spoken of melting their cancer with love, and others have melted out of their body in profound peace.

Having entered directly into the sensations and thoughts and feelings of the mind/body one may breathe mercy and compassion into illness just this much through the opening to the heart. One may breathe the discomfort of illness into the heart point as a means of purifying and releasing the long held. Illness, floating in the luminescence of being, breathing love directly into the sensations surrounding illness in the body, drawing loving kindness in with each breath, breathing love directly into dis-ease.

By sending love with each breath into the once-abandoned area of discomfort, one's whole life heals within them. Caressing the area with care and mercy, with forgiveness and love, a powerful purification opens and softens that area. The body floods with warmth and light, sensations arising and dissolving in boundaryless awareness. The Great Peace arrives, sitting light as a hummingbird, probing the heart of a newly opened blossom. Then one may experience that there is no longer a need to send love into the area but that whenever awareness is brought into the space of discomfort, love is received. By focusing on injury or illness with a deeper connectedness to something essential, something very close to unconditional love is found right there in the center of discomfort. This experience has been likened to finding a luxurious oasis in the midst of a parched and undernourished wasteland. Many have said that their wanderings in the wilderness of the mind and body germinated a whole new ecology of life. Begun as an impoverished pilgrimage into the unexplored, it quickly became the most fruitful experience of their lives: One patient spoke of this transformative process as leading from "a great dryness of the heart to a deep moistness of the spirit." She said it was like watching lifeless sand transformed into the richest loam, nurtured with nothing but her love and attention.

This healing comes not from "being loving" but from being itself, which is love. It is not a case of "being clear" but of clear being. This healing is not about being anything else but being itself. Nothing separate, no edges, nothing to limit healing. Entering, in moments, the realm of pure being, the gateless gate swings open—beyond life and death, our original face, shines back at us.

PLEASE CALL ME BY MY TRUE NAMES

Do not say that I'll depart tomorrow
because even today I still arrive.

Look at me: I arrive in every second
to be a bud on a spring branch,
to be a tiny bird, whose wings are still fragile,
    learning to sing in my new nest,
to be a caterpillar in the heart of a flower,
to be a jewel hiding itself in a stone.

I still arrive, in order to laugh and to cry,
    in order to fear and to hope,
the rhythm of my heart is the birth and death
    of all that are alive.

I am the mayfly metamorphosing on the surface of the river.
I am also the bird, which, when spring comes, arrives
    in time to eat the mayfly.

I am a frog swimming happily in the clear water of a pond.
I am also the grass-snake who, approaching in silence,
    feeds itself on the frog.

I am the child in Uganda, all skin and bones,
    my legs as thin as bamboo sticks.

I am also the merchant of arms, selling deadly weapons
    to Uganda.

I am the twelve-year-old girl, refugee on a small boat,
who throws herself into the ocean after being raped
by a sea pirate.

I am also the pirate, my heart not yet capable of seeing
and loving.

I am a member of the politburo, with plenty of power in
my hands.

I am also the man who has to pay his "debt of blood" to my
people, dying slowly in a forced labor camp.

My joy is like spring, so warm it makes flowers bloom in
my hands.

My pain is like a river of tears—so full it fills up all
the four oceans.

Please call me by my correct names so that I can hear at the
same time all my cries and my laughs, so that I could see
that my joy and pain are but one.

Please call me by my correct names so that I could become
awake, so that the door of my heart be left open,
the door of compassion.

Thich Nhat Hanh

CHAPTER 9

Forgiveness

The beginning of the path of healing is the end of life unlived. As awareness deepens, each moment is received anew. Entering the process as complete beginners, we take each breath as though it were the first, watching each thought as though it were the last, becoming wholly alive. Recognizing that to finish business means the end of relationships as business, not a totaling of accounts, not awaiting another's acceptance or forgiveness, we cultivate compassion. When we have touched another with forgiveness, we no longer require anything in return. Our business is done.

One of the first steps on the path of healing is the deepening of forgiveness. Indeed, after awareness has brought us to the path of healing, it is forgiveness that softens the path and allows continued progress.

As awareness becomes yet subtler, able to discern even the muffled whispers of the mind, we are confronted with what a dying musician friend called "the Unfinished Symphony"—the dreams and longings that have played themselves out unabated just beneath the surface of our worldly persona—the unfilled, the uncompleted, the oft-resented inheritance of a life only partially lived. Many, coming upon long unresolved issues and old holdings, find it difficult to simply let go. The holding around the unresolved, the unapproached has become so cramped close that it seems to take considerable effort to soften it back to its natural openness. But forgiveness acts almost as a kind of lubricant to allow the yet held to slip lightly away.

Indeed, in theory it would be ideal to just let go of heavy states such as resentment or fear or guilt. But in practice we discover that the considerable momentum of our identification with such feelings is not so easily dispersed. Before we are fully able to just be mindful of such feelings, to just let them be without the least tendency to cling or condemn, it may well be necessary to deepen the practice of forgiveness—to actualize the potential for letting go that the open-handed acceptance of forgiveness offers upon meeting the gavel-fisted judgment of the often unkind mind.

It is in passing through the holdings around the heart that the power of forgiveness becomes most evident. Forgiveness allows us to let go of the curtains of resentment, the filters to life that have kept us so lost in the mind. Forgiveness softens the clinging and allows our holdings to sink a bit more deeply into the healing heart.

Cultivating forgiveness daily softens our life. It holds the possibility of freedom from the ancient incarcerations of the judging mind. Forgiveness allows anger to float in a merciful awareness. It makes room for life. It is the nature of the unobstructed heart which dissolves separation and allows mercy and awareness to go beyond the conditioned. It is a cultivation in the mind of the spaciousness of the heart.

The traditional manner of practicing forgiveness is to first extend it to someone you have some resentment for and to touch them with the possibility of forgiveness. Secondly, you picture another who is unforgiving toward you, and you reach out with an openness to be forgiven and a willingness to let go of the unfinished business of the past which separated your two hearts. Then, lastly, forgiveness is sent to oneself. Truly we have been waiting our whole life to hear "I love you" in our own voice. One cannot deeply receive love from another until they have received it from themselves. Indeed, the Buddha said that no matter how hard one searched, one could not find anyone in the universe more deserving of love than oneself. Practicing this meditation for fifteen minutes a day seems to broaden the path of healing and allow a bit more easy going.

In working with each of these meditations, our own natural wisdom recognizes yet other levels at which we may enter our healing, using our own great genius to guide us. Though the forgiveness meditation is very powerful in the form it has most usually been practiced, we discover yet another aspect of its healing when we begin to send forgiveness directly into the center of discomfort. It is to touch with forgiveness that which we have so often touched with condemnation and profound resentment which allows the miracle of healing, of balance, to enter fully into each moment, into life itself. All such practices are adapted to our immediate needs seeing with soft eyes the next appropriate step. Relying on nothing of the past, we enter profoundly into what is needed as it is needed, the ocean of awareness dissolving our footsteps behind us, leaving no trace, but only the ground beneath our feet, this very instant in which all that we have ever sought is to be found.

So we direct forgiveness into each moment of mind/body experience. We do not lean toward or pull back from any aspect of the mind. Nothing is hindrance. We are learning to keep our heart open in hell.

So we see that cultivating forgiveness is a skillful quality to finish business, to soften the clingings of the mind, and open the holdings of the body so that a conduit can be established between the heart and the disheartened. Directing forgiveness into the body, the resistances to life dissolve, pain diminishing, healing permeating to the center of each cell.

The practice of forgiveness opens the mind to the natural compassion of the heart. Practiced daily, it allows ancient clingings to dissolve. But in the beginning forgiveness may have something of an odd quality about it. One needs first to recognize that guilt arises uninvited. It is important to use forgiveness not as a means of squashing guilt, or even upleveling the unforgivingness of another, but as a means of dissolving obstructions. At first one may feel they did nothing wrong, so why ask for or send forgiveness. But emotions are not so rational; they have a life of their own. We ask for forgiveness and offer forgiveness not because of some imagined wrongdoing but because we no longer wish to carry the load of our resentments and guilts. To allow the mind to sink into the heart. To let go and get on with it.

If at first forgiveness feels a little awkward, please remember that forgiveness is not a condoning of the unskillful act which has caused injury, but a touching of the actor with mercy and loving kindness. We cannot condone rape, but we may in time be able to touch the rapist with some understanding, lessening our own fear, opening our life a bit more. Forgiveness benefits oneself, not just another.

Although we may open our hearts to another, it is a means of letting ourself back into our own heart. Indeed, forgiveness may be felt across hundreds of miles and even acknowledged, but that is not the primary purpose of this meditation. In fact, to wait for such acknowledgement is an example of how we continue unfinished business. Forgiveness finishes business by letting go of the armoring which separates one heart from another. As one teacher said, "As long as there are two there is unfinished business. When the two become one, the heart whispers to itself in every direction."

In the deepest stages of forgiveness, one finds there is no "other" to send forgiveness toward, but just a sense of being shared. The one mind, the one heart in which we all float. Then, as in unconditional love, there is not forgiveness *for* another but forgiveness *with* another.

Many years ago, during a very difficult time in my life, sitting very alone by a pond in a redwood forest practicing the forgiveness meditation, the practicer disappeared, and all became forgiveness: the trees were forgiveness, the boulders, the pond, the salamander crawling across my sneaker. The world became an all-accepting love. And in my mind a voice whispered that I was forgiven for everything I had ever done. To which the mind responded, "Oh, but that's not possible, there has been so much." To which the heart replied, "You are completely forgiven, it is all done. If you want to pick it up again, that's up to you. But it's all yours from now on." How difficult it was to accept, to allow such an enormous forgiveness into my heart, and how healing!

Let me share with you a few examples of individuals who found the application of the forgiveness meditation a skillful means toward healing.

Chuck was a young fellow whose shoulders were slumped so far forward when we met him that his body resembled a question mark. He was bent under the strain of great resistance and guilt. "I have a brother who is kind of nuts. On a couple of occasions he has carved himself up real badly. Cut off his penis and stuff like that. Almost bled to death twice. He's been in and out of mental institutions for years. The last time he was out, he moved to where I was living, and he would call me every day and tell me about the hell he was living in. For an hour or so every day I would talk with him, but his pain was more than either of us could bear—there was nothing I could do but sit with his awful torment and be there. I was really beyond my edge. I finally got an answering machine and would listen to all his messages as they came through. Sometimes he would call eight, nine, ten times an hour, and I would be just sitting there with a bottle of Jack Daniels feeling so awfully guilty for not being able to help more, and would get drunk. I didn't know what else to do."

Having experienced the forgiveness meditation for the first time during a workshop, he sensed the possibilities of a healing. He said that toward the end of the meditation a shudder ran through him as he saw the coldheartedness with which he related to himself and others. "This load of anger at myself for being so inadequate and useless."

With minimal instruction he took on a daily forgiveness practice, "Forgiving my brother's craziness and my intolerance toward all the pain I have inside." He said that as he began to relate to his pain instead of from it, with a forgiving softness he began to recognize how the path of the spirit is such a creative one and began to trust himself and sense what was right for him. "I never trust myself like that. I have always treated myself kind of like an unwelcome stranger, so when I begin to send forgiveness to myself, it is easy to see myself as someone else in pain, and that little bit of space gives me room to forgive." As his meditations continued, his body slowly began to straighten. As the forgiveness sank deeper, he saw himself not as an "other" but as the mind suffering to be free, and he began to let go of the past. Ever so slightly his ability to bless and learn from his pain increased.

About a month into the practice, he said, "I think I will continue with this meditation for some time. It might actually allow me to come home. To step back into the living room and sit down to share supper with my agonized family."

Mary had been doing the meditation about six months when we met her. "At first it put me straight in touch with how helpless I felt about all the wrongs done to me and all the wrongs I have done to others." But she said that as she continued the practice, she was gradually able to make room for helplessness, to touch it with forgiveness, and to explore its nooks and crannies. She said that in time the state of mind of helplessness no longer made her feel helpless. That whenever that feeling of helplessness arose, her heart seemed naturally to go into a rhythm of forgiveness. "I used to be so afraid of being helpless that I felt paralyzed. But when forgiveness touched this helplessness, all the urgency went out of it." She said that she believed she would never be overcome by helplessness again because "there is always something I can do about it. I can always open to how it is right now."

Describing the slow unfolding of this practice, she said, "Sometimes this meditation works better than at others. But it always puts me in touch with the value of forgiveness. It usually shows me what blocks me. Sometimes it's so difficult to forgive someone because I have so much anger at them. I guess it's just pride. But forgiveness has taught me to let things be a little bit more, and I have to go through that anger gently and remind myself that I am doing this meditation, this forgiveness for me, not for someone else. I wouldn't be at all surprised if others benefit from my forgiveness, but primarily I do it for me and my life has been a lot easier lately."

Dorothy had been sexually abused as a child. When the meditation was first offered to her, she didn't feel quite ready for it. "I don't know if I am ready to let go of my anger." She trusted herself enough to realize that she didn't *have to* forgive anyone, but she felt the cage about her life tightening.

Watching others about her who had similarly been abused as children, working with the forgiveness meditation, letting go of levels upon levels of holding and fear, of anger and self-hatred, she began to sense the release possible in the practice.

Encouraging her to trust herself deeply, we suggested that she use the forgiveness meditation as an "experiment in truth" to discover for herself whatever use, if any, this technique might be for her particular predicament. Giving herself a kindness she had seldom known, she trusted her process sufficiently to just take a mini-step over her fear and anger into the possibilities of forgiveness. She did not jump headlong into the deep ocean of her profound inner injury but instead waded in "just this much," ever so slowly, wakefully.

A few weeks into experimenting with the meditation, she related to us an experience that, she said, "blew my mind and mended my heart." Comprehending the skillfullness of starting slowly, she had been sending forgiveness into the slight injuries and minityrants she had known, when all of a sudden her father came toward her in her mind. "My mind said, 'I don't want to forgive him!' There he was sitting in his old chair in the living room, and I was sitting in front of him and I had a knife and I just began to stab him. I stabbed him everywhere. And then my mind, sensing this was a safe arena for experimentation, said, 'Why don't you just try it, Dorothy? Just try it.' So I said, 'I forgive you,' and all of a sudden it just flooded into me. He was sitting there and he just started crying. It was really beautiful. He asked me to get up on his lap, and my first response was, 'Are you kidding?!!!' And then my mind said, 'Just try it.' So I got up in his lap and he just held me. I was just a little girl with her father. I couldn't believe it. It was so healthy." Astonished that her father could be touched by the possibility of forgiveness so easily, it occurred to her that there was yet someone else who she was more frightened of: it was the nasty father in her, The Judge. So she asked The Judge to have some forgiveness. "I really get myself coming and going. Somehow everything is always my fault. But I felt it was worth a try. Surprisingly enough, The Judge didn't judge me for asking his forgiveness. In fact, I had a feeling he wanted to be forgiven."

Although in future sittings she found her father was not always so easily forgiven, each moment of such forgiveness was a moment of healing. About a month later, now deeply into the practice, she shared with us her experiences of meeting the baby she had aborted some years before. "My first response was to withdraw. I had been told to talk to it before, but I was never ready. But I heard it and we talked many times, and it forgave me. It told me that it loved me, and it told me that what I did was okay. It was remarkable! And when it said, 'Forgive yourself,' I began to see myself as that little infant, so in need of protection and care, and I sent myself that love. I forgave myself for never ever being enough. And my whole body began to glow. Then, at times, it was like I was out floating in the universe just loving the world, and the world was just so different. I felt such peace. And there is still healing work to be done because it scares me a little to share all this with you because—just because."

The injury done to Dorothy may take years to heal, but each day is a day of being closer to her true nature.

Samuel, dying at age eighty-six, after a life in which his main preoccupation had been commerce, spoke of his death in terms of a business deal. Having been almost obsessively involved with making his small factory a success, much of his family life had been pushed aside to concentrate on his goal. He had few friends. His drive to be a "business success" had resulted in a good deal of unfinished business. Having had three small strokes within the month, having died on the emergency-room table and then been revived, he said, "I've got the strongest, strangest feeling that I'll be going out of business very soon." The suggestion that he forgive those he mumbled were "bastards and sons of bitches," he had at first refused, saying they had done him wrong and had earned his anger. But then, sometimes, when forgiveness was mentioned, a soft smile would spread across his face, and he would say, "I guess you are right. What is the use now? It only aggravates me."

For most, finishing business usually means the end of relationships as business. But for Samuel, whose obsession with business kept him ever distant—having exchanged business for relationships —the finishing of business meant the end of business as relationships.

Taking his metaphor of going out of business for death, I spoke with him in terms of "balancing the ledger" in a way that seemed to focus him on the possibility of forgiving others and perhaps even acknowledging that he too might wish to be forgiven. Suggesting he no longer needed to merchandise his life, that his business had succeeded and no longer needed all of his attention, I spoke to him in loving terms of merger. "It looks like you are being bought out by the Man upstairs." And he smiled his loving smile, dreaming of a penthouse office with his name in gold on the door. In the days that followed, aiding Samuel in his life review, commenting again and again on how sympathetically he had done business, what honest commerce he had purveyed, a certain trust and confidence in the life just past could be seen in the increasingly deep receptiveness of his gaze.

Although the word "forgiveness" was not one he was altogether comfortable with, that quality of spaciousness became very attractive. "What am I knocking myself out for with all this business? Maybe it's time to retire." His anger at the past was dissolving.

Having had another stroke and gone into a coma, he awakened for a moment one afternoon, looking straight into my eyes, and said, "You will pardon me if it takes a little while to transact business with the Lord. He runs the place. But I think we can do business." And he resumed his coma with a smile.

Lennie was dying of AIDS when we met. Having already practiced the forgiveness meditation with a gay-consciousness group for some time, he approached us for further instruction. We met every few days to meditate together and deepen his trust in the process. Very quickly his practice deepened to an all-encompassing compassion. He was ripe. His heart burst open. "I feel this meditation is a key part of my healing. It helped me find a way through the anger. It is one of the few processes I have ever been through that acknowledges the anger without making it worse or having to hide it. It gave me confidence that there is a way out of this pain. If I had tried this ten years ago, I probably would have thought I had to forgive myself for being gay. Even five years ago I probably would have thought I had to forgive myself for getting AIDS. But now I think I can just forgive the AIDS. I mean to send forgiveness into this AIDS, into this situation which has changed my whole life, is really exciting.

"I don't know where this forgiveness thing will take me, but I am willing to go. Because I don't know when life begins and I don't know when it ends, but I know that the opportunity to tell the truth is spectacular and forgiveness takes me closer to that. And I know that gay men are exquisite, sensitive, beautiful, vulnerable, loving, tender, generous men who are now dying with very little forgiveness from others or for themselves."

Lennie now offers free forgiveness workshops in the gay community. It has been five years since his original diagnosis.

Caroline began the forgiveness practice about two years ago. About six weeks into it, she was drawn to a daily mindfulness meditation which has brought considerable healing into her life. "At first the harder I tried to forgive, the guiltier I felt for not being very forgiving, but then I realized I was being too hard on myself and really didn't have to forgive that fellow who raped my sister." So she started focusing on the little insults that often caused her to close and watched, fascinated, as her capacity for forgiveness gradually increased. "Now at times I can forgive that fellow, but the meditation hasn't made me stupid. I'm not about to go and knock on his door and tell him so." Her forgiveness did not condone rape; she forgave the actor, not the action. She said she had learned to forgive the cruel but saw no reason to forgive cruelty. "I was so outraged when my sister got raped that I just hated this world and wanted to kill the guy. But forgiveness helps a lot. In fact, now I find I can even forgive God and I often can feel her arms around me. I have never felt less alone. I have never been happier. Forgiveness is a miracle!"

A FORGIVENESS MEDITATION

[To be read slowly to a friend or silently to oneself.]

Begin to reflect for a moment on what the word "forgiveness" might mean. What is forgiveness? What might it be to bring forgiveness into one's life, into one's mind?

Begin by slowly bringing into your mind, into your heart, the image of someone for whom you have some resentment. Gently allow a picture, a feeling, a sense of them to gather there. Gently now invite them into your heart just for this moment.

Notice whatever fear or anger may arise to limit or deny their entrance and soften gently all about it. No force. Just an experiment in truth which invites this person in.

And silently in your heart say to this person, "I forgive you."

Open to a sense of their presence and say, "I forgive you for whatever pain you may have caused me in the past, intentionally or unintentionally, through your words, your thoughts, your actions. However you may have caused me pain in the past, I forgive you."

Feel for even a moment the spaciousness relating to that person with the possibility of forgiveness.

Let go of those walls, those curtains of resentment, so that your heart may be free. So that your life may be lighter.

"I forgive you for whatever you may have done that caused me pain, intentionally or unintentionally, through your actions, through your words, even through your thoughts, through whatever you did. Through whatever you didn't do. However the pain came to me through you, I forgive you. I forgive you."

It is so painful to put someone out of your heart. Let go of that pain. Let them be touched for this moment at least with the warmth of your forgiveness.

"I forgive you. I forgive you."

Allow that person to just be there in the stillness, in the warmth and patience of the heart. Let them be forgiven. Let the distance between you dissolve in mercy and compassion.

Let it be so.

Now, having finished so much business, dissolved in forgiveness, allow that being to go on their way. Not pushing or pulling them from the heart, but simply letting them be on their own way, touched by a blessing and the possibility of your forgiveness.

And now gently, giving yourself whatever time is necessary, allow the other person to dissolve as you invite another in.

Now gently bring into your mind, into your heart, the image, the sense, of someone who has resentment for you. Someone whose heart is closed to you.

Notice whatever limits their entrance and soften all about that hardness. Let it float.

Mercifully invite them into your heart and say to them, "I ask your forgiveness."

"I ask your forgiveness."

"I ask to be let back into your heart. That you forgive me for whatever I may have done in the past that caused you pain, intentionally or unintentionally, through my words, my actions, even through my thoughts."

"However I may have hurt or injured you, whatever confusion, whatever fear of mind caused you pain, I ask your forgiveness."

And allow yourself to be touched by their forgiveness. Allow yourself to be forgiven. Allow yourself back into their heart.

Have mercy on you. Have mercy on them. Allow them to forgive you.

Feel their forgiveness touch you. Receive it. Draw it into your heart.

"I ask your forgiveness for however I may have caused you pain in the past. Through my anger, through my lust, through my fear, my ignorance, my blindness, my doubt, my confusion. However I may have caused you pain, I ask that you let me back into your heart. I ask your forgiveness."

Let it be. Allow yourself to be forgiven.

If the mind attempts to block forgiveness with merciless indictments, recriminations, judgments, just see the nature of the unkind mind. See how merciless we are with ourselves. And let this unkind mind be touched by the warmth and patience of forgiveness.

Let your heart touch this other heart so that it may receive forgiveness. So that it may feel whole again.

Let it be so.

Feel their forgiveness now as it touches you.

If the mind pulls back, thinks it deserves to suffer, see this merciless mind. Let it sink into the heart. Allow yourself to be touched by the possibility of forgiveness.

Receive the forgiveness.

Let it be.

And now gently bid that person adieu and with a blessing let them be on their way, having even for a millisecond shared the one heart beyond the confusion of seemingly separate minds.

And now gently turn to yourself in your own heart and say, "I forgive you," to you.

It is so painful to put ourselves out of our hearts.

Say, "I forgive you," to yourself.

Calling out to yourself in your heart, using your own first name, say "I forgive you" to you.

If the mind interposes with hard thoughts, such as that it is self-indulgent to forgive oneself, if it judges, if it touches you with anger and unkindness, just feel that hardness and let it soften at the edge. Let it be touched by forgiveness.

Allow yourself back into your heart. Allow you to be forgiven by you.

Let the world back into your heart. Allow yourself to be forgiven.

Let that forgiveness fill your whole body.

Feel the warmth and care that wishes your own well-being. Seeing yourself as if you were your only child, let yourself be bathed by this mercy and kindness. Let yourself be loved. See your forgiveness forever awaiting your return to your heart.

How unkind we are to ourselves. How little mercy. Let it go. Allow you to embrace yourself with forgiveness. Know that in this moment you are wholly and completely forgiven. Now it is up to you just to allow it in. See yourself in the infinitely compassionate eyes of the Buddha, in the sacred heart of Jesus, in the warm embrace of the Goddess.

Let yourself be loved. Let yourself be love.

And now begin to share this miracle of forgiveness, of mercy and awareness. Let it extend out to all the people around you.

Let all be touched by the power of forgiveness. All those beings who also have known such pain. Who have so often put themselves and others out of their hearts. Who have so often felt so isolated, so lost.

Touch them with your forgiveness, with your mercy and loving kindness, that they too may be healed just as you wish to be.

Feel the heart we all share filled with forgiveness so that we all might be whole.

Let the mercy keep radiating outward until it encompasses the whole planet. The whole planet floating in your heart, in mercy, in loving kindness, in care.

May all sentient beings be freed of their suffering, of their anger, of their confusion, of their fear, of their doubt.

May all beings know the joy of their true nature.

May all beings be free from suffering.

Whole world floating in the heart. All beings freed of their suffering. All beings' hearts open, minds clear. All beings at peace.

May all beings at every level of reality, on every plane of existence, may they all be freed of their suffering. May they all be at peace.

May we heal the world, touching it again and again with forgiveness. May we heal our hearts and the hearts of those we love by merging in forgiveness, by merging in peace.

CHAPTER 10

Exploring Grief

Along the path of healing that leads into the heart, one is often called upon to examine grief. Grief is the binding alloy of the armoring about the heart. Like a fire touched, the mind recoils at losing what it holds most dear. As the mind contracts about its grief, the spaciousness of the heart often seems very distant.

Some believe they have no grief. This is another aspect of our rigid denial and self-protection. Some indeed may say, "I haven't lost anyone—why should I be grieving?" If only it were that simple.

Most think of grief as a momentous sadness but it is a lot subtler than that. Everyone has grief. Everyone seems to have some unbalanced tally sheet with life, some unfinished business. An incompleteness with the past and with ourselves, a fatiguing self-consciousness, the predominant theme of the unfinished symphony of mind's yearning.

Our grief manifests as a self-judgment, as fear, as guilt, as anger and blame. It is that insistent mercilessness with ourselves and a world which we hardly let within. Our grief is our fear of loss, our fear of the unknown, our fear of death. Grief is the rope burns left behind when what we have held to most dearly is pulled out of reach, beyond our grasp.

At the most microscopic level one sees that the tendency of the mind to hold, to cling and condemn, to judge, is an aspect of grief. A feeling of "not-enoughness" that longs to become otherwise.

As we begin to direct the energy of forgiveness to ourselves and others, voices may arise that try to block that way of giving and receiving. These voices tell us that we are unworthy and useless. It is where we feel separate from ourselves, so many parts of mind pushed away, so little heart allowed to express itself. We wonder, looking into the warped mirror of our self-image, why what is reflected back seems so distorted, so unacceptable, so unwhole, and unlovable.

But even grief is workable. Opening the heart to the mind's pain, we find space to explore mercifully. Then, instead of constantly appraising what looks back, we observe, we begin to look directly at what looks. We watch the watcher. We enter the eyes of discovery. And gently approaching the long-accumulated density of our grief, so long reacted to with aversion and disgust, we discover the unexplored territory between the heart and mind. And we acknowledge, with the sigh of letting go, how often we have distrusted what we feel. Examining *what* we feel, not analyzing why, we discover the labyrinthine patterns of our grief and unfinished business, the skeletons of so many moments of life which became lost by the wayside. And the darkness of a thousand moments of helplessness and hopelessness is illuminated in a clear and merciful awareness. That which has seemed so untouchable in the past is cradled in the arms of forgiveness and compassion, and the armoring begins to melt. The path to the heart becomes straight and clear, recognizing how this exploration of our grief, of the ways of our old suffering, opens the path to joy. Those who know their pain and their grief most intimately seem to be the lightest and most healed of the beings we have met.

Gazing into the mirror of our self-image, of the mind's thoughts of itself, we no longer seek some solid entity, some unchanging "me" and "mine." We do not shrink from the nature of impermanence, which is constantly causing hairline fractures in the image of our long-suffering self. We see how our attempts to keep it together, to stay in control, have intensified our grief. With a deep willingness to surrender, to let go, to listen to the "still small voice within," we allow facades to crumble. We enter directly into our grief, encouraging it to reveal its deepest nature. So we discover what lies beyond a lifetime of holding: our healing and the finishing of our most subtly unfinished business.

One fellow with terminal cancer noticed that in trying to heal himself he had learned to *appear* well but never how to *be* well. He said he had been pretending his whole life that he wasn't sick. He spoke of noticing an ache in his chest just over the heart, which was becoming more intense as he worked with the grief meditation and the exploration of his stomach tumor. One day, when the pain in his heart was particularly apparent, he decided to address it directly. He spoke to it, asked it how long it had been there. To his surprise the ache responded, saying, "I have been here all your life. But this is just the first time you ever noticed me." The difficulties in his stomach put him in touch with an aching in his life which had always been submerged. He realized that he couldn't disregard it any longer. He began to speak to his pain as if it were his only child, to relate to it with a new loving kindness, to make room for it in his heart. And he noticed that the pain decreased in direct proportion to the open space he was able to create for it.

Many find correlation between the pain in the body and the holdings in the mind which block entry into the heart. For those who have discovered the connection between the pains in the body and the pains in the mind, the exploration of grief has been a very practical path toward decreasing discomfort and increasing healing.

A friend of ours who has for several years experienced intermittent acute discomfort from a crushed disk that pressured the nerves in her arms, told us how the exploration of her pain put her in touch with a grief she had never recognized. Often awakened by discomfort, she noticed that at three o'clock one morning she awoke, addressing her pain with "Damn it! That pain again!" But she decided on this particular morning that instead of damning the pain she would relate to it with something new and spoke into it words of kindness and nurturing.

Speaking gently to this pain, which had always seemed so unreachable, so impossible to change, she saw the eyes of a starving child, the eyes so often seen on television and poster campaigns to feed the needy around the world. And in a flash she recognized the parallel between her previously untouchable pain and her feelings of helplessness in the face of the enormity of the suffering in the world. She experienced a correlation between her increasing back pain and all the pains of the world that she was unable to ease. She saw that the relationship to her pain had somehow reflected her feelings of impotence about the ten thousand children who starved to death each day. And she recognized that, indeed, she was not without something to do about it all.

So each morning, at whatever time she awoke, she would whisper into her pain, "Good morning, sweetie, how are you today?" She talked to it with loving kindness, recognizing the necessary balance that *did not invite it to stay* but no longer pushed it away. She greeted it as one would a colleague at the breakfast table. Not wishing her occasional pain to become a chronic difficulty, she did not make it the love of her life but instead allowed the love in her life to exclude nothing. She used her pain as a means of focusing compassion on the predicaments of the world. Sending forgiveness and mercy into the pains of the world, she felt that no pain in her body was unapproachable by love. And she let the pain of her body, of the world, float in her heart. Her exploration of this deep grief leading to an ongoing practice of service to all she met. In the years that followed, she no longer held so much to a philosophy of life as she made her life a statement. The compliment now most often extended to her is "Thank you for being."

The power of the work of seeing deeply into the nature of our grief cannot be underestimated. One fellow mentioned after discovering a skin cancer on his cheeks and lips, "I guess after the death of my daughter I just didn't know what to do with all that I felt. I had always been told to keep a stiff upper lip and tough it out, so I just swallowed it down. I thought I had to put her away so I wouldn't lose face, but just look at what happened." He said that each time he looked in the mirror each blemish reminded him to let his daughter come back into his heart so he could feel their connection again. As he began to talk to his daughter in his heart, to acknowledge the enormity of the pain of their separation, he said he encountered "so much sadness, so much unlived."

Over the last eighteen months, his grief work has opened him in a way that had previously been disallowed. Opening his heart in hell, he became healed. And that cancerous self-image, which kept him from grieving, has abated some. "Now it doesn't hurt my face to smile or cry, and Beth and I can just sit like we used to in the woods behind our house and watch the birds together." He speaks of being able to see his anger or fear or grief in the same way that they silently watch the deer nibbling at the underbrush. Now that he has made room in his heart for his grief, he sees that he and his wife and children and friends and the thoughts of his dead daughter are "just another of God's creatures come to visit for a while, come to remind each other of the preciousness."

The application of the grief meditation, the intense work of opening our heart in hell, has been most useful. By finding the touch point of grief, one discovers the touch point of the heart. Once again, our greatest suffering leads us toward the possibility of our greatest liberation. There is not somewhere else to go. One is constantly arriving. All the work is done in "just this much."

All of us have grief to explore, the grief of incompletion, of not having what we wish, the loss of face or actually the loss of facade, the despair of no control in the shifting sands of impermanence, in the ever-varying winds of constant change in an unknown universe. It is the death of friends. It is the loss of one's pet as a child. It is good friends moving away and old pains returning. It is all the moments of being unloved. It is the millions abused by those in power. It is that half of the world goes to sleep hungry. It is the impermanent body. It is the loss of faith. It is all the things of Column B, the world-weariness, the fatigue of the struggle, the loss of love, the carelessness of certain actions that congeal around the heart. It is the ordinary grief, our unfinished business, our daily dying out of life. It is all that remains unlived in the preciousness of just this much.

Often, however, it takes the loss of a loved one for us to notice the grief that has always been there. But even in the intense grief experienced in the death of a loved one, we recognize that nothing in grief is new. Grief is just old mind never before so intensely experienced. The ancient guardians of our self-image, the blockages of the heart, become uniquely evident. The fear, the self-judgment, the heaviness of body dense with doubt, the guilt and anger of so many lost moments, feelings of failure, trepidation, loathing, dread, and helplessness arise from just beneath the surface to present themselves in a blaze of anguished feelings. None of these qualities or experiences are new, though few have appeared with such intensity before. Little of our ordinary grief has been acknowledged.

In intense grief of loss we rediscover, unmistakably this time, the grief we have always carried, the ordinary grief that inhabits and inhibits our life. Some call this ordinary grief *angst*. Many experienced it as discomforting self-consciousness. Some experience it as jealousy, others as nationalism. But always it is accompanied by a deep sense of isolation and separation. It is the daily narrowing of perception which allows so little of life directly in. It is the envy and judgment of a lifetime, that everyday sense of loss. It is our homesickness for God.

I would like to add here that many people we talk with tend to equate death with God. Death is not God. Coming home is not something we can only do later but something available to us right now, in each moment we are open to. To the degree we appreciate the light now, we will stay with the light then. Death is not God, any more than a magic trick is the magician. And just as a magician might show you after performing a trick how it was done, so too perhaps after death we might gain insight into the trick itself. As the death trick loses its mysteriousness, it tunes us deeper to an edgeless entry into the mystery itself. God is not someone or something separate but is the suchness in each moment, the underlying reality. Like birth or illness or old age, death is just another event along the way. In fact, like birth, illness, and old age, death has a universal quality—it is nothing special. It is as common as God, inherent in every moment.

As Kabir says:

If you don't break your ropes while you're alive,
do you think
ghosts will do it after?

The idea that the soul will join with the ecstatic
just because the body is rotten—
that is all fantasy.
What is found now is found then.
If you find nothing now,
you will simply end up with an empty apartment in the City
    of Death.
If you make love with the divine now, in the next life
    you will have the face of satisfied desire.

So I ask you, please do not mistake death for the divine. Do not be looking elsewhere for your true nature. Do not think of it as something coming, but instead recognize it as the ever-present possibility in each moment. If we do not examine the grief of our homesickness for God now, we will always be looking elsewhere for our healing. Death is not going home. Our home is the heart, our real nature. God is "just this much," the vast spaciousness of our inherent nature, luminous and whole, the heart of the moment.

Grief takes many guises. It is not a single state of mind but a generic label for a very specific process. During a conscious living/ conscious dying retreat, after a particularly intense morning of investigating grief, a number of people came up to share their experiences. The first fellow who approached seemed quite agitated and said, "I am not grieving, I am not sad about the death of my father. I am angry as hell." The next woman who came up said, "I am not feeling grief, I am feeling anxiety." The next person said, "Well I don't know if it's grief but I sure feel kind of lost." The woman who approached next said, "What I am feeling isn't grief, it's guilt." Another spoke of shame, and the person following shared the deep self-doubts which had arisen after the suicide of her brother. Each felt they weren't "grieving correctly," but for each this was their process. These different states were the armoring that grief puts us in touch with. Each person was expressing the quality of the mind which had always blocked their deeper entrance within. For most, grief is more a word used to describe a feeling of being overwhelmed by loss than it is a definition of the multiple moods which constitute this most natural process. All of their feelings, all of their states of mind, were aspects of grief. There is no doing it right; there is just being with what is as wholeheartedly as the moment allows.

We expect our grief to be something special. In fact, our grief is as old as our self-image, so familiar in fact that we often do not recognize it when it affects us. It has been there all our lives, but it is only with the impact of unmistakable loss that we acknowledge it for the very first time. Perhaps if we recognized our ordinary grief sooner, we wouldn't be so overwhelmed by all that we have denied for so long. Opening to the little grief, the little losses, the little deaths, we make room for the greater griefs, the greater losses, the greater death. By making room in our heart for the lesser holdings, we cultivate the strength and presence for the greater.

Of the thousands we have worked with who were in the midst of deep grief, not a single person has said that the experience was altogether new. It was the same sadness, only deeper. It was the same anger, the same frustration, the same anxiety. The only thing that seemed to be new was that these feelings so powerfully arisen into consciousness, could no longer be denied.

We have somehow wrestled our common everyday grief into submission which is actually a submersion. We have learned to cope. This means, "I won't feel too much as long as I don't hurt too bad." It is quite a trade-off.

But when some loss arises that we simply cannot deny, when it is our parents who have died, our husband, our wife, our lover, when it is our children's death, our best friend's, when it is our own body going through sickness and decay, then the ache we have carried for so long can no longer be ignored. Then the pain of a lifetime can no longer be suppressed. Feelings of separation or doubt or fear that have often caused us to withdraw from life and hide in safe territory are experienced in all their painful reality.

Grief is a process; it is not a single emotion, any more than anger or fear or doubt is. These are just sloppy labels we use to dull and remove ourselves from the intensity of so much work that is left unfinished, so much pain and fear and remorse gone uninvestigated. Someone asked the other night, "Do I have to get rid of my anger before I can get into my grief?" Anger is our grief, and until it is acknowledged and investigated, it may be difficult to get into the feelings that lie beyond. For some it may be that until they explore whatever anger is felt toward the individual who died, they will not be able to experience the unfolding of accompanying states and moods of their grief. Unexplored anger may separate one from the deeper levels of their grief in the same way it has always separated them from the deeper levels of that person who is now grieved.

Actually that feeling of not grieving correctly, of being separate from grief, is grief itself. It is that feeling of separation from ourselves and others to which the word "grief" can be most accurately applied.

In our inquiry into the nature of mind, we quickly recognize just how much of a sense of separation resides there. It is in those feelings of isolation, which the imagined self takes on in the identity of "I am this body, I am this mind," that our ordinary grief is most evident.

When we begin to acknowledge our everyday sense of isolation from that which we love most and wish so dearly to merge with, we begin to let go of the grief and pain which always existed around our heart.

When someone says they can't get into their grief, perhaps what they are saying is that they can't open to their anger, their fear, their doubt. They have put so many parts of themselves out of their heart, they have been coping with the mind so long, that now, with the death of a loved one, they are overwhelmed by the intensity of such feelings and find very little space in which to explore, to experience, to allow the history of their grief to manifest.

The acknowledgment of this long-held suffering is the first stage of healing into grief. We can no longer deny the reality of the long-submerged and, as in any healing, the first step is acceptance. We cannot let go of anything we do not accept. Investigation deepens our letting go. The fear which has always guarded these heavy emotions from exploration now becomes an object of examination and acts as a guide into new territory. Fear becomes an ally which whispers that we are coming to our edge, to unplumbed depths, to the space in which all growth occurs. We discover that we have never learned how to allow ourselves to be overwhelmed, how to let go of control, how to go beyond the pain we have become so accustomed to. So we continue to examine our resistance to life, our ancient griefs which have so profoundly dulled our perception and limited our experience to just old pathways of silent suffering. In a very real way, when we are in grief, we are no longer so blind to our blindness.

It is at this stage of recognition, of acknowledgment, and the slow acceptance of the condition that we find ourselves in that tenderness is most necessary. It is a tenderness that simply allows us to feel what we feel, the compassion with which we allow the process to unfold as it may. Go slowly and with great gentleness into the dark night of the mind that's been confronted with loss, with all the losses that each loss puts us in touch with. Entering our grief directly, we see so clearly, perhaps as in no other process, our capacity to heal the past. Each loss offers us a remarkable opportunity of healing every loss. In every loss is recapitulated all previous losses.

Our grief is the reservoir of loss, a considerable pool of all the losses past and all the confusions present stored away without resolution. Often, from this deep underground pool of loss, feelings of helplessness and perhaps hopelessness arise. Our grief drains us and leaves us feeling only half alive, only partially able to heal.

We often wonder if one would feel the attenuated suffering we call grieving, if there were no residual grief beneath it all. It is not as though we wouldn't miss our loved one but instead might skip the middleman of the mind and go directly to the heart's sense of ever-connectedness.

Grief has the potential to allow us to see how cramped we have always been. In acknowledging the pain, we can open past our long-held resistance to the unpleasant, to life itself. We can dissolve old partiality in a great wholeness, able to let old pains be, to let them go, without clinging or suppression. It clears the way for life to reenter—a willingness, a noncondemning that allows the healing to go so deep. It means meeting "just this much" with mercy and awareness, recognizing that we don't need to change anything but rather to add mercy and awareness to this moment so that what is can be as it is.

When we allow ourselves the feelings that arise around the loss of a loved one, we notice, unmistakably, a feeling of being distant from him or her. The first stage of grief is characterized by the experience of separation, of the loved one not being there, of the loved one's absence. Within that experience of separateness, one notices a quality created not only by death, but by a sense of separation that has always existed throughout life. Many people have told us, "I am not sure if I am grieving their absence now or *my* absence then." Our feelings of separation are *the* feeling of separation.

In many ways grief, in its initial impact, connects us to the place where separation always existed; it drops us into the mind, into that level where we *thought* that person more than experienced them. For instance, in the grief following the loss of our child, we may repeatedly imagine how we are not going to see that child grow up, how we are not going to see them get married, how we are not going to have grandchildren. If it is our lover, our husband, our children, our dear friend who has been lost, we may feel how we are unable to share their growth, how we are not going to see them become what they had always wished to be. There is a profound feeling of not having. We can perhaps see how our loved ones always act as a mirror for our heart, how they allow us access to ourselves by reflecting back to us the love within. We see how they are a connection with that place within us that is love. So, when a loved one is lost, we grieve deeply the loss of connection with ourself.

So, in the early exploration of grief, we come across feelings of separation, a sense of "I and other." These have always been felt but seldom acknowledged, except when heavy states such as anger or fear or envy or doubt magnify the distance between the heart and mind. We come across the levels of remorse, of guilt, of self-doubt which may naturally follow. We are not taken by surprise but instead can watch each state in its unfolding, allowing deeper and deeper insight into the process. We can see that grief too has its own nature, its own tone of voice, its own texture, its own patterns in the body and tape loops in the mind. And hard as it may seem, we begin to make friends with our grief and thus are reminded of how long we have forgotten, locked in our own little cage, reaching through the bars, hardly able to make contact with another. In this seeing we are set free. The past no longer compulsively creates the future, and we see yet another alternative to our suffering. We acknowledge with deep forgiveness how much self-mercy it takes to be fully alive and how difficult it is to live solely in the mind and still be able to breathe another into our heart.

Several years ago, a friend's eight-year-old daughter disappeared. For a year he went crazy, out of his mind, which means he was actually thrown *into* his mind. Unbearable feelings of separation, of infinite loss, of helpless inability ever to experience her again overwhelmed him. But he and his wife saw all too clearly what such a sense of separation could lead to and worked very hard to meet this pain with something gentler. Knowing how easily these feelings could pull the family apart, they recognized the need to honor the intensity of the pain. Slowly, they allowed the pain into their heart without trying to change it. They didn't try to work it out too quickly, but simply opened to be with it. They used the only method that works in life—the braille method—feeling themselves along a moment at a time and allowing the next moment to arise as it would. They made contact as best they could with the ground beneath their feet. Just taking a breath at a time, letting the pain tear their hearts open. Acknowledging the depth of the separation that the mind so often insists on, they died into their grief. When the grief manifested as feelings of separation, they did nothing to separate themselves from it but instead tuned deeper.

A year and a half after her disappearance, he spoke of what he had felt in his initial grief—not only of how his daughter had been separated from him but how often they had previously been separated by what he had considered life. "I was always the daddy that knew, and she was always the child who needed to learn, so many roles and posturings. But I am learning something other than that now. I am learning something other than being separate. I am learning that we are inseparable."

In the life review that grief so often stimulates, he saw many moments when he and his daughter were a father knowing and a daughter not knowing. A big body and a little body, a grown-up and a child. And he met whatever feelings followed with a deeper kindness for them both. He drank deeply of those memories when each was only a heart, just love that went beyond separate roles and identities and curled up within each other's being. His relationships with his other children, with his wife and friends, became so precious, so deeply connected that they didn't try to stop or control the pain but simply shared it. The deepest kind of healing occurred, a deep finishing of business with themselves. As they allowed the pain in, it moved through, and he spoke of experiencing during those times of deep self-acceptance, beyond feelings of separation from his dead daughter, moments of an inseparability that they shared. He entered the second stage of healing into grief. When the mind sinks into the heart, we no longer feel so separate but recognize how connected we have always been and always will be.

As he let himself be taken care of when that felt right or let himself take care of others as that felt appropriate—allowing himself to be massaged when he felt like it and not to be massaged when he didn't, trusting himself moment to moment to see what was appropriate for him—he moved more deeply through all that he had for so long denied himself entrance to. Screaming when he felt a scream, not screaming when the scream did not enunciate itself. He gave himself permission to be with the constantly changing flow of feeling. When it was time to play, he played. When it was time to be silent, he was silent. He noticed the guilt for not feeling bad enough when he felt good, as well as the guilt for feeling too bad when he was down. He watched the process with mercy and care and let it open his heart. Later his wife said, "This almost seems to be more than I ever could have asked for. That we could experience this now. Somehow I feel we are healing together. What more can we give to each other?"

As the process of grief deepens, as the mind begins to sink into the heart, we see the power of opening into our pain with mercy and awareness. It may take months, it may even take years. The heart has its seasons, and even as the mind sinks into the heart there may be times when one can touch their pain with care and tenderness, and times when once again the mind interposes its long-conditioned "shoulds" and tension and control.

As the mind sinks into the heart there are moments when we feel how inseparable we are and have always been. Perhaps even a sense of connection that existed even before we were born, a sense of the deathlessness of our essential oneness.

When the grief sinks so deeply into the heart that we can accept even this much pain and touch what that murdered girl's mother called "our shared divinity," we are healing to the core of life. Even though one may still feel terrible at times, the healing continues. We are not surprised at how little capacity we have at times to remain open, not surprised at how it changes, how our healing comes and goes. We notice how there may be moments or whole days of great openness and a deep sense of connection, but upon awakening the next morning we discover that the heart is seemingly inaccessible— a density where just a few hours before had been considerable spaciousness. As the healing discovers itself, drawing from beyond all previous resources and unimaginable tenderness, we make room in our heart for ourselves even when our heart is closed.

At this stage of our grieving, of our healing, nothing can take that sense of beingness away. We are inseparable, and our connection is recognized beyond and before time.

Perhaps a greater tragedy than the loss of a child or the death of a dear friend is how often we feel this communion missing from those with whom we share our life.

For each and all of us, our work is to heal the grief that separates us from those we love so that we may begin to experience our wholeness and share it now in this moment.

For many, the healing that occurs through the exploration and recognition of grief does not begin until loss has arisen. But for some there is the profound recognition that the work we do to meet the pain now, the suffering now, finishes our business and allows each moment to be new and fresh instead of a continuation of the old pain, the old separation and grief that has always so limited our experience of life, of ourselves and each other.

Meeting the grief in mind, meeting the grieving world with a bit more wisdom and forgiveness, we enter the healing moment fully alive.

INTRODUCTION TO
A MEDITATION ON GRIEF

The armoring around the heart is the accumulation of our grief, all the moments we have put ourselves out of our life, all the times we have given ourselves and others so little mercy. On the way to healing the mind and body into the heart of the matter, our grief must be explored to go beyond the holdings of old mind and open in a brand-new way to the potentials of this very instant. Some may be led to this meditation at first because they sense there is some unfinished business with a parent's death many years before or the pain of the illness of a loved one remaining in the foggy shadows of the suppressed. Some will be drawn to this meditation because of the pain of unfulfilled dreams, the multiple losses of a changing world, the unnamed, unlabeled grief we all carry. It connects with the tears unshed, the laughs unlaughed, the moments unlived. One need not have experienced the death of a loved one in order to find this exploration a very useful endeavor. It makes room in our heart for our pain, for our joy, for our life.

There is a point on the chest, on the sternum, roughly between the nipples about two or three inches above where the rib cage comes together. It is the focal point for this process. Investigate the breast bone to find this point of sensitivity. It is a place where we hold much grief. It may be extremely sensitive. For many when they find it, it will be unmistakable. There may even be a slight indentation there. Take a moment to explore the breast bone to see where it may be evident. Some may find it immediately. For others it may not be as obvious. In this case you "sense" where it may be, mid-sternum, and work with whatever sensations arise there. This point has correlations in many healing technologies. In acupuncture it is "Conception 17." It exists in all traditions which view the body as an energy system. It is the heart center.

After you discover the grief point place your thumb onto it. As you push into this point with your thumb, you will feel something pushing back. Obviously there is the sternum, the bone plate, but there is also something subtler which is received—a desire to protect yourself, to stay in control, to push away feelings. All the moments of hiding, of protecting ourselves from life, add layer upon layer over the heart of the matter. Thousands of such moments accumulating to become thick as armor. A density of self-protection and an unwillingness to directly enter and emerge from the pain so long suppressed, which pushes back as you push into it. A resistance to life. A resistance to birth. A resistance to healing that asserts itself like a shield against the light. Living in the shadows instead of entering directly the suchness of "just this much." The resistance of a lifetime pushing back against the thumb probing the grief point, opening the way to the heart along the pathway of sensations created.

If you have long fingernails, be careful to use the pad of your finger and not press in with your nail. It doesn't matter whether you use the tip of the finger or knuckle, just as long as you can exert pressure so as to bring attention to that area. One of the qualities to be aware of as you start to push into the grief point, to touch the grief, is that the pressure doesn't turn investigation into punishment. You want to push in, to stimulate that point to feel the pushing back not to cause pain. This is not an exercise in endurance. This is an exercise in opening. We don't have to cause ourselves any more pain to be aware of how much pain already exists. A simple pressure exerted in that very sensitive area connects the mind/body with the heart center. On the way into the heart, the millions of times we have abandoned ourselves becomes all too evident. Gently exert pressure to bring oneself wholeheartedly awake to the grief we have carried for so long and the vastness which awaits a merciful awareness.

If you are a grief counselor or are working with someone who is unable to get in touch with their feelings, only after you have made this meditation your own would it be appropriate for you to press into the heart of another. Only after you have done it so many times on yourself and thereby made it yours. You are not being showy or trying to help. You are that being. And your finger touches your heart in their chest. Before giving this meditation to anyone else, because it is so extremely powerful, do it on yourself, work with yourself. The fear we have, the unwillingness, the lack of steadfastness in opening to ourselves in this often difficult work of letting our heart be torn open to ourselves may become very distinct and allow much insight. Then you can be there for another's grief because you are there for your own. Then you have room in your heart for another's pain because you have room in your heart for your own.

One of the remarkable qualities of this meditation is that when you have completed your process and taken your finger away, you may still quite possibly feel distinct sensations in the grief point. This is when the grief point becomes the touch point for the heart and becomes the place where you continue to breathe compassion in and out of the heart.

A Meditation on Grief

[To be read slowly to a friend or silently to oneself.]

Let your eyes close.

As your eyes close and you feel your body breathing, let your hand, your thumb, press into that point at the center of the chest between the nipples where it feels so sensitive to the touch. As sensitive as we are. And push into it.

Feel all that pushes back. Feel all that tries to resist, that denies the pain. All the armoring. All the resistance to life.

Push into it. Let the pain into your heart. Breathe that pain into your heart. All those moments of self-hatred, all that anxiety, all those times you could just jump out of your skin.

All those moments you wished you were dead. All held there, all pushing against the pressure, all denying life. Let the heart break.

Breathe the pain into the heart. Let the pain in.

Let yourself in.

Push into it.

It is so long since you have entered fully into your heart.

Feel the grief that lies there just beneath the tip of your thumb. All the loss. All the moments you couldn't protect yourself or the people you loved.

The helplessness. The hopelessness.

Feel it, breathe that pain into your heart.

Let go of the resistance. Let go of the self-protection.

It is just too much suffering to be locked out of your heart. Nothing is worth it.

Push resolutely into your heart. Not causing yourself pain but creating deep attention to whatever arises there.

Breathe in that pain.

Acknowledge that place which knows that all your children, all your friends will die some day.

The place that knows you might die and leave so much undone.

All the things you didn't say, all the love you didn't give, all the pain you have held on to right there pushing back.

Breathe through it, push into that pain.

Let it in. Let it into your heart.

Don't hold on.

Let it in.

The ten thousand children starving to death at this very moment.

The pain of mothers with empty breasts trying to feed starving children.

The pain.

All those feelings of having been misunderstood, of having been unloved right there in the midst of these sensations.

And how hard it is for us to love, how incredibly hard it is to keep the heart open.

So frightened, so doubtful, so scared.

Let the armoring melt into the center of your heart without force, without punishing yourself. Draw the pain in, draw it in with each breath.

With each breath let your heart be filled with yourself. So much has gone unexpressed. Layer upon layer covering the heart. Let the pain in.

Make room for the pain. Breathe it in. Breathe it in.

Let the pain come and let the pain go.

Have mercy.

Have mercy on yourself.

Let the pain out.

Breathe it in and breathe it out.

So much held for so long.

Let it go. Breathe it out. Let yourself into your heart. Make room in your heart for yourself.

Have mercy on you.

Let it come and let it go.

Let the thumb push into the armoring that guards the feelings of loss and grief there. Focus the attention like a single point of light in the center of the pain.

Go deeper.

Don't try to protect the heart.

Maintaining a steady gentle pressure at the center of the chest, feel the suffering held there. All the loss held, all the fears, the insecurity, the self-doubt.

Surrender into the feelings. Let it all come through.

Allow the pain into your heart. Allow the pain out of your heart. Each breath breathing awareness into the heart, each exhalation releasing the pain of a lifetime.

Let yourself experience it all. Nothing to add to it. Nothing to push away. Just see what is there, what we have carried for so long. Feel the inevitable loss of everyone you love. The impotent anger of being tossed into a universe of such incredible suffering.

The fear of the unknown. The ache of the loss of love. The isolation.

Let go into the pain. Breathe into it. Allow the long-held grief to melt.

Bring it into a soft awareness that dissolves the holding with each breath. Let yourself be fully born even in the midst of the pain of it all.

Let your heart open into this moment.

Allow awareness to penetrate into the very center of your being. Use the sensations and the grief point as though they were a conduit, a tunnel into the center of your heart, into a universe of warmth and caring.

Feel the heart expanding into space. The pain just floating there. Fear and loss suspended in compassionate mercy. Breathe into the center of the heart.

Let go of it. Let the heart open past its longing and grief.

Now take your hand away and fold it in your lap.

Feel the sensitivity remaining, throbbing at the center of your chest as though it were a vent into your heart.

Draw each breath into that warmth and love.

Breathing in and out of the heart.

Breathing gently into your heart.

CHAPTER 11

Connecting the Heart with the Disheartened

For many, to soften the belly and explore moment to moment the holdings in the mind/body may seem very unattractive. To open to levels of armoring around the heart, the grief, the anger may even seem extreme. Cultivating awareness and mercy to embrace suffering with spacious acceptance and tenderness is a new idea for many. To discover the breath inside the breath, the very beingness out of which life originates, may seem bizarre, even useless, in the face of their discomfort and confusion.

But for some, something in the heart is drawn toward using illness or injury as a teaching that stimulates the possibility of deeper levels of healing and love. We have seen many people start to direct awareness and mercy into their mental and physical wounds, their illnesses, and deeply affect the course of their cancer, their degenerative heart disease, their depression, their fears, their AIDS, their ALS, their multiple sclerosis. Though all did not experience their body as healed, many began to experience, for the first time, a new satisfactoriness in that which had always seemed so dissatisfactory. Something within began to change its relationship to mental and physical pain, even if illness did not change its relationship to the body. For many, whatever originally drew them to a healing became less of a problem and more the focus of a new participation in life.

It is not difficult to recognize how merciless we are with ourselves and how deeply conditioned we are to escape. As in the image of hitting our thumb with a hammer or stubbing our toe, filling that area with disgust and aversion, ostracizing it, when it needs most the heart's connection, imagine just allowing these sensations to be received and felt fully in a merciful awareness. Just letting the sensations be there experiencing themselves floating in compassion, met by a softness and care that didn't create or hold to pain, but simply accepted the moment as it is. Imagine how much it might affect our daily lives if we connected the heart with the disheartened!

We have seen many who began to send love into their tumors, heart disease, chronic pain, and watched their cancer or illness melt away. We have also worked with many whose greatest pains were mental or emotional, who also found considerable relief and a sense of completion using such bolder moving techniques as the grief or heavy-state or heart-of-the-womb meditation to clear their path— for example, the mother with a Down's Syndrome child, who went so deep within herself to discover that what had seemed like "life's greatest curse" was indeed "the most remarkable blessing of my life." Using the grief meditation, and eventually the letting-go meditation, she worked hard to release whatever separated their hearts, and reveled in the communion with her ever-smiling child. Not calling on the techniques again until three years later when her daughter unexpectedly died. She said her pain was beyond description. In her note telling us of the memorial service, she added, "I have your book out again, it is soaked with tears."—The healings in the father of the dying child, who said that finally he could let the pain in and stay bedside for the last few days of an all-too-short shared life.—The sexually abused woman who said, after several weeks of working with the heart-of-the-womb meditation, that she could now "stand in the light" and no longer had to hide in the shadows of the doorway to her heart.—The Vietnam veteran, who met his pain in his heart and can now walk without a cane and counsels other "still wounded" veterans.—The parents who worked so hard to open themselves to forgiveness after discovering they had unknowingly passed a crippling genetic disorder on to their suffering child.—The fellow who, as a child, waited impatiently for his younger sister's leukemia to finally remove her from the house, who worked for months with self-forgiveness so he could ask, without guilt, to be forgiven for putting her out of his heart.

One may enter almost any pain in the mind or body and discover around it the shadow of some associated feelings. Perhaps a bit of anger or shame or guilt encompass it. A vision of oneself as a failure or perhaps a sense of not-enoughness. The mind may say, "I deserve it," or "How stupid could I be to let this happen to me?" or "This is what I get!" We are so merciless with ourselves. We often find so little room for ourselves in our hearts when we most require it. So much of our mental and physical pain is touched with resistance and anger, so little of ourselves available to healing.

Imagine hitting that mental or physical thumb and letting the pain in. Not isolating it to the pulsing thumb but feeling the throbbing in our whole body. Watching the waves of sensation spread out across the ocean of the mind/body, accompanying their momentum into the subtlest ripples, at the ever-dissolving edge of consciousness. The tiniest wavelets, the least ruffling, received with the same tenderness with which one might welcome one's only child. Embracing those areas in the mind/body.

Many such healings of the mind into the body can be clearly seen in the following chapter on great injury.

There is nothing to judge in the anger or fear that may surround our pain—of course it's there at times, Big Surprise! No blame. But uninvestigated and stuffed below the level of awareness, they burn the heart and make our pain inaccessible. So much self-hatred gathers about the pain. So much to repel healing. But heartfully explored, the blockages to healing become the guideposts of the path of healing.

Many years ago, just as AIDS was first being diagnosed, we met Bill. He came to a conscious living/conscious dying retreat and was the first person to stand and say, "I hear in the group story after story about cancer, and it makes me jealous. I am envious of those who have a disease you could go to a doctor with and be treated with kindness. And there might be a fifty-fifty chance of the treatments curing you. But I don't have cancer. When I go to an M.D., I am seen as a contagious leper. I am seen as incurable. I am looked at by many people as though I were some smelly piece of garbage that needed to be dumped as quickly as possible. If I went to a doctor tomorrow and was told that my diagnosis of AIDS was incorrect and I only had cancer, it would be one of the brightest days of my life. Imagine the diagnosis of cancer making you happy! I am in a real fix, and I don't know how to fix it! People were saying things like God was punishing me for being gay, and others were saying the same thing but just in pseudo-hip holistic terms like 'You created your illness, now uncreate it!' They were making me feel so terribly helpless and vulnerable and unhealable." People were pouring so much hatred and fear into his body that it reinforced the place within him that was all too ready to touch his pain, his body, his illness, with dread and castigation. He was thoroughly disheartened.

At that time various opportunistic infections weakened his body and created considerable discomfort. He spoke very little during the retreat. But something was cooking deep inside him, and by the end of the six-day intensive there was a light shining in his face that had not been evident before. Bill told us that in the course of the retreat, he "got it." His priorities had changed. He showed me a few red lesions on his leg, the signs of Kaposi's sarcoma, and told me that he had been "a real body person," had thought more of his body than his mind or heart, before this illness and that these blotches were a considerable embarrassment to his self-image. But something had deepened in the course of sending a merciful awareness and loving kindness into his illness. He saw that he wasn't just a body. He saw the power of touching with kindness all that he and so many others had touched millions of times before with lust and fear and aversion. He said he felt reborn.

After the retreat, he went through a period of about six weeks of near ecstasy. "I hope everybody can get born before they die." This period of six weeks was perhaps the happiest in his life. And then the pain returned. Considerable rectal discomfort, fissures, and complications distracted him greatly from his all too new practice of sitting meditation. For ten days he was quite depressed and understandably contracted considerably around his pain. He said he was losing his birth until once again he surrendered his distrust and judgment and just let the pain in, let the AIDS in, let life back into his heart. And soon he came to see that his work with even these new levels of discomfort was birth too and that all the pains were the labor pains of getting born. Supported by his long-time friend and lover, Andy, and a group of caring friends, he was encouraged to relate to his pain with the same loving kindness he received from them. Allowing mercy to receive that which had been rejected, he started once again to send love into his pain. Examining moment to moment the area of his body from which the greatest discomfort arose, he let the pain talk to him, listening with the intensity and love that the Quakers necessitate for hearing the "still small voice within." He said, "As bizarre as it sounds, I am listening to the still small voice within my anal sphincter. There is no place we can't find God." He said he saw shame, fear of failure, and a deep disheartenment that he should be so ill so soon. But hearing these voices, and seeing these qualities as if they were in the body of a dearly loved one, he began to send forgiveness into his pain and it dissolved. "I don't wish to be crude," he said in his genteel way, "but I saw that what I had to do was take my ass into my heart. I can't exclude anything anymore."

Discovering for himself, within himself, that touching the holdings around his pain with forgiveness dissolved the resistance and the pain itself, he let the healing in and continued on wholeheartedly with his life.

The following is what Bill called "An open letter to my brothers and sisters." It was written in June 1983, a short time before he died.

"Dear Friends,

Six or seven months ago I lay in a hospital convinced I was going to die. AIDS, cancer, and pneumonia all seemed to be fighting to claim my life. At that time I felt very terrified that I would die and go to hell or just not go on at all. But my time had not come. The time since then has been a precious gift in which a great healing has occurred. After months of medical treatment, followed by months of holistic treatment and months of spiritual work on myself, I am free.

My lover's remarkable support, a spiritual guide, a meditation partner, several meditation retreats, support from wonderful friends, and a lot of work within my own heart has left me at peace.

For many months, my idea of healing was that of curing my body. I gave it my very best shot and I am proud of that fact. I was even given several months of relative health and energy. At that time I often expressed my certainty that I could heal my own body with my own powers. I still believe these healing powers exist, but as my physical health reached a point where optimism about my health would have had to become self-denial, I realized the need to accept my own impending death.

I also realized that self-compassion meant feeling in my heart that even physical death was not a sign of weakness and failure. This seems to be the ultimate act of self-acceptance. I thank God for it.

One other thing that I have learned is that any time you know absolutely you are right, you can be sure you're not. Rightness is just our trying to prove that someone else is wrong. But we often confuse being right with truth.

So in these past six months I have started my own production company which produced a calendar of my own photography. I have worked in the community to heighten awareness of this disease. I have grown closer than ever to my lover, family, and friends. I am very proud and thankful for these things. Most importantly I have come to accept myself exactly as I am. This is the greatest gift of all.

And so my healing has occurred. Soon my body will drop away from me like a cocoon and my spirit will fly like a butterfly—beautiful and perfect. I don't claim to know exactly where it is that I am going, but my heart tells me it is filled with light and love.

An open heart is a much greater blessing than death is a tragedy. Let us all take comfort in this knowledge.

> Love,
> Bill"

Bill's healing had gone deep. Discovering himself in mercy and awareness, he had trusted his own process and used his creative energy to develop the path that was necessary. Along the way he had developed a meditation mantra which he would use for long periods in whatever activity he was engaged. Having been deprived for some time of the sitting posture because of the complications of his illness, he found a mental repetition that would keep him present. Bill's meditation mantra was: DROPS, an acronym for "Don't Resist or Push, Soften." As Bill started to make room in his heart for his pain, he made room for his joy as well. The healing of the mind became his greatest happiness and whether or not it manifested in the body became secondary. He entered life so deeply he went beyond death. His healing was unlimited; he left no traces of unfinished business, no broken hearts, no closed minds—doing what he could to finish, to touch with love that which he may have touched with confusion in the past. His was the path of forgiveness and mercy on a body which he often treated with severity and disdain. He connected the heart with the disheartened.

Some time after Bill's death, our friend Daniel Barnes invited us to visit 5B, an AIDS ward at San Francisco General Hospital. I could see Bill's face softly smiling and hear him whisper that all should visit so we would not imagine that this suffering is happening to someone else but could see ourselves in those pained faces. So that we can no longer be innocent bystanders to a process unfolding in the body we all share. I could hear him say, "Don't live your life in safe territory, live as though you were on 5B!" So no one's suffering is put out of our heart, and we don't touch the pain in another's body, in another's mind, with fear or rejection. So that everyone might touch everything we share in all our bodies with a merciful awareness, forgiveness and loving kindness. Then who could suffer from that case of mistaken identity in which the pains of the world are thought to be happening to someone else.

A sign of Bill's healing, and many of the healings we have shared in, is that those friends and attendants closest were healing as well. Two years after Bill died, Andy, his lover, dying from AIDS as well, after coming to two or three retreats, knew that was all he needed and continued peacefully with his life. He had been healed so deeply by Bill's death that his heart seldom closed and his work with others was rarely interrupted. Just as Andy received the healing heart from Bill, so he passed it on to the next in line, blessing his new lover as he died. Conveying the healing to the next in line—connecting the great heart with the greatly disheartened—trusting the process, letting go lightly, entering life renewed through the portals of death.

A Meditation on Connecting the Heart with the Disheartened

[To be read silently to a friend or slowly to oneself.]

Let your eyes close and bring your attention to the sensations that accompany each breath.

As awareness begins to establish itself in the moment, allow it to approach the area of discomfort.

Just feel what is there. Nothing to change. Nothing to do about it.

Just sensations arising in the moment.

Just let it all be as it is.

As awareness approaches the area of discomfort, is there any tension noticed, any rigidity that it must pass through on the way to the discomfort?

Is there a pushing away of this investigation?

Just notice whatever resistance might arise.

Notice what limits the approach of awareness.

Is there a quality of holding surrounding the area of discomfort?

Just examine it. No need to change anything.

Just receiving the present as it is.

Nothing to define. Just allowing a willingness to know, just allowing a not knowing, to receive the moment, to express its nature.

As awareness makes contact with the sensations that arise in the area of discomfort, what else arises to block the moment-to-moment experience of sensation?

Does thought interpose itself? Do feelings interfere with the direct reception of sensations? Do other images arise?

Take some time to explore the tone of voice of any interposing thought.

Do these thoughts repeat themselves?

Do certain feelings seem to be associated with sensations we have labeled as "discomfort"?

Nothing to create, just receiving the moment as it presents itself in a receptive awareness.

Are there other sensations which predominate? Sensations of tension or stiffness around discomfort? Are these sensations the same as pain or different?

Is there a sense of urgency?

Stiffness? Resistance? Holding?

Just noticing whatever arises in an expanding awareness that does not resist resistance or hold to holdings.

Is there a density, a shadow that obscures the clear reception of sensation?

Is there a texture to whatever holdings may be noticed?

What blocks the moment-to-moment reception of sensation?

Notice whatever qualities arise in the mind to repel awareness, to deny pain, to resist the moment.

Just watching whatever may limit the entrance of awareness into discomfiture. Whatever may disallow mercy.

Now allow the body to soften around whatever hindrances, whatever holdings have presented themselves.

Let the body begin to cradle discomfort as if it were embracing a sick child.

Nothing to push away. Opening moment to moment all around sensation.

Allow awareness to meet whatever arises with a merciful softness, a willingness to touch the suffering. A willingness to let it be, to let it go ungrasped.

Acknowledge whatever attitudes, feelings, or thoughts arise into awareness as it approaches yet more deeply the center of the area of sensation.

Just let the sensations be there as they are.

Moment to moment.

Whatever arises into awareness, just let it be there.

Notice how thoughts of "pain," "tumor," "cancer," even of "healing" may tighten the area.

Let these mental images come and go. Notice whatever expectation creates tension.

Notice even the subtlest body reaction to these mental states, to these thoughts and feelings.

Notice how even an instant of relating to sensations with fear creates constriction and intensifies discomfort.

Watch the mind as it becomes body moment to moment.

Watch the subtlest, the slightest beginning of the hardening-around sensation that reacts to any hard thought.

Notice the relationship between thinking and tension.

Notice what amplifies discomfort in the area of sensation.

And begin to soften yet more deeply.

Notice how softening lets it all float in edgeless awareness.

Nothing to hold to, pushing nothing away, let the moment be received without interruption.

Pure awareness touching pure experience.

Notice how even the least pushing away amplifies discomfort.

Notice how a deeper softening, a greater letting go all around sensations, allows them to float.

Allow each sensation to arise and dissolve in soft open space.

Receive each particle of sensation as if for the very first time.

Acknowledging even the slightest tension or holding in a soft allowing awareness, let the healing in.

Notice any thoughts or emotions that predominate. Investigate whatever seems to close down on the sensations, to enclose them, to limit access to their deepest nature.

Opening moment to moment at the very edge of unfolding sensation.

Opening all about sensations to allow them to float.

Noticing any repetitive thoughts that conflict with this opening.

Notice whatever qualities arise in the mind to repel a deeper investigation. And let them float as well in an awareness that has room for it all.

Are there feelings, moods held in the body, associated with discomfort? Fear? Grief? Guilt? Expectation?

Is there shame or anger or doubt?

Is there anything that limits the full entrance into the moment-to-moment sensations generated in that area? Or is it just space in which sensations appear and disappear in rapid succession? Or is it both?

What seems to be going on there?

Nothing to create.

Just receiving each sensation, each feeling, each thought that arises in choiceless awareness.

Just letting it all come and letting it all go. Watching the process unfold.

What is the direct experience of sensation, of thought, of feeling, arising in the mind/body?

What is it to be alive, to experience?

Now just open space receiving the constant flow of change in the area of sensation.

Vast space receiving moment-to-moment change.

Nothing to hold to, nothing to change. Just change unfolding all by itself.

Each sensation dissolving in edgeless space.

Arising and dissolving in infinite space, in infinite mercy.

Watching the mind become body moment to moment.

Watching the heart receive it all. Entering the moment directly. Awareness, sensation, experience.

Now allow the attention to come back to the gentle flow of the breath.

Just more sensation, feeling, thought dissolving in mind/body.

Just this moment forever.

CHAPTER 12

Great Injury

With no intention to particularize or isolate our pain or predicament but as a powerful example of the hidden wounds we carry, and
the power we have to heal them, we share here some of our work
over the years with sexually abused women. It displays how even our
greatest pains and injuries can, in time, be brought within the spacious heart.

   Some years ago, during a workshop, after a particularly intense
letting-go meditation, a few people were gleefully sharing out-of-
the-body experiences which had spontaneously occurred in the
course of the exercise. They had, as they put it, "floated free, and
watched it all from above," the body of awareness momentarily let
loose from the earthen body of flesh and bone. Their excitement
filled the room with new possibilities and something of a lust for
"mystical experiences." Many were losing their perspective of "just
this much" as old mind leaned out from its merry-go-round to
snatch at yet another brass ring which it still hoped, just this once,
might be made of gold. The room was thick with spiritual material-
ism.
   Then one woman raised her hand and said, "You know, I think all
these out-of-the-body experiences are real nice, very flashy, but they
are not of much interest for me. I'd like an in-the-body experience
for a change. I'd like to trust life enough to be able to stay in my
body, to not always be on guard, to not always tense as if someone
were going to jump out of a dark hallway and do me great injury."
Several women in the room nodded in agreement. Each had been
sexually abused as a child. Each had found that the body was an

unsafe place to be. To be in the body was to be a target. For these women out-of-the-body experiences were somewhat beside the point. They were not so much interested in what it might be like to die as in what it might be like to be fully born.

Later that afternoon, after the forgiveness meditation, a woman in her midtwenties took me aside and said, "I have no more room in my heart now than I had in my body when I was two years old and my father raped me!" And instantly the connection became clear between a woman's spiritual heart, her "upper" heart if you will, and the heart of the womb, her "lower" heart. Clearly many women's upper hearts had become inaccessible when their lower hearts had closed due to abuse and frightful mishandling.

Spending some time that afternoon with the woman whose upper heart had shut down when her lower heart had been raped, closed, we began to discover together the seeds of what would become the "opening the heart-of-the-womb meditation." Sitting under a giant redwood, we worked together with the forgiveness meditation, particularly focused on herself and localized in the womb area to bring some light into the tension and fear that naturally resided there. At one point she laughed and said, "You know, some people seem to just let go and go out of their bodies. But I have to let go a whole lot just to get into mine." She said it frightened her even to think of her womb much less to approach it with any forgiveness. But as the afternoon went on and the meditation began to sink deeper, she became a bit more present, sitting a little easier within, and a certain softening of the heart was reflected in the body as the hopelessness and helplessness so long stored in her womb began to be released with deep sobs. She held her knees and began to rock herself back and forth. She was beginning to relate to herself as her only child. After some time she asked if she could put her head in my lap. As we held each other and rocked back and forth, she whispered that I was the first man she had allowed to hold her in almost fifteen years. And relating to herself with a mercy she had seldom known, she cried out to her father-abuser, "How could you have done this to me!? I am just a baby! I am just a baby!" Having for a moment let go of the enormous fear and guilt and distrust which had so long blocked her upper heart by being held so tightly in her womb heart, she was able to reenter her two-year-old body and begin again from there.

By the time the sun set, her long hair soaked with tears; a capricious wave of her arm indicated a body which felt tons lighter. Hers was the beginning of the agonizing shedding of the armor developed at a very early age and once much needed for physical and psychological survival. At the time, this closing down had been the only way out of an impossible situation. She had no choice. But now she was finding that what had been functional in the past made her nearly dysfunctional in the present. She spoke of how many times her heart had been closed in unsuccessful relationships over the past several years. She felt she had been "closed down" and couldn't open to others for longer than she could remember

Her eyes began to fill with tears again, but these were not the tears of an hour or two before, they were not the deep sobbing of release. They were tears of joy, the in-breath that follows the out-breath. After an afternoon of sending forgiveness and softness into the womb, she said she felt perhaps the possibility of not remaining closed the rest of her life. Drawn by her experiences that afternoon, she continued to spend at least fifteen minutes a day with both the forgiveness and the rudimentary form of the womb meditation which had developed during our session together. Soon she was spending two half-hour periods each day sending loving kindness and mercy into her lower heart and beginning to feel it open as she shed image upon image of the pain she had held there for so long. In the next months she found others to share with as well and began to surface back into her body. A year after beginning to "get to work on my own," she is in the longest relationship she has yet experienced and speaks now in terms of long-range commitment.

In the course of our work together that afternoon, it became abundantly clear that women have two hearts, two sets of smooth muscles in the body—the heart and the womb. Many years ago, when women used ergot as a means of aborting a pregnancy, they would occasionally experience heart palpitations as well. This is because ergotrate is a spasmodic for the smooth muscles of the body. In the case of a woman, these are the womb and heart. This connection between the womb and the heart was never so clear as with our friend's sharing about the early enormity of her injury.

For many women I suspect the upper heart has been closed by rough handling in the lower heart, in the area of the womb. Having been treated unconsciously, unkindly, maliciously, coldly, in the lower heart, a thick armoring of distrust and fear has barred entrance to the spacious heart of being.

It seems that all women have been touched roughly in the lower heart by one means or another. Some by sexual abuse as children or adults, others by rape, others by insensitive lovers or the uncaring touch of medical personnel. All are abused by the soft pornography of the advertising industry and the hard-core smut which does such violence to us all. Each at one time or another has been seen as an object. If a person sees you only as a body, they can't see your heart, your mind, or your spirit. You become another log thrown on the fire to warm someone's desire system. The greatest abuse is to be treated as an object, to be put out of one's heart. It is this preexisting condition that allows all cruelty and abuse to occur. Without seeing someone as an object, as "another," intentional abuse cannot occur. For some women it has been the forcible roughening of the sensitive heart which has caused a callus over the trust and openness that allows hearts to meet and merge in love, in living relationship, both the hearts between people and the hearts within people. For others it has been a callous lover or a cold speculum. It seems that most women have been subject to some level of abuse that has touched their lower heart and left their upper heart that much less accessible.

From these understandings arose the following meditation. It is preceded by a slow and gentle coming into the body with a long softening and opening to sensations beginning at the top of the head and moving ever so slowly and mercifully through the various parts of the body. It is suggested that those who find this meditation appropriate might explore carefully the "Opening the Body" chapter, which follows and speaks more precisely of the process of opening the body in soft belly. Also, the "Sweeping the Body Meditation" chapter can encourage the establishment of awareness and mercy in the body. At retreats we will often begin the opening-the-heart-of-the-womb meditation" by a forty-five-minute slow Sweeping-the-body meditation. I think for general use that is not as necessary as a shorter softening of the body and a tender reception of the sensations generated in the area of the womb.

In the sweeping-the-body meditation, the attention moves gently and lovingly and protectively through the body to allow awareness, particularly an awareness that has been frightened out of the body, that has found the body an unsafe place to be, to reenter and establish itself in mercy where much dullness and difficulty may have existed before. Indeed, many of the women who have spoken to us of their lower heart being closed have also mentioned various physical difficulties they felt were somehow linked to this lower closure, including pains in the feet and knees and hips because of a difficulty in staying "grounded" in the body. Others mentioned a decrease in menstrual difficulties as the meditation brought healing and made their body more available for safe inhabitation. Some women have used this meditation to create a "hospitable womb," which has allowed them after several unsuccessful attempts at pregnancy to let an embryo take root there. Others are using this meditation to dispel fibroid tumors or yeast infections.

In this slow sweeping through the body, the awareness reestablishes contact with being in a body. Then slowly the awareness is brought, with a tenderness beyond imagination, perhaps beyond all previous history, that moves gently and mercifully with profound awareness and not the least increment of time or rushing, up into the vagina. Gently, through the folds of the flesh and the muscular ripples into the womb stopping at any point to dwell in love and awareness on the sensations received. Examining the tree of life there, the fallopian tubes spreading out like branches to bear their ovarian fruit. And within each ovary at birth, all the eggs, all the possibilities of birth and rebirth, as seed potential there. All life discovered at the center of the sparkling moment. Healing, touching with mercy and care, that which may so often have been approached with hardness and thoughtlessness. A profound forgiveness entering the body in the womb. A forgiveness that allows us to reenter our lives. A forgiveness that is for ourselves, though it may touch and heal others. A forgiveness that is primarily for our own healing and therefore tends to heal all we come into contact with.

The men who enter this practice will find it as exquisitely useful as the women. To discover the vagina, the womb, the ovaries and eggs that exist within us all brings us into our humanness and allows us to more fully occupy our incarnation. After such meditations, we have had men come up to us and say, "I'll never touch a woman roughly again," tears pouring from their eyes, filled with remorse. Not rapists, not abusers, but husbands and boyfriends acknowledging the pain we all carry. Men have the potential for getting as much healing out of this as women. There is something for all of us in this meditation. See how it might bring you deeper into the refuge of the heart, the body a safer place to be, the lower heart opening, softening, allowing, releasing, making room for you in your womb in the same way we need to make room for ourselves in our heart. This is a powerful healing meditation in a root energy. Sexual energy is a primal force in one's life.

For those who are reading this, men as well as women, please suspend old mind's knowing/doubts so that whatever healing is available in this concept and practice may be applied as needed. This frightful contraction, the result of great injury, which closes the lower heart and leaves the upper heart so isolated, is not solely the domain of women but is a universal condition. The reason these ideas and meditations arose in the realm of women is because that was our experience at the time. Indeed, this issue about healing great injury is no more a woman's issue than a man's, but this is a powerful example of the work we can do on ourselves to finish business with the past in awareness and mercy. It is an instance of how even the "dead spots" in our life can be resuscitated. Men have no less suffering and no less pain around issues of injury or cruelty. But their suffering most often arises from other forms of trauma. Although we have worked with many men who have been sexually abused, it is predominantly our work with women which has given rise to this material.

For those who have been sexually abused, this meditation can be extremely difficult at times. One woman told me of doing it twice a day for about twenty minutes at a time and finding it to be quite a grind in the beginning, often the least pleasant part of her day. "But I know there is nothing else I can do right now that will do me as much good." The difficulty in doing this meditation defines the condition we find ourselves in. There is so much fear to be approached before we can see beyond fear. After about two and a half months of working with this meditation, she told us, "A miracle happened the other day. I walked into the kitchen, sat down at the table, and looked up and saw the wall. I just saw the wall! I was just here in my body, in the world, in my heart. I saw the wall as if for the first time. I was just here. It was the most wonderful experience of my life!" As her lower heart opened, her upper heart became visible to so many that she was drawn by other women to counsel and share the profound and difficult work she had done with herself, on herself. She is now a much sought-after therapist for abused women.

A year ago, just before a talk in a California auditorium, a woman came up to me with a big smile on her face and said, "I am pregnant, and it's all your fault." As my right eyebrow arched, she continued, "In the last nine years, I have had six miscarriages. I think my womb was just plain discouraged. All the abuse and sexual confusion when I was a child left me with an angry womb. Nothing could have lived there. But after working with the meditation for some months, life has come back into my body."

Many of the women working with this meditation find it useful for reasons other than just the balancing of great injury or sexual abuse in the past. As mentioned, many women are working with this meditation as a means of healing fibroid tumors, cervical cancer, herpes, PMS. For many, along with other treatments they are working with, the opening-of-the-womb meditation allows a deepening receptivity of whatever other healing method is being employed. A deepening that allows the healing to be received at yet another level.

Certainly the meditation doesn't work for everyone, and it may not even be right for everyone's temperament. But for those who find their heart drawn to it, who feel some resonance inside that this may be a way in and through at last, it is worth experimenting with for at least a month. To test, to explore, to allow the possibility of healing. To discover that healing may even be possible, even in the aftermath of great injury. To experience the tears of joy our friend wept when that which seemed so unworkable sank into the heart of healing. It is remarkable to find a tool that works in this world of half-truths and superficial approaches to deep pain. If it works, use it, make it your own, share it with your brothers and sisters in similar pain.

In entering into this meditation wholeheartedly, we become part of the solution instead of continuing the problem. We break the conspiracy of suffering passed on for generations; we stop the war. We become responsive to our pain instead of reacting to it. We begin to stop the suffering now by making room in our hearts for the pain we carry and the work of a lifetime. None of us has anything better to do, and if we don't open now, life will never get better. We'll get smaller and smaller because we have to contract in order to find safe territory. We each will close all our hearts. There is no urgency, but we can't waste a moment more with letting the pain we carry go unexplored. Our children do not need to inherit their parents' confusion. We can stop the war now. But it is not easy. Things are workable if you are willing to enter into them, but if we are not willing to put our heart into our pain we will always feel kind of heartless and we'll always be in pain. Finding our way back into our womb, back into our lives, we take birth, whole at last, able to breathe soft breath in soft body. Able to be.

It might be said here that sexual abuse is being used as an example of the great injury many have experienced in the course of a lifetime. It is not the only abuse that leaves us unwilling to be fully alive, to be present, to take risks. But it is such a clear example that I think analogies can be easily drawn. For instance, in the course of our working with those in grief, many have approached us to say that they feel something is the matter with them because they have so little feeling upon the death of a parent. They think their heart has gone cold, but in actuality some great injury in the past originating from that parent has caused them to grieve their loss many years earlier. The children of alcoholic parents, for instance, occasionally notice upon the death of that parent that there is not much feeling of deep loss. Their grieving perhaps begun at five or six years old at the loss of that person to parent them. Many daughters who had been sexually abused experienced a feeling of relief and safety upon hearing of the death of their father. Certainly, in these cases there is not a feeling of loss so much as a feeling of relief and even a deeper sense of self-trust and wholeness now that the abuser, the "un-lover," is absent. Indeed, one might hear of the death of a lover who long ago betrayed one and feel little or no grief because their loss had already been grieved for so long. Death is not the greatest loss. The greatest is the separation of hearts in the world, which leads to the separation of hearts in our body.

In the case of any great injury, whether it is sexual abuse, the abandonment by alcoholic parents, or the infidelity of a committed lover, forgiveness may be very difficult if not impossible at first. Similarly entering the womb with gentleness and loving kindness may take a while. Again one does not go to the 500-pound weight to improve one's capacity for lifting. Working with the lighter weights, we find entrance, touching with mercy the lesser abrasions and holding so as to approach the greater. There is no rush with forgiveness. There is no forcible entry. One works with this meditation slowly and as feels appropriate. There can be no force with this process, just a gentle allowing of forgiveness and mercy to fill the empty spaces, the deadness in our mind and body. And a recognition of the importance of timing. For some, to try to forgive too soon will cause a hardening in the process, a self-judgment that will just leave them more deeply abused than before. One forgives as one can in one's own time, without the least obligation. Always the work is to remember that before we can encourage another to open their heart, we must open our own. That all of our hearts need to open before we will be able to receive the heart of another.

This meditation offers the possibility of moving through the pain of the mind locked in the body to experience the one heart we all share. In the same way that our physical heart is a manifestation of the spiritual heart, our womb is a manifestation of the Mother Of Us All.

As with the forgiveness meditation, it might be useful to share the experience of some who have worked with the opening-the-Heart-of-the-Womb meditation.

ANN

"During the womb-heart meditation, I had a wonderful experience. Sweeping down the back was wonderful. I had a perfect spine. But when we started moving down the front, I had horrible black holes with yellow light around them. I heard a voice say to just watch them, and they just got smaller and smaller and went right up my heart. But I couldn't find a womb where anything could grow. I kept looking and looking. And finally I saw it. It was like a shriveled-up prune, and I thought, 'What's that?' And I just kept looking at it, and all of a sudden there was a seed there and then a baby, and it just kept growing and growing and I felt real joyful. And all of a sudden I saw the baby, and it opened its mouth like a bird saying, 'Feed me, feed me,' and I saw there was a snake wrapped around it, the same snake that always wraps around my throat in my dreams. But it didn't frighten me this time. I just undid the snake and played with it. And I saw that every time I got frightened of the snake, my womb would close and the baby would gasp for breath. So I saw that I had to pet the snake or else I would starve the baby. And then, when you said bring the heart and the womb together, the baby opened its arms and it just embraced my heart. It was a remarkable experience because for years I have spent thousands of dollars trying to figure out what was wrong with me, so many problems around food. And this whole thing of eating and purging. I saw that I was strangling my baby, baby me, I was strangled with fear. I felt so helpless, so without willpower. Every time I hated my hunger, it strangled me all the more and starved the poor baby in me. When my heart touched my womb, I saw what I was starving for.

"Yesterday, when you said something about the stomach being the center of control, that place which turns the whole world into itself, my heart was pounding so hard. Just as it is right now. I feel so alive. I feel wonderful."

FRAN

"One of the main reasons I came to this retreat was because I had heard about the work around this meditation and I felt it was right for me. I had heard about the woman who had gotten pregnant after her many miscarriages, and I sensed this might be a way for me to have a child after all the miscarriages and difficulties I have gone through. It is a long story, but what happened was that a while before the meditation I was working with my grief point down by the river, and I was overwhelmed with feelings of grief and felt as though I just couldn't move, I was so heavy. But then a fellow walked by who had shared very openly in the workshop, and I thanked him for what he shared and I sat there and I trusted him and he was a man. It was very different. And everything was just happening inside me, but I didn't get very frightened. I sort of trusted it. And the more I trusted it, the more that I saw what I needed to do was trust. And then something happened that was really neat. After I spoke to this fellow I realized that I had missed the meditation, and I said, 'Oh shit! That was the one I came for and I missed it!' But for a change I thought, 'Well, that's all right, I'll just do something else.' So I was sitting by the river under the trees, and there was this huge tree above me and I began to see the trunk of the tree just like you had described the uterus in the meditation. I saw that it was all closed off, but then I remembered that fellow and that little bit of trust, and then even this closed-offness seemed pretty okay. And while I was doing this I heard two children coming toward the river and my first reaction was, 'Oh shit! a distraction,' and then I said, 'Wait a minute, wait a minute. Everything is working out so perfect. This is perfect too.' And there coming toward me were those two children and I was trying to get in touch with my uterus, thinking the children were going to block it. But again and again my mind kept saying, 'Two beautiful children, two beautiful children.' My mind actually began to laugh! And I started to laugh out loud, and the children came over to play and sat in the creek right next to me and I felt myself real easily slipping off the bank, plop, into the water, and it was like we were all in the womb together, so soothing. And I realized maybe for the first time that I really didn't need the mother who wasn't there for me in the first place. I was the mother. And I felt like I fell in love with something, with everything."

CARLA

"I was sexually abused as a child and raped twice as a teenager. And when we started to get into this meditation, I felt like I was going to throw up. Even as we started to go into the sensations in the head and shoulders, I could hardly stay there. It was terrifying to be inside this body. But I tried to stay with it because I am sick of being so separate, so I listened very carefully and tried to stay with the experience.

"But as I got more into my torso, I was surprised at how little feeling there was. It was a kind of deadness where it was all right to injure myself as I have done so many times in the past. And I could see how I was trying to feel through all this deadness. The level of anesthesia was shocking! But I could really *see* why I had tried to hurt myself so often before. I was just trying to be alive, to feel. I was so angry, I just didn't know what else to do. But something in this meditation was different. I can't believe it. My pain told me it was okay to be alive. It actually told me that. It is really okay to be alive! I mean, it's all right even to be in pain, isn't it? Of course it is! It is all right. It is all right. I don't have to hurt myself to feel my pain. In fact, for a moment when I was frightened, I felt a kind of hot tingling in my gut. I never felt that before. Then I wasn't so scared and just looked at all those empty places in my torso, and it all felt okay. But I didn't wish for more pain when I saw how much pain there already was. I actually felt some kindness for that person in pain, and it turned out to be me.

"Just so much was happening as we started to approach the womb —God there was so much happening! I could actually feel me. That might sound dumb, but for me it was a new experience. I have been so closed off. Maybe that is why I have had so much trouble with my knees. I can hardly find my place on the earth. But in the womb I found myself. I was really there. It was so exciting. But there were still all kinds of deadness and insensitive areas. It was very spotty, this contact, but it was the most contact I have ever had.

"And then, all of a sudden, in the womb, in the middle of the deadness, I experienced my mother and instead of hating her, for the first time I experienced how mothers of abused children deaden themselves. How they put themselves to sleep and allow the abuse to happen. They lie to themselves, and they put a great deal of energy into perceiving the adult as perfect without flaw. And that was one of the places where the self-destructive energy came from. I was trying to see the adult without flaw, which just left me the battered and flawed one. I had deadened myself to try and make it all okay, to see as my mother saw, to deny the abuse. But all these dead spots showed me how dead I was. I think maybe I forgave my mother some because she disappeared in one of those dead places, she disappeared into the numbness, and all of a sudden my whole womb began to tingle. It felt like conception."

ZENA

"When you said earlier today that we were going to do this meditation, I thought that would be an interesting one for me because I don't have a uterus. I had my whole reproductive system removed about a year and a half ago because I had ovarian cancer. But as I went through the body, I imagined it was there. I enjoyed remembering the receptivity that took in sperm and egg. The fallopian tubes that were so mobile and ready to take in anything. And then I went through a sadness and a grief that they were gone, but then I thought, 'Oh what a wonderful time to reseed my heart,' so I said to my womb, 'Oh come back, just for a moment. I still need you a little bit for this minute.' And again the whole receptivity thing was experienced. It cradled my heart. And then I could say goodbye to it. Oh and I forgot, somewhere in there, with some effort, I had the fallopian tubes touch even my cancer lovingly. My womb is gone. But during the meditation I certainly experienced what you refer to as the second heart space. That receptivity, that acceptance of it all. Oddly, I wasn't even angry at my cancer. I wasn't angry at anything. I didn't feel deprived, I felt thankful."

ROBERTA

"During the meditation I had an awful experience. Everything was going fine until all of a sudden I remembered twelve years ago when I was giving birth. I was in my tenth month, and the doctor knew I was having a difficult time. Then my labor stopped and I became very frightened. And he told me to 'stop being such a baby' and handled me very roughly. It was just a horror show. And in the meditation I could feel all that anger, actually all the hatred at that doctor because his mishandling almost killed us both and left me with all kinds of problems with my uterus. During the meditation I could feel all this anger at him. It was really terrifying how much anger there was in my womb. And then I remembered another doctor who raped me once, and I was hysterical and all, carrying on, and he said, 'Oh calm down, it's just flesh and flesh, you're not a virgin, you've had children, you know what it's all about.' And all this hatred was there in my womb. All this hatred that I had always felt was for men.

"But what I experienced during this meditation was this horrible anger at all these doctors, the ones who were cruel, the ones who abused me, and all the other doctors who just forgot I was a human being. But I must say something very strange happened. In the midst of all that hatred, something inside of me burst. Something inside of me began to laugh and clap, and I realized that I don't hate men, I hate doctors! That may sound kind of weird, but to me it was very freeing. Anyhow, it's a beginning."

DON

"I experienced quite a bit during that meditation, but most of all I want to say that I feel my womb, I feel my openness, but I am abused too. So many women look at my penis as if it were an instrument of destruction. All the missiles, all the bullets, all the swords, so many weapons shaped in that same form. I am just sick and tired of having that part of me which is capable of expressing great tenderness, seen as a weapon, a destroyer, instead of as a lover. I can't blame them for feeling this after these days of sharing about abuse and hearing women's agony around such heartless treatment. But I am a human too and I hate those who have abused those I love and cannot love me back because of it. I hate the abusers."

VALERIE

"Something helped me tremendously today to validate the experiences in my body and just step aside from the debate that constantly goes on in my head. As we were exploring so lovingly I quit blaming myself for feeling so helpless about being abused. It was such a relief for me to just say that at times I feel helpless, and quit trying to do and undo all those things in the past and make it all better, to just accept the heartbreaking pain I feel at times. Something in me just quit blaming and feeling all caught up. The situation with my dad is hopeless. He doesn't drink anymore, but he has forgotten much of what he did to me so I am left feeling to blame for all the anger I have always felt. Nobody will acknowledge it, so it's almost like I did it to myself. But I am not to blame. No one is to blame; there is no blaming. It was hard as hell to go beyond blaming to the next place. But it's so good to be here if even for a few minutes.

"I probably feel right now more peace and space in myself than I have felt in a long time, maybe ever. What is happening in me is that I feel the tiniest little opening of compassion for those people who abused me because all of a sudden it came to me that they couldn't have had any knowledge, any truth about love themselves, and how painful and sad that made me feel for them. It's like the line from that poem you read us by Thich Nhat Hanh, the Vietnamese monk, about the sea pirates who were killing all those innocents. He understood them as 'hearts who were not yet able to see.' I think that's my real forgiveness for all of them, for all of that, to see how blind their heart must have been to have created so much pain. Seeing this allows me to come back into myself, and right now I can give myself the love I know they missed."

ELIZABETH

"After the meditation I felt like I just wanted to be quiet, so I went for a walk in the woods. I felt kind of soft inside. It was a new feeling for me, and the woods were so beautiful and the birds were singing. And I came around a bend in the trail and there was this huge ponderosa right there in front of me. And it was beautiful and I was looking at it, but all of a sudden I just saw it! I just saw the tree. I don't think I've ever seen a tree before. It's like you say, my life has always been an afterthought, but I was just there and this tree was just there. And it made me think of the woman who came down for breakfast and just saw the wall. When you told that story, I didn't quite get what you meant. I can't really express it. But if when I go home I can just see my husband the way I saw that tree, I know things will be different. He has been very understanding, but I've always been a little cold to him. Maybe I'll be able to see him without all the fears that his 'maleness' brings. I wasn't sexually abused as a child, but I am still fearful of the power that men have over women. I think there is something in me that has been frightened to come out all these years. I am the last one who ever would have thought they had anything to do with this meditation. But I think it may make our home a happier place to live."

MARNIE

"I was really surprised by this meditation. I thought I would find all kinds of darkness and deadness in the womb. But instead it was just filled with light. It was so hospitable. I couldn't believe how easy it was to touch myself with mercy, to feel my whole womb as forgiveness. And I sure could feel the connection between these hearts. There was so much light in my lower heart, the womb, that there seemed to be light everywhere. And I think somehow in there I forgave myself. During the forgiveness meditation, when we came to the part of sending forgiveness to ourselves, it was very difficult for me. But in the womb meditation I was just there, kind of like how Elizabeth saw the tree. I saw me. I was just there. It was just forgiveness. I didn't have to try and do anything. I just can't believe the womb and the heart actually are one. This is a wonderful meditation, and I can't wait to get home and share it with my husband. We have been thinking about having a child, but there has been something in me that was reluctant. It made me kind of queasy thinking about trying to protect and nurture a child in this crazy world. But there is more trust in me than I imagined. Even fear isn't as deep as I thought it would be. I just can't believe it, I am going to be a mother. It's just like Ondrea says, 'Nothing is too good to be true!' This may sound like nothing to you, but it's a whole other world for me. I almost said, 'Goddamn, I am going to be a mother!' But my womb said, 'No, no, it's God bless, God bless!' "

After the meditation a woman took us aside to share her experience. "I was shaking with so much energy. So much had been released and tears were pouring out all over the place when someone came up behind me and put their arms around me and tried to rock me and I didn't feel like it at all. It scared the shit out of me, and I felt myself close right down. It was an old familiar feeling. I didn't trust them. It didn't feel right." She had been touched with pity instead of love, and it frightened her. It sounded as though the person who approached may have had a need for her to be otherwise. They may have touched her tears with fear instead of love, with need instead of blessing—they perhaps reacted instead of responding. Not trusting their own pain, they didn't trust hers.

All mental wounding, from sexual abuse to racial harassment, results in distrust. That is why it is of such prime importance that therapists who wish to serve those with such deep mental wounding clear themselves of "healers' disease," the need for someone else to be different as a means of bargaining with their own sense of helplessness and unworthiness. It is by understanding the intention behind our touch that we break the knee-jerk emergency reaction to suffering. It defines the importance of the work on ourselves, which allows us to touch with love that which has been fearfully rejected. It is another example of how working on ourselves is of benefit to all so that we do not touch with need but instead offer love.

Those who have been sexually abused are extremely sensitive to being touched. It is especially frightening to be touched with need because that is what a rapist does, an abuser does, a torturer. And no one is so sensitive to the difference between being touched with love and being touched with need as someone whose mind or body has been abused.

This process is another example of how we can heal by not distancing the heart from the unhealed. In self-forgiveness and kind deliberation, the womb and the heart become one. Just as the mind sinks into the heart in the healing of grief, so the heart sinks into the body as a part of the healing of our mind.

Rumi says:

> We are the mirror as well as the face in it.
> We are tasting the taste this minute
> Of eternity. We are pain
> And what cures pain, both. We are
> The sweet, cold water, and the jar that pours.

Opening-the-Heart-of-the-Womb Meditation

[To be read slowly to a friend or silently to oneself.]

Find a comfortable place to sit in a quiet room and begin to bring a soft awareness into the body.

Beginning at the top of the head, allow a merciful awareness to gently receive the sensations arising—the softness of the scalp against the skullcap, the roundness of the brow. Releasing any tension around the eyes, allow this gentle awareness to move slowly through the face. Receive the soft flesh of the cheeks, the tingling at the tip of the nose, the warmth of the ears at the side of the head. Feel the muscles of the jaw begin to soften as they let life in, in mercy and loving kindness. The tongue lying gently within the mouth. The weight of the head perfectly balanced on the willing muscles of the neck.

Allow awareness to receive the multiple sensations that arise in various parts of the head and face before it proceeds downward into the throat and the neck and in the darkness of the throat unsaid, the often swallowed away, touched by deep acceptance and kindness. The tension of the unloved dissolving in mercy and self-care.

Feel the long muscles that extend from the base of the skull soften as they spread out into the shoulders, gently cradling the head on the neck.

And in the darkness of the throat the long unsaid, the often swallowed away, touched by deep acceptance and kindness. The tension of the unloved dissolving in mercy and self-care.

Sensations floating in a gentle comforting awareness which receives the body as living suchness, pulsing, vibrating with aliveness.

Feel how the shoulders support the arms that cradle the sides of the body. Feel the strength in the shoulders, the musculature, the bones, the tendons that so easily allow their remarkable capacity for movement.

Feel how this miracle of life extends down each arm filling the palm, vibrating to the tip of each finger.

Feel how life animates the muscles, the tissue, the flesh that comprises the shoulders, extending down the arms into the hands.

Feel the capacity for movement, for service, within the hands' ability to reach out and to touch, to bandage and to caress. Feel the aliveness of the hands scintillating in each palm.

Notice how the arms embrace the body.

Feel the chest rising and falling naturally with each breath. How the breath breathes itself in trust, each breath following the last effortlessly. Feel the heart beating within, the lungs gently opening with each breath.

Notice any sensations around the grief point, at the touch point of the heart. Soften any holding there. Let sensations float in a new mercy, in a deeper kindness toward oneself.

Notice that wherever awareness enters, life is to be found. Feel the varying densities of different areas of the body. Feel its warmth or coolness. Feel the pressure and release that awareness allows as it opens the body. Wherever awareness is directed, healing arises.

Now allow this gentle awareness to move toward the back. Beginning at the top of the spine where the neck spreads out to form the back of the shoulders, allow this healing awareness to gradually receive one vertebra after another in loving kindness moving from the first to the last vertebra one at a time gently descending the back.

The miracle of the spine supported so perfectly by the flat muscles of the upper back extending down to the long lateral muscles of the lower back. Feel the tissue, the flesh, the remarkable support of the back.

Let your attention move gently to the base of the spine, approaching the lower torso.

Just notice in mercy and awareness whatever sensations, thoughts or emotions arise as you approach the lower torso.

Now let the attention return to the chest area and proceed gently down the front of the body receiving the ribs as they spread out like a protective canopy above the open softness of the stomach and belly.

Allow the belly to soften, to receive healing there. In soft belly there is room for it all. In soft belly is the possibility of completion.

Feel the breath breathing itself in soft belly. Feel the muscles rising and falling all by themselves with each breath. Just breath breathing itself in soft belly. Just life continuing to heal itself.

Continuing gently across the pelvic area notice whatever tension or thoughts arise. Feel this whole area in softness and mercy. No force, just a gentle allowing of sensations to present themselves as they will. Softening lower belly, softening the hips, softening the buttocks.

Allowing awareness to gently move through, let the sensations in the upper legs, knees and feet, be received in whole body. Letting awareness pass tenderly through the genitals continue through the upper legs, thighs, and calves as it slowly moves to the soles of the feet.

Feel the strength and durability of the legs and knees, and ankles and feet. Feel their capacity for movement.

Feel the preciousness of each step they are able to provide.

Feel the quality of tingling and vibration in the lower body. Feel both legs, feet, knees, hips, as an aliveness, a presence in the body.

Feel the rootedness with the earth at the bottom of each foot. Its trust.

Begin gradually to allow awareness to fill the legs, gradually moving up from the soles of the feet to the upper legs.

Allow awareness to gradually gather toward the inside of the upper legs. Feel the area between the knees, the sensation of space, the tingling of skin and muscle. Feel the space between the upper thighs at the very top of the legs.

Let your attention move up to that space at the very top of the legs, where the left leg meets the right leg. Feel the space between the upper thighs at the very top of the legs, where they connect with the lower torso.

Gently.

Gently moving toward the area between the legs.

Just receiving very tenderly whatever sensations are generated there.

Allow this soft awareness to receive the sensations there at the labia with great mercy and tenderness.

Allowing the awareness to gather as it will without the least sense of rushing or urgency, allow a merciful exploration of the entrance into the body.

Feel the ruffled fringe of flesh that protects that tender entrance of the body.

Just allowing awareness to gather there at the opening into the body.

With mercy.

Tenderly moving through the shadows and light into the area of the vulva.

Feel the muscles there, their capacity to receive.

Their capacity to feel.

Their willingness to be this holy body we all share.

Gently allowing the light, the mercy to enter into the vagina.

This moist, merciful entrance.

Touching so tenderly with mercy the subtle wrinkles, the subtle muscles of the vagina.

Allowing awareness to soften and receive life as it enters the body.

Allowing mercy to receive the sensations in the vagina.

Moving so tenderly into the cervix and muscles. The tissues softening to receive this sweet heart expanding into the dome of the womb.

The cave of life.

Feel its spaciousness, its openness. Its homeness.

Let awareness start to receive the womb with mercy and loving kindness. For yourself. For this tender heart.

Let your womb fill gradually with the light of your mercy for yourself.

Let the heart of the womb open to receive its own nature once again, to come home to itself, to make room for you.

Let the soft light of that heart shine there in the womb.

Opening the womb of mercy, of forgiveness, of compassion for yourself.

Letting the womb soften, letting it open.

Letting it just be at last. In loving kindness, in gentle healing mercy.

Sense the fallopian tubes are extending like branches from this tree of life, the strong trunk of the vagina opening through the cervix into the great dome of the womb, its branches extending like arms embracing itself.

Feel the loving kindness slowly expanding in the womb, filling it with a healing mercy and gentleness, slowly extending life into the branches of the tree through which the essence of all life has always passed.

Allow the light of the womb to move gradually into each of the fallopian channels.

Feel the feathery subtlety there like leaves flowering at the end of the fallopians and feel the ovaries like fruit filled with seeds shimmering at the end of each branch.

Allow the light of this heart to bring mercy to itself.

To heal itself in loving kindness, to allow itself its own embrace, its own fulfillment, its own completion.

Feel the light, warm golden light filling the womb, filling the branches of the tree, shimmering in the ovaries, sparkling in the seeds within.

Feel the whole womb, the whole tree of life filled with light. Filled with mercy. Filled at last with tender mercy.

With tender care.

Let the womb fill with love for itself, for all sentient beings.

And let the heart meet the womb, let the heart gradually sink into the womb, the upper heart and lower heart forming one shimmering star of being, of kindness, of completion.

Let it be. Allow.

Allow your hearts to meet.

Let the heart sink into the womb, let it receive itself in wholeness, in mercy, in joy.

Allow the light to be.

May we be free of a past of pain and confusion.

May we let our wombs, our hearts, be filled with their own natural light.

May we be whole unto ourselves.

May we be at peace.

May all beings be free from suffering.

May all beings know the joy, the healing of their true luminescent nature. May we all meet in mercy, in noninjury, in compassion.

May we be healed. May we be at peace.

May all beings be free.

May we all be free.

PLEASE TAKE A FEW SOFT BREATHS
AS WE MOVE
FROM ONE LEVEL TO THE NEXT.

AS IN GROWTH, OR DYING,
WE NEED LET GO
AT THE EDGE
TO CONTINUE FURTHER.

TRUST THE PROCESS
LET GO LIGHTLY
PASS ON GENTLY.

CHAPTER 13

Whose Body, Who's Ill?

Invited several years ago to lead a workshop with a well-known healer, a few minutes before we began, a newspaper reporter approached who asked, "Are you the healer or the one who helps people die?" To which I heard myself respond, "I don't know."

It was not unlike the question, "Should I continue healing or let myself die?" It came from the same separation between life and death, the confusion which keeps our healing so shallow and our life so partially lived. Both questions presuppose death to be opposed to life. They are asking, "Should I live or should I die?" But life is process, and death is but one event during this enormous unfolding. It is not a matter of life *or* death, of healing *or* dying, but simply of life which includes death, healing which excludes nothing. It means living our death, healing our dying.

After the workshop, Ondrea and I explored the newsman's question. It was at some levels as unanswerable and as naturally evident as a Zen koan.*

It was clear, reflecting on the reporter's question that the work we are discovering even at this writing is not about being a "conscious dier" or a "holistic healer," but about being another pilgrim on the

---

* N.B. a koan is a mystery conundrum, a contemplative device used in the Zen tradition to empty the mind and clear the heart. Perhaps the most famous koan is "What is the sound of one hand clapping?" To which a friend with great jocularity snaps his fingers as if gesturing "Eureka!" These are not questions, they are challenges to become who we really are. It is said that the greatest of koans is "Who am I?" Its levels and levels of unanswerableness force us past death and other such concepts in the mind to enter the indefinable deathlessness of being. Seen as a koan, "Should I live or should I die?" is not a question but a call to awaken, secret passwords into the moment, a reminder to die into our life and to "outlive our death." "To be or not to be?" is the toll collector's riddle as he requires us to relinquish our suffering if we are to continue to the other shore.

path, brailleing our way toward the truth: creating the body moment to moment in the mind, reflecting mind instant to instant in the body. All so clearly recognizable against the spacious backdrop of awareness, the opening heart, the impermanence of the moment.

On the pilgrim's path, all credentials are just extra baggage to lug along, more a source of fatigue than satisfaction. Any identifications at all, even those such as "dier" or "healer," are seen as more models, just more concepts and dreams, the separatisms of mind, the identity to which our suffering clings. Someone different to be, someone special to suffer. For whenever there is this specialness and separatism, whether it be fear or pride, ecstasy or infatuation, doubt or confusion, to the degree there is identification with these qualities, to the degree there is a sense that these qualities are all we are, there is a blockage to healing, a limited access to the universal. Caught in the small mind, we have so little room in the small body.

So there arises yet another question: "What keeps us in this very instant from discovering what direction our natural healing might take?" And instantly the heart whispers that it is the mistaken identity of "I am this body" which keeps us so small. The same narrow identification we find so present in the mind/body of "I am this pain." It is the same *my* body, *my* pain that takes illness or injury as a personal failure. But when awareness comes to see it as *"the* pain in *the* body," there seems room for healing in the Greater Body, in the Greater Mind. Then the edges of our old identifications with ourselves as pain and illness soften as the mind/body is allowed yet a deeper expression of the vastness and balance from which healing may be drawn.

So it has been for those who began to see that it is not "my mind, my anger, my fear, my difficulty healing," but instead began to relate to all these previous blockages and hindrances to healing as *"the* mind, *the* anger, *the* difficulty in healing." They started remarkably not to take their suffering so personally. As each began to see it as *the* mind instead of *my* mind, it all became so much more workable. They began to relate to the mind instead of from it. Then the mind and body became a classroom instead of a prison cell.

This investigation may at times even allow one to see that the body has cancer or pain or some imbalance but that who we really are is just a temporary tenant of this rented domicile. Seeing the body as solidified mind we watch the mind in order to unlock the body. Or more precisely, unlock identification with the body as all that we are. We go beyond death or even birth to define the indefinable essence of being that hums at the very center of life, the melody of the spheres that resonates in each cell. It is a silent watching of all the changing conditions in the mind/body which leads to a recognition that we are, as a friend put it, "creation constantly in the act of unfolding."

When we question the nature of the mind's incessant identification with the experiences of the body and the contents of thought, we enter into the very moment in which existence is to be found. We discover the spaciousness in which all these forms of thought and sensation are unfolding. We touch "the ever-trusting," the "ever-open." When we go beyond definition, trusting that spaciousness in which all wisdom arises, the edges dissolve into being itself. The stillness in which all activity floats, the formlessness that defines form.

When we let go of everything that blocks healing, only the healing remains, only our essential nature. We are all healers who need healing, but it seems so often to be a question of trust. Because letting go means letting be, and few trust what it is.

Many who entered physically and mentally into the heart of healing began to have a different sense of who they were. They no longer held so to "I am this body," because "I am this body" is the same as "I am sickness, I am pain, I am unhealed." They loosened their grasping to "I am this mind" because "I am this mind" is "I am fear, I am death." They no longer navigated by a sense of someone to be, of something to lose, of failure and loss. It was no longer the sickness of the imagined separate insisting on its separateness. Nor the increasing accumulation of grief and disappointment and sense of disconnection from the source. From the healing that seems always just a breath away or, perhaps more accurately, the healing within this very breath.

But if I think I am this mind/body, will I not imagine you to be equally lost in that mind, that body? How will we ever join in the shared heart of healing? How will we ever let go into the universal healing that awaits? Seeing healing does not mean creating anything, even a new body or a different mind, but only the discovery of what already exists; we come to recognize that awareness itself creates the balance we call healing, and wisdom is a sign of our deepest health. We discover the healing which is always present when we aren't identified solely with this body or mind or any separate aspect whatsoever with any model of who we should be or who we are or even what illness might be. Seeing illness as a teaching instead of a curse, we learn to let go of a lifetime's denial of pain and confusion, to see the deeper illness, the sickness of separation from ourselves, the nausea and discomfort that leaks into the separation between the heart and mind.

When we closely attend to the sensations and reactions of the body, we come to see in the body, solidified mind—a kind of perpetual reference to the past. A catalog of old imprints and deep conditioning, a reference library of the illusion of separateness held solid in the once flesh. In this exploration one discovers the states of mind and holdings which reinforce the idea, "I am this body. I am this mind." But when we allow the mind to sink into the heart, we enter life at a level where healing is appreciated in whatever form it takes.

To see for ourselves with clear attention what is "real," never settling for a single answer, but always continuing deeper through levels and levels of understanding so that the healing can penetrate to the very marrow of existence. So that the imbalances conditioned in the mind/body can be exposed to the light of the ever-uninjured within, the deathless.

Those who start this investigation of what illness might be open the gates of healing. When we get up in the morning and don't take anything for granted that day, when we want to see whether life is real or just a dream, then that day becomes very precious, unforgettable in these tens of thousands of forgotten days. Days where we have brought so little attention, so little tenderness to ourselves, so little of that joyous bewilderment of not knowing, of being willing to participate directly, of taking nothing for granted. Seeing that even the word "real" changes meaning from moment to moment as awareness enters deeper, as mercy melts resistance and our edges dissolve into the unknown.

As we look into our conditioning, we see how profoundly incised in consciousness is the concept that healing is the absence of disease. This old conditioning creates the old mind of a relatively low realm for healing. It is by healing that we heal: it is in the moments when the mind has gone beyond its identification with the body that we see the uninjured, the whole, the edgeless nature of that which inhabits the body and experiences illness without itself being ill. With each moment of this seeing beyond illness comes a reconditioning which meets the old mind of "I am this body, I am this mind," with a new inquiry—"Whose body? Who's mind?" And seeing yet further that the body belongs to itself and the mind has a mind of its own, we enter the undefinable center of consciousness—awareness, the light by which consciousness is illuminated, experienced directly as our essential "am-ness" as we come to ask who indeed is body, who indeed is mind. Whose who?

Among the first steps of healing is to let go of our definition of what we imagined healing might be. Our healing is a meeting of the old with a newness. It is a letting go of the ancient numbness with which we react to our suffering, a relinquishment of clinging and identification with our incessant mercilessness and judgment, our momentous resistance and fear. It means not thinking our healing but being it.

We have seen among the "very healed" many that nonetheless experience illness. Many holy women and men, many saints and adepts, bodied with disease. That even what appears to be "enlightenment" does not preclude the possibility of suffering in the body. Indeed, most of my spiritual teachers have experienced illness of one sort or another—Neem Karoli Baba, known as Maharaji, suffered what appeared to be a heart attack; Ramana Maharshi died of cancer, as did Nisargadatta. Suzuki Roshi also died of cancer, as did Ramakrishna and Vivekananda. And such living contemporaries as Kennet Roshi, Aachan Cha, Bill Kwong, and Seung Sahn have been confronted with such as cancer, strokes and heart failure. Indeed I am told that when Seung Sahn, the extraordinary Korean Zen master, experienced fibrillation due to a diabetic condition, when asked by concerned students what was the matter, he said, "It is okay. My heart is only singing." This is a heart which is diseased but a healed heart if ever I've seen one.

Experiencing the illnesses of such spiritual friends and teachers, noting their remarkable responses, has helped us to let go of any half truth or concept about the cause of illness or what true healing might be.

From this vantage point we get a glimpse of what the deepest healing available might be: the healing that begins with the ability to learn from disease in the body, to "take the teaching" from illness. The healing are those who allow love to replace fear in meeting the unknown and allow awareness to enter resistance. In an odd way, one might say that healing is not so much changing the body or removing illness as it is allowing all of it into the heart. It means not even getting lost in identification with old doubt or fear, but seeing the content of each moment with the deep acceptance of "Big Surprise!", doubt again, fear again. It isn't the first time, and it certainly won't be the last. Then *"my* doubt," *"my* fear," *"my* resistance" only remind one to investigate more deeply, to more mercifully enter the moment of *the* mind, *the* fear, *the* resistance we all share. The exploration of our identification with doubt or fear or the old clingings that have always amplified pain give rise to a new confidence. Another moment of trust to take one step, to open just one millisecond more to that from which we have always withdrawn. To open to the old in a new way, to experience the fear, the anger, the love, the mercy. Healing becomes deeper as that which blocks healing becomes more clearly seen.

Seeing that it is not *"my* body, *my* pain," but *the* pain, brings up the question "Then who is in this pain, *the* pain?" So we look to see "who" is ill, "who" is suffering, which one of our many changing selves and personality aspects is the source of this discomfort. We see a thousand thoughts and sensations in quick succession arising and passing away in the edgeless spaciousness of pure awareness.

As we look to see "who" is looking, "who" is healing, "who" is healed, the mind simply states, "I am," with no explanation. But who is this "I am" to which the mind refers? Is it some part of oneself that needs to be healed? Some idea of oneself? Is it just some old dream, just an afterthought, some constantly reinforced illusion to which all the pains of a lifetime adhere? And how do these pains attach to this "I am"? How do they conclude, "I am this suffering" or "I am this cancer"?

We notice that whenever we say "I am this" or "I am that" that something just doesn't feel quite right. That somehow we feel incomplete. That there is no this or that which can quite define the all of what "I am" refers to. That any identification at all leaves us feeling kind of compressed and dull, grieving some deeper spaciousness that goes beyond definition. That the "thises" and "thats" of "I am a carpenter, I am a mother, I am a man, I am a woman, I am a person with cancer, I am a parent, I am a spiritual seeker, I am a healer, I am someone who helps people die consciously, I am the body, I am the mind" are all just more dark lenses which obscure the clear seeing of edgeless being.

All the thises and thats to which we have adhered for so long and that we have thought we should be just leave us feeling more like imposters, more incomplete. Nothing we can attach to this "I am" seems sufficient. That essence to which "I am" refers goes beyond all definition and limitation. We see that the idea "I am this" leads to the belief "You are that"—it is the very definition of separateness, the creator of I and other, the basis of all fear, the distance of the mind from the heart. When the "I" of being this or that, the personal, the sufferer falls away, all that is experienced is the "amness," the universal, the ever-healed, beingness itself.

In fact, if we were to write a list of all the things we thought we were and had, it would be a compendium of our distance from our true nature, from God itself. But with this "don't know" trust in the process of investigation, we discover this involuntary, unconscious blocking of our natural ability to heal.

Going deeper, as we experience the "I" separating from the "am," we loosen the sticky quality which holds so to our recurring discomfitures. There becomes less and less for fear or confusion or even pain to stick to, less of someone to be afraid. As one ex-cancer patient said, "It is not so much a process of losing oneself as it is of finding out what is there in the first place."

And as we go yet deeper, beyond "I am this" to just "I am" and investigate, to what does this "I am" refer? "I-ness" begins to separate from "am-ness," and the various "who's" of our imagined self dissolve. And we experience the many masks of our overacted melodrama falling away in a clatter to the theater floor and the heart turns to the mind and says, "That's okay, just leave them for the sweeper!" Then this "I am" becomes not an afterthought but a direct experience of being itself, and we see dissolving one after another in a succession of ghostly incarnations all the images of ourselves that have grasped so long at definition and have suffered so unbearably. We see each image of ourself simply as another thought, a bubble in space constantly reborn as another idea of someone we imagine is experiencing it all. But as we stay with this willingness to experience life directly, to constantly ask, "Who is in pain, who suffers, who heals?" the painfully separate "I" dies, and only the ever-connected peacefulness of "amness" remains. Healing with each breath, we go deeper. The experiencer and the experienced dissolve into the very moment of experience itself unfolding in spacious being. No definitions to create, just the moment unfolding, clearly demonstrating that all preconceived answers are just old problems, another shallowness that limits the deepest healing. Letting go of our separate identities, our credentials, our masks, our hearts' armorings we awake from the under-dream of a separate suffering self into the amness of pure awareness.*

When that part of the mind which wishes to define itself by creating identities, credentials, someone to be, a body to be in, is the least assertive, the healing that seems to go on about us and within us is the most intense. The less of the separate "I" there is to be identified as a healer or as someone who needs to be healed, the more there is available to healing. And the less there is to obstruct the place within that is already and forever beyond illness and beyond need of healing. The center of the universe, the center of the heart.

---

* For a more detailed explanation of the "Who am I?" investigation, please see *Who Dies?*

The clear bead at the center changes everything.
There are no edges to my loving now.

I've heard it said there's a window that opens
from one mind to another,

but if there's no wall, there's no need
for fitting the window, or the latch.

Rumi

CHAPTER 14

Taking Your Medicine

As an example of how we can use even the seemingly insignificant aspects of the healing process as a means of powerfully connecting the heart with the disheartened, let us explore the usual "unconsciousness" with which we often take our medicine.

To clarify our relationship with the body of illness, or the injured mind, and to bring the distress of "my pain" within the sacred moment of the immediate present—the healing spaciousness of "the pain"—the way in which we take medication becomes a matter of much importance. By converting mechanical unconscious pill swallowing to a momentary ritual of awareness, it becomes a sacred act by which many begin to comprehend the teaching that medicine symbolizes. By breaking our addiction to automatic action, a desire of the superficial to be healed from outside itself, we enter into the direct participation in our healing from within. Then taking medication is not an act of distancing from our illness but a means of opening the channels to healing, of taking the medicine deep within, of letting the healing enter. It becomes an act of discovery instead of subtle helplessness and shadowy despair. Taking the medicine within instead of from without, we discover how deeply we wish the healing and at how many levels we might draw our sustenance.

To take our medicine in a sacred manner is to parallel the highest level of the American Indian shaman consciousness, which sees experience *as* medicine. The degree of a medicine's power to heal is predicated on the intention behind it. The Sioux speak of acts of love as "good medicine" and acts of distrust or fear as "bad medicine."

Recognizing that each moment holds the potential for injury or healing, we use here the word "medicine" to include any methods from wheat-grass therapy to open-heart surgery, from prayer to meditation. We see medicine not as the curse of illness but as a teaching of aliveness. It is not, "You had your fun, now take your medicine!", not the deep conditioning of medicine as punishment. It is not at all the bitter pill so often referred to, but rather medicine as the sweet potion of the release of suffering into liberation and wholeness. It is medicine as an opportunity for awakening.

Because each suffers, to some degree, from a case of mistaken identity—mistaking thinking for our true nature, feeling for our true body, the givens of personality for our true nature—it is not uncommon for us to relate to a treatment for an illness as though it were the illness itself. We often gulp down our aspirin in order to swallow back our headache. But to relate to these aspirin as a teaching is to make yet more space for the dull pain in our head. There is a saying, "Don't mistake the finger pointing to the moon for the moon itself," which means don't confuse the body of illness with the heart of awareness, don't mistake what catches our attention with the attention itself. This case of mistaken identification is perhaps why so many spiritual aspirants become so stiff, taking on the method as personal self rather than as a means of letting go of this separateness.

Thus taking medicine, using each treatment as an act of consciousness, we come to experience the "healing before healing." The moments of wholeness experienced on the way to total wholeness, perhaps akin to what Zen Master Suzuki Roshi called the enlightenment before enlightenment. Moments of seeing clearly before our sight is completely clear. The don't-know openness of the complete beginner spontaneously experiencing sudden wordless understandings arising in a clearing mind and opening heart. The pure joy of our innate wholeness, glimpsed if even for a moment, blossoming in the vast spaciousness of being. Each flower recognized by its momentary fragrance and texture, ripening into the fruits which will finally be tasted fully. In these fleeting views of our potential for healing, these healing moments, we experience a glimmer of our true nature.

It is here we see it is not our methods of healing, either physically or spiritually, which do the work for us, but rather the intention and intensity with which they are applied. We don't expect our healing to come simply from our methods or medications, but rather from a willingness to let them in fully. Seldom is this phenomenon more noticeable than in the taking of medicine. We swallow our headache aspirin unable to separate our pain from our desire to be painless. How often do we take our aspirin or chemotherapy or treatments with any degree of awareness? How much more often do we just swallow down our unwellness and our medication as well? How seldom do we directly participate in our healing instead of letting some method or medicine do it for us? Do not mistake ideas about healing or medication or cures for the healing itself.

To take our medicine consciously is the difference between a temporary cure for distress and the long-lived spaciousness of our true healing. Medicine as chemistry alone is the materialized longing for things to be otherwise. It holds the potential for causing the mind/body to cultivate and intensify resistance and despair as well as gratitude and trust. The attitude with which medicine is taken is the intention toward healing which allows deepest access to our deepest imbalances. For some the fear, anticipation, and helplessness with which they take medicine may indeed block healing.

Perhaps to some degree in our culture we have lost the healing within healing. At other times and in other cultures, beyond the powerful influence of the medical physician's mind/body technology, when one took a medicine, all about them prayed that change be accomplished in grace. So, for many, the half dozen moments each day when medications are administered have become the most heartful moments of the day. We are often told by individuals who use this technique of focusing on their medication and guiding its entrance into the body that as they took a few minutes of silence and reflected on what they wanted from the medication, they felt a connection with the area of illness and could sense the most skillful means of directing lovingly the healing within. Some began to visualize the medication sinking into the area to be healed in the same way that the mind sinks into the heart. Many spoke of receiving more healing from each tablet or injection received. As one fellow put it, "I always wanted to get my medication out of the way. I never paid any attention. Medication time was kind of like a station break —it identified who I was—a cancer, an aging man, a pain—but I was always waiting for the main program to resume. I didn't feel like listening to another test of the emergency broadcast network. I wanted it all to go away, so I tried to tune it out. But I saw that I was kind of in collusion with the tumors because I really wasn't doing anything to help my healing. It was my throat that led me to it. I was always worrying about taking my pills, trying to remember the schedule, hoping they would work, anxious that I needed something stronger. I could hardly get them down, I gagged, they scraped my throat. The whole thing about medicine made me uptight. I just chugged them away without a thought to what I was doing. I had to relax or choke. I noticed that if I just took a minute beforehand, maybe taking a sip or two of water, seeing how many sips it took before I could really taste it, there was more presence for what was happening. As the pills went down, they were actually welcomed in.'' Eventually his three-minute meditation on medication, as he put it, became a half dozen ten- or fifteen-minute meditations each day. "Now I look forward to my medication. It is a perfect excuse to heal."

It might be mentioned here that the following meditation is applicable to more than simple swallowing of medication in pill form. Many use it during radiation treatments or chemotherapy. One mother, who must daily pound on the back of her child who has cystic fibrosis to clear her lungs of breath-denying mucus, said that the use of this meditation allowed the powerful striking of her palm against her daughter's often-exhausted back to become less an act of violence and more "the thud of blessing," "kind of like the Zen Master's stick which wakes me when I go on automatic—when I am somewhere else dreaming instead of just there in the room with my distressed child. I used to hate that sound, but now these treatments have become deeply meaningful to us both. Somehow that intenseness is softer than I ever could have imagined and more accurate." Now she takes a moment to put on some music before the treatment, to massage her daughter for a while before and after, to allow a consciousness of love to enter into a place that had previously been anticipated with fear and trembling. Now she sees the treatments not as a necessary evil, but as an essential goodness. It has taken her a while to make this leap of faith between the profane and the sacred, between automatic despair and loving application, but she and her daughter are much the better for it. Her daughter says the treatments are no more fun than they ever were, but they are a lot less unfun. "My mom used to hold me so tight after the treatments—it was always like she was apologizing, and it kind of scared me. But now she rocks me in her arms and sometimes even hums to me."

So this meditation can be used to direct any form of healing into the area that healing is wished for. Use your own genius to see how it might best be applied for your temperament and needs.

Meditation on Taking Medicine Within

[To be read slowly to a friend or silently to oneself.]

Sitting comfortably in a chair or lying easily in bed, pick up the medicine container and just feel it there in your hand. Feel its shape, its denseness, its texture, its quality of coldness or warmth.

Let your hand make contact, feel the sensations generated there.

Let the fingers open the container with awareness. Notice any strain or urgency and soften all about it.

Feel the medications, the pills, as they drop onto the palm of your hand.

Take a moment to look at the pills.

Take a moment to notice if the pill is regarded wholeheartedly as a medium of healing, or if there is a modicum of shame or failure that accompanies it. Focusing on the healing quality within the medication, look on the medicine as a healing potential.

Let the body open to receive the healing within.

Sense the treatment's potential to enter fully into the area of discomfort, its power to bring equanimity and balance.

See the pills there in your hand. Feel their slight weight against the sensitive nerve endings in your palm.

Listen to the medicine. Does it have something to say? What is its tone of voice? Is there any sense of helplessness in your relationship to the medicine? Just notice it.

Meet with mercy and awareness any resistance we may have previously ingested along with our treatments. Look on these medications with loving kindness and gratitude.

Thank the pills for whatever healing they may have to offer and place them gently in your mouth.

Feel it on your tongue, feel the liquid taken to swallow it entering across the lips.

Feel the tongue moving the pills into position to be swallowed. Feel the swallowing.

Let the pills be drawn past the heart into the awaiting stomach.

Sense the movement of the pills down your esophagus, gently received by the body.

Feel the medication settling into your stomach, radiating like a soft golden light. Feel the medication conveyed into the place of need.

With loving kindness direct its healing quality to the area of greatest need. Feel the area absorb the healing.

Let it in.

Receive the medication as a blessing.

Find an image which opens you to the healing in your medication.

See it as a gift from a great teacher, as a sacred communion between the outer and inner worlds, as the smile of unbearable compassion on the soft face of the divine mother, as a flower from a dead lover.

Let it in. Absorb it.

Allow the loving kindness to combine with the treatment that directs it into the area which calls for healing.

Allow the medication to be drawn in, mercy and awareness binding to each molecule sent wholeheartedly into the cause of suffering.

Feel the medication dissolving the resistances of a lifetime, dispelling the tension and difficulty around illness.

Feel it entering directly. Feel it melting injury and illness.

Let the medication heal you.

CHAPTER 15

Opening the Body

Most healing techniques deal only with the body. They are an attempt to reestablish balance *in* the body *through* the body. But, as many patients have somewhat angrily pointed out, much of what they did *for* the body was done *to* the body. They "forced" diets, they "endured" chemotherapy, they "tried to squeeze in some time for meditation." To enter what they were told was a healing modality, they hardened themselves to the mind/body. They did what they thought they "should." Little credence was given to the powers of the heart. They did not discover who they already were. The effort with which they attempted to direct their healing energy became a force which closed their body instead of opening it.

When many become ill, they attack the body with new strategies they hope will restore health. The energy, directed toward their illness was very skillful, but their effort, the urgency with which they applied this energy, was not. Energy, the scintillation at the center of each cell, the vibrational sense of life in the body is the vital quality which fuels the unfolding process. Effort is the will to direct that unfolding. The necessity for energy and effort to be balanced is a prime requisite for healing. Many have the energy to heal, but their effort is askew. An analogy might be that energy is like fire, while effort is the way fire is employed. Fire wrongly used can decimate a forest. Fire appropriately applied can create a fire break, a burned strip, which stops the further progress of the forest fire.

The difference between energy and effort is important to recognize. When we have tasted deeply of the crystalline waters of our true nature, our life becomes effortless. There is no need to push the river. But one of the ironies of healing is that it takes effort to become effortless. A balanced effort is one in which our concentration and mindful awareness is balanced with a soft acceptance and willingness to investigate lightly the pains of a lifetime without clinging toward them or condemning them away. A balanced effort does not exert energy to force conclusions. A balanced effort is a constant remembering to open gently into the moment, to approach life wholeheartedly. Then effort does not reinforce resistance or become its collaborator, repelling healing. When our effort is goalless, when there is no attachment to results, to the fruits of our labors, then our only work is to be with the energies of the present. Whenever we are exerting effort, the quality of judgment rises concomitantly in the mind. To the degree we wish to, for instance, play the piano well, we will imagine we are playing poorly. The harder one tries to accomplish anything, the more one has a tendency to calibrate success. But in attempting to enter directly the energy of the mind/body, one may experience in a balanced mind and opened heart how sensation, though labeled pleasant or unpleasant, hot or cold, moving or still, is all essentially pure energy. Indeed, when we start to see energy in the mind, we begin to see process, watching each state of mind dissolve one into the next; the same energy which propels thought moves the stars across the sky. In focusing on the quality of energy in the mind/body, we enter the realms of creation constantly unfolding.

To understand our effort is to investigate our intentions, to recognize our motivation for directing energy in the first place. One might ask, "Why do I want to heal?" Is it just to continue feeding old mind's way of becoming the world? Or is it to discover life anew? To replace with love that which has so often been touched with fear? Is it to live a life of deeper awareness and mercy, or to continue living with such great effort and disappointed expectation?

To understand energy is to enter into the process itself. To feel the vibration pulsing in our tissues, to watch the mind unfolding, to recognize the body as an opportunity to awaken to that which goes beyond the body, the pure energy of pure awareness, that which we call life and whose absence from the body we conceptualize as death.

So we must see how we apply our healing techniques to the body. And to see their results. Do these techniques harden the body for healing or do they soften it to healing? Do we heal at the expense of all else, pushing all those away who do not see things our way? Or do we, using everything as an opportunity to awaken, open to new possibilities of seeing? Once again it becomes clear that it is not the technique but how it is applied that heals. Because energy is the nature of our innermost reality and effort is the expression of our outermost personality, to bring these two into balance is to merge who we really are with who we wish to be. Each moment energy is directly perceived as change, as process; a spacious awareness results in which effort naturally comes into balance. Seeing the perfect unfolding, nothing is noticed to be absent, and nothing additional is required. Each moment of such inner harmony is a healing moment; it allows once again the mind/body to be received in the heart.

One woman we worked with some years ago, in attempting to heal her cancer, undertook the regimen of a particularly arduous nutritional system. She forced herself to drink a glass of raw vegetable juice every hour. And twice a day she said she had to "confront" a glass of raw osterized liver, which she could hardly "force down." Her relationship to her technique was blocking its capacity to heal. She continued to get sicker. The resistance and despair with which she applied the method seemed to block her healing. She was trying to push through the technique in order to get to the other side. Until she came to a point where she saw that her relationship to her method of healing was not unlike her relationship to that which required healing. She hated her method as much as she hated her cancer. She saw that it was just not going to work and searched her heart and mind for a clue to how she might open to her chosen method. And she came upon the idea of taking the raw liver juice not as a punishment but as a gift. She began to see it as the Eucharist. And then twice each day she drank of the blood of Christ and found a sweetness in the body beyond the bitterness of the mind. She put a good deal of effort into softening the body so that the energy of this technique might penetrate more deeply.

It is not unlike that story of the fellow who could not open to his radiation treatments until he saw them as a natural exudation from the palm of Jesus. His healing technique was no longer a war with himself but an opening to the divine within and all about him.

Energy is the nature of the system. Effort is how we use it. In all healing techniques there is energy but how it is applied is for many the degree of its efficiency. Our effort is our attitude toward life. If we have always met life as a struggle, thinking of ourselves as war- riors in a battle instead of pilgrims on a path, healing will continue to make life an emergency. But when we soften to healing, when we let the mind/body float in the heart, the potential for reestablishing balance in the body greatly intensifies.

And so most of us need to learn to open the body to healing. And each of us is given the perfect receptor of that openness. Keeping soft belly is the primary foundation for opening to this level of being. For it is in the belly that we have so long attempted to control the world. It is the nature of the belly to turn the whole world into itself—all that we take in as food from the outside is converted to the body from the inside. It is the nature of the stomach to turn the world into itself. Indeed, we live in a culture which holds its belly in, which tightens the abdomen for appearances and some imagined strength. Perhaps the worst advice one can be given is to tighten the belly, to appear flat-stomached. The belly is our center of control and holds much tension.

To give our healing every opportunity, it is our sense that those who wish to open the body into healing should not wear tight clothing. Nothing to restrict the even rise and fall of the breath deep in the belly. The belly should be allowed its deepest breathing, its greatest sigh. It is unwise to hold it flat for "beauty's sake." Indeed, this suggestion to allow the belly to be—loose and open instead of constricted and held in—may at first rub noticeably against our conditioning to "look good." We may mistake ourselves for our belly. It is not uncommon to notice an attractive person enter the room and hear a few sucking wind through clenched teeth as their bellies mysteriously retreat within a sagging sweater. It is the "I am this body" contraction in the mind which tightens the belly and makes healing a tug-of-war. A war nobody wins. A war in which all is lost.

To just let the belly be, to take a full breath allowing the abdomen to rise as it will, to fall as it must, is to come back into the body as a hospitable residence. In soft belly there is room for everything. In soft belly fear and joy float, no contraction, no clinging or condemn- ing. In soft belly, in open belly, we make room for life, we make room for healing. Even if one's effort were only to come back to remember to soft-belly a thousand times a day, there would be much benefit. In soft belly we see years of holding—plates and plates of tension—falling away. In opening deep softness into the belly, one may notice that even the slightest thought can harden the belly. Indeed, we have become so accustomed to hard belly that it takes much remembering to soften back into our natural openness. Baby's belly is soft; Buddha's belly is soft. Before the accumulation of tension and after the release of such tension, the belly remains naturally open and soft. Even in meditation one may notice that the least bit of thinking, of holding to thought, tightens the belly. The grasping aspect of mind reflected in the closing belly. For this reason soft belly can be used to encourage an open body, which loosens tension and opens the mind, and in turn clears the way to the open heart.

The belly can be used almost as physicists used to use the Wilson Cloud Chamber: to create a soft mist in which the subtlest motion of otherwise invisible particles could be instantly identified not by weight or shape but by the unique trail each left through the cloud. The belly becomes like a diagnostic mirror in which we see how a lifetime of liking and disliking, of tension and resistance, has created an elaborate labyrinth through which each perception must wander. How each moment of life must run the gauntlet of our fears and distrust, of our limited opening to what is. In held belly we see old mind. But in soft belly lies the possibility of new mind creating a new body. In soft belly deep energy is allowed effortlessly to arise.

In soft belly the heart's armoring becomes clearly evident. Indeed, the ever-varying density of such shielding can be determined from moment to moment by exploring the hardness of the belly. Stratum after stratum of fear and unworthiness, compacted by a deep resistance which longs to manipulate the givens of the moment. In hard belly can be found almost the exact opposite of the "don't-know" wonderment which allows our natural wisdom and healing to arise effortlessly.

In "don't-know," the belly softens to the miracle of the moment. Indeed, in the "Who am I?" practice that seeks to experience life directly rather than using some imagined "I" as middleman, we notice that even in asking "Who is asking?" the belly automatically softens to allow the investigation in.

The softness of the belly is a good indicator of our openness to the moment. When we are at peace, the belly is soft and open. When we are not, it is tense and held. In soft belly even the subtlest obstruction to the heart may be noticed. In letting go into soft belly, we open the body and loosen our grasp on the mind to expose the heart of essential healing.

A Meditation on Softening the Belly

[To be read slowly to a friend or silently to oneself.]

Take a comfortable sitting position and allow the body to breathe all by itself. As awareness deepens sensitivity to the breath in the body, gradually allow the motions of the abdomen to be noticed with each breath.

Let the breath breathe itself in soft body.

As awareness enters into the tissue of the belly, feel whatever tension or holding is evident there. Soften into the muscles, the tension of the belly. Let the muscles soften. Let go of whatever tension arises there. Let it float in soft belly.

In soft belly we have room for all.

Completely let go of holding in the belly. Let it be full. Let it be round.

Let the breath enter fully through the body down into the belly. Each breath raising the abdomen, expanding the musculature. Each exhalation, abdomen falling, tension dispelled.

Just breath pushing belly out with inhalation. Letting belly fall with each out-breath.

Belly breath.

Soft belly receiving the breath as it is.

Notice how even a single thought can recreate tension, holding in the belly.

Coming back to soft belly a dozen times a minute if need be, open the belly to life.

Opening the body to healing.

Just soft belly.

Each breath so full. So deep into soft belly.

Letting go with each out-breath.

Levels and levels of letting go in the belly.

Smooth breath breathing itself deep in soft belly.

The belly receiving the moment as it is, open, tender.

In soft belly floats it all.

In soft belly there is room for pleasure as well as pain, fear as well as joy, doubt as well as confidence.

In soft belly there is room to give birth to ourselves. In soft belly the old hardness floats in a new softness.

In soft belly no control, no holding.

In soft belly floats the world.

In soft belly the sadness of a lifetime—the grief and tension dissolve.

In soft belly so much space, such tender mercy.

In soft belly we are born at last into our healing.

CHAPTER 16

Reading the Body

In the context of opening the body, it might be useful to discuss a meditation practice used in the southern Buddhist tradition. It is the practice called "sweeping the body." It is a sweeping of attention through the body in a very precise and organized manner. It is a long gentle scanning of awareness from head to toe, a fine-tuning to the full range of sensations available to awareness. It allows us to read the map which conditioning has imprinted in the body. Moving very mindfully from one area to another, one discovers areas of high sensitivity as well as areas of low sensitivity. The body emitting all kinds of sensation—one area pulsating strongly, another only slightly vibrating; one area warm, another cool; one area scintillating, almost ecstatic, perhaps another withdrawn and almost morose. Most areas alive with sensation, a few seemingly deadened with little or no sensation available—a dullness, a numbness, an area of unfinished business, perhaps. Injury to the mind/body can leave an area insensitive, unwilling to stick its neck out once again. A woman who has been sexually abused may at times find the womb area numb, as might someone who has not dealt with the grief of a hysterectomy. A fellow who has attempted to stay in control his whole life, carrying the weights of the world, may find his shoulders burning. When awareness encounters a numbness in the mind/body, love gravitates to the lowlands of our most noticeable holding. And in each area of high sensitivity, moment to moment, mountains of sensation arise.

Just as some areas of the mind are found to be well developed and others deeply submerged, so in the body this same high and low terrain of sensitivity is discoverable. Exploring the field of sensations we label "body," areas of pleasure or pain are instantly recognizable from within. And we discover it is not just the mind that hides but certain areas of the body have also withdrawn to some degree and thirst for a merciful awareness to bring them back into the greater body we all share. Which is not to say that areas of high sensitivity in the body are in any way superior to areas where little sensation may be received—each one an opportunity for awakening. Sweeping through the body, microscopically exploring what is, we receive life as it has developed in the body. Wherever the attention is focused, sensitivity germinates and life gradually reinhabits that area.

These areas in which little sensation is received help to define "the unfelt" in our lives. They are the parts of the body that reflect the unfinished business of the mind. They display a condition that is waiting to ripen, much as Thich Nhat Hanh refers to the sea pirate's heart as "not yet able to see." Often, when awareness enters these areas, sensation spontaneously arises and gradually integrates that part of the body into the greater body. It is interesting to note that in exploring these dead places, as awareness deeply enters, we may discover anything from a far-flung joy to an intense pain. Our numbness covers our sensitivity. We give up life in increments and die a piece at a time.

In the course of this meditation, one may discover unknown pains and joys—areas of tension as well as areas of high receptivity and openness. As one teacher pointed out, "It is not so difficult to be out of the body as it is to be in it." Very few have taken birth fully, fully entered their mind or body. This meditation allows awareness to meet the body not as idea but as the direct experience of the field of sensation. It is not the idea of leg, or arm, or foot, it is the experience of the sensations generated within. It is the leg as reality instead of as dream. It allows direct access of the healing energy focused by awareness in an area that calls out for such attention.

It may take anywhere from a half an hour to an hour to scan the body adequately. To move ever so slowly from the crown of the head through the brow, the eyes, the cheekbones, the jaws, the tongue within the mouth, the teeth, the lips, the chin, the skull within the enveloping tissue, the muscles of the neck, etc., down through the body—torso, hips, legs, through each toe to the very sole of each foot.

It allows us to meet the body in intimate detail. To see that what we call body is actually a map of sensations floating in awareness. It allows us to see past "I am this body" to the vibrating "am-ness" in which even the dullest sensation can be resuscitated. Attending from place to place to the undernourished and starving, as well as the loving and present, we open the body to its full potential, reading its map, following the path of healing.

SWEEPING-THE-BODY MEDITATION

[To be read slowly to a friend or silently to oneself.]

Allow the attention to come gently to the top of the head. Tuning to the level of sensation generated right there at the crown of the skull.

Maybe even feeling the soft scalp against the hard bone of the skull.

Let your attention gradually gather at the very top of the skull.

Gently. Receiving sensation generated by life in the body, focus now at the very top of the skull.

And allow the attention to open to include the sensations all about the top of the head, the scalp. Maybe you can even feel the softness of the scalp as opposed to the hardness of the bone just beneath. Let the awareness be that subtle.

And let the awareness move to the brow, the forehead, receiving whatever sensations arise.

Let the awareness include the eye sockets, the bone, cartilage, the flesh that surrounds the eye, sensitive, full of sensation, full of feeling. Just receiving what is happening, nothing to create. And see if you can feel the eyes themselves within their sockets. It may take a moment as awareness sweeps from one area to another for it to gradually focus there. Don't force. Just moving and receiving whatever presents itself.

Feel the cheekbone.

Feel the ears.

Let sensation present itself in the ear. Does the top of the ear feel any different than the bottom? Exploring minutely, receiving gently.

The jawbone. As it moves below the ears, angles forward to form the chin. Feel this bone. Feel inside this bone.

Feel how the jaw forms the mandible in which teeth are set.

Starting in the lower mandible, the lower set of teeth, see if you can move your awareness gently from one tooth to the next across the bottom section of your mouth.

Just allowing sensation, not creating, not grasping. Just noticing its qualities or even its absence wherever awareness alights. Nothing to judge, no one else to be, simply receiving the body as is in a merciful awareness.

Let the attention move to the upper teeth, moving one by one across the roof of the mouth.

And the tongue as it lies in the mouth. Are there more sensations toward the tip of the tongue or does it change as we move back into the throat?

Gently receiving sensation generated by life in the body.

Feel the whole mouth.

Feel the front of the face. The brow, the eyes, the nose, the lips, the teeth, the tongue, the jaws, the ears. Just face sensation, awareness.

Feel the skull behind the face. Whole skull, whole sensations arising in the face, in the skull, in the head.

Let the attention move into the throat, receiving whatever sensations arise there.

Feel the front of the throat. The windpipe. Feel how the neck extends down to an indentation that spreads out to form your shoulder. That continues down to create your chest. Awareness moving slowly down the front of the neck, spreading out, experiencing the shoulders and the upper chest.

Let the awareness receive the sensation of the right arm as it hangs from the shoulder. Feel how the shoulder supports the weight of the arm, holds it, allows it.

Feel the security of that shoulder socket. Its readiness to move, its ability to support weight. Its strength.

Let the awareness gradually move down the right arm from the shoulder to the elbow, through the muscles and tendons of the upper arms and biceps, just slowly moving, awareness softly receiving the body as sensation.

Feel the elbow, its hardness, pointedness, flexibility.

And allow awareness to continue from the elbow to the wrist of the right arm. Feeling the multiple sensations that may arise, moving through the bones and tissue of the forearm.

Feel the wrist, multiple bones connected within muscle and tissue so supple, so perfect this wrist. So useful, so ready to help. And allow your attention to come into the palm of your right hand.

This hand that gives, this hand that receives. Allow the awareness to gradually move from the smallest finger to the thumb, one finger at a time, gradually receiving the whole hand in sensation.

Allow the whole hand, wrist, arm to be received. Feel the whole right arm as sensation, as merciful awareness receiving the body, receiving sensation moment to moment in soft awareness.

Let awareness explore the whole arm up to the shoulder . . . and begin moving slowly across the upper chest to the left shoulder, and begin gradually to allow the awareness to move from the shoulder through the biceps of the upper arm to the elbow of the left arm.

Feel the elbow, its hardness, its flexibility, moving to the wrist, to the forearm of the left arm, feeling the miracle of the wrist, its flexibility, its ability to give and let the attention move into the palm of your left hand.

And slowly move the awareness from the smallest finger to the thumb of the left hand, one finger at a time received in soft awareness.

Then feel the whole hand, thumb and fingers, palm, bone, tendon, muscle, this hand that serves, this hand that receives, this miracle of life vibrating in the palm of the left hand.

And let the attention include the whole left-arm weight of the arm in the shoulder. Muscles of the upper arm, elbow, forearm, the wrist, the hand.

Feel the sensations generated in the left arm.

Now feel how both the left arm and right arm lie at the sides of the body, feel their strength. The right arm and left arm, how they cradle and protect the sides, how they hold the body in constant embrace.

Move down between the shoulders into the chest, feeling the muscles of the chest, the weight, the substance of flesh of the matter, of living suchness vibrating there in the center of each moment received in the area around the heart, the nipples and chest.

Feel the abdomen, the diaphragm rising and falling all by itself with each breath. Perhaps awareness can even receive the connective tissue that attaches the muscles of the diaphragm within the body cavity.

The abdomen generating sensations with each breath.

The flesh that overlays the muscle and tissue of the abdomen. Let the awareness gently move through layer after layer of skin, tissue, muscle until it is receiving the sensations generated by the organs within the body cavity.

The liver, stomach, lungs, kidneys, bladder. Feel the intestines, feel the spleen, feel the pancreas there perhaps as a weight, as a mass but in subtle, gentle mind perhaps receiving various sensations from various organs. Let the mind be very still and receptive inside dark body cavity, receiving the sensations of the organs of digestion, of breath, of blood, of life.

Feel the whole torso. This strong body. This body of life. This body of being.

Now gradually bring your attention to the back of your neck, to the top of the spine. Vertebra to vertebra down the back, feeling the muscles of either side, the connective tissue, the shimmering channels of nerve and blood and being. Gradually moving down from the neck to the tip of the spine.

Moment-to-moment sensation, moment-to-moment body received in the heart of the matter, in pure awareness.

Some areas are more sensitive; generate more sensation than others; just notice and allow awareness to move slowly through the back to the base of the spine.

Feel the pelvic area, the sensitivity. Is the guardedness there? Is there openness?

Feel the hips that support the tissue, that allow us to sit erect, feel the muscle bands of the lower back, softly receiving sensation, receiving life in the moment, awareness and feeling meeting moment to moment in this precious body.

Feel the fleshy cheeks the body cushions itself on. Feel their graciousness, their support, their comfort, the protection there that allows us to sit.

Gently allow the awareness to move to the right hip.

Receiving whatever sensations that arise there, creating nothing, receiving life in the body. Sensation as we move down the right leg to the knee, through the strong muscles of powerful tissue of the upper leg, the heavy bone of the thigh, the deep muscles that convey blood and life through the body.

Let the awareness settle for a moment in the right knee to continue down through the lower leg to the right ankle. Allow the awareness to be focused, receptive, alert.

Feel the quality of awareness to absorb, to simply be with life unfolding as sensation in the body and let the awareness move through the ankle into the right foot.

Feel the bottom of the foot.

Notice how sensations in the bottom of the foot may differ from sensations in the top of the foot.

Allow the awareness to move from the smallest toe to the biggest toe, gradually receiving whatever sensations spontaneously arise to meet awareness as it moves gradually from the smallest toe to the largest toe of the right foot.

Feel the whole foot. Its ability to support, move forward and backward.

Its ability to take us where we wish to go.

Allow the whole right leg to enter into the field of awareness, receiving sensations from these thick muscles and powerful bones of the leg, of the knee. Through the lower leg and ankle, through this agile foot.

Whole right leg received in gentle awareness, in receptive awareness.

Gradually allow your attention to come to your left hip, receiving the hardness of the bone.

Sensations within the bones of the hip and upper leg. Layers of sensation through layers of bone and tissue and flesh. The multiple sensations that create the feeling, the experience in the left leg, in the knees.

Feel the knee's ability to move, its ease, its functional quality.

Left leg received as sensation moving through the lower leg to the ankle.

Multiple changing sensations. Bone and flesh. Tissue and ligament. Skin and muscle.

Let your attention come through the ankle into the left foot, noticing the different qualities of sensation in the foot.

Moving from toe to toe, awareness gradually receiving sensations generated from the littlest toe to the biggest toe of the left foot.

Feel the whole foot there. Strong and flexible, supportive, capable.

Allow the attention to open to receive all the different sensations arising in the left leg from the hip to the tip of the largest toe. Feeling all the various levels of density, of softness.

Tinglings and vibrations that are the experience of the sensations in the left leg.

Allow both the left leg and the right leg to be received in awareness.

Multiple sensation coming and going in the hips and knees. The feet, legs, and thighs vibrating with aliveness.

Let awareness continue to fill the body vessel, moving upward from the toes, through the knees to the hips, and up into the body cavity.

Feel awareness as it continues through the abdomen into the chest and shoulders and arms.

Everywhere awareness reaches the sensations of life are released.

The body filling with awareness. The body filling with sensation. Attention filling the body to the top of the head.

The body vessel filled with luminous awareness from the tip of each toe to the peak of the roof of the skull.

Whole body tingling, scintillating. Sensations of prickliness or dullness, of movement or stillness, of heaviness or lightness, of warmth or coldness, generated from one point to the next. Each area blessed equally.

Whole body filled with soft awareness receiving life as it is.

Moment-to-moment sensation arising and dissolving in vast awareness.

Whole body alive in living awareness.

Whole body filled with presence. Whole body filled with mercy and awareness.

CHAPTER 17

Healing Directly

Having begun to remove the blockages to healing by investigating the holdings in the mind and learning to soften and open the body, to enter the heart of "just this much," we become able to approach illness or discomfort directly with a merciful awareness that brings balance to all it touches. Exploring the ever-varying densities of the mind/body, the spirit of healing reveals itself moving through ancient encumbrances, silhouetted in the open doorway to the heart.

At first there are many depths of exploration and meditation on the blockages to healing, the clinging and condemning of the mind/body, and varying levels of awareness and resolution. Sinking through levels of old mind, we approach things directly in their essence. Having made contact with the sensations through so many moments of keen-eyed, mindful observation, we are allowed entrance directly into the areas of holding and pain. We go beyond what at first were thought of as stages of healing into the unending process of our natural birth into being.

This process, begun for many by a few minutes of exploring the individual sensations that comprise the experience of discomfort— like examining each unique luminescent snowflake passing by in the midst of a gray flurry, watching each melt in the palm as another glides in to replace it—develops into more moments of mindfulness and mercy as the passageway to the heart expands to establish a conduit between the sensations in the body and the spaciousness of the heart. Then, with a few breaths into the heart, we reestablish contact with something yet deeper than who we think we are, the breath of love, the breath of mercy directly entering the body.

At this point one may look back at the work that has been done and discover that it has not consisted of steps toward a goal or rungs on a ladder but instead of a single unfolding, a continual birthing, a path that presents itself from moment to moment with each step fully taken. A continual deepening of insight into the cause of suffering and the source of healing.

For the last few years we have been developing a meditation to integrate the levels of healing into the mind/body. This meditation first approaches an area of discomfort with tenderness and begins to soften all around it. To let the sensations float. Entering directly into moment-to-moment sensation, participating in its very nature, the area of sensation fills with a soft mercy and gentle caring.

The meditation is begun by settling into the body and gradually approaching with tender awareness what has been armored by resistance and fear. It is a gentle moving toward that which defines the blockages along the way as well as recognizes the power of letting go.

Softening the area, allowing sensations to float, awareness is then directed toward the center of sensation. One begins to sense life even in an area which may have been disregarded or the object of confusion and long ago walled off. Instead of becoming more an object of tension or confusion, this investigation of the qualities of discomfort or its equal and opposite numbness becomes the subject of a healing awareness.

As sensations become directly available to awareness, we explore their texture, their warp and woof, their comings and goings—the voice within and the attitude surrounding. These sensations which the mind has pulled back from so many times are received moment to moment in a new exploration of the unfolding.

The softening space developed around sensation is filled with heart. Mercy and care receiving each moment as it floats in edgeless awareness. Holding dissolves in vast space. Things arise and disappear just as they are without the least clinging or condemning. Even holding seen as just another bubble floating in the vastness. Nothing to push away, nothing to pull toward. Nowhere to go, no one to be, nothing to do, and nothing left undone. Just this moment forever. Just the merciful healing of merciful awareness.

In the beginning of this practice it may be difficult to make contact with an area so long isolated by the armor of our aversions. But it is not advisable to rush healing. As when working with pain one approaches a step at a time, work with the meditation for ten or fifteen minutes and then take a break and go fully back to the breath for a while, softening the belly and watching breath from that softness. Not attacking the area even in the slightest we swing back to the healing or pain meditation for whatever period feels appropriate. While some areas of the body seem almost to sing in the light of awareness, other areas may be difficult to contact directly. If upon first approach toward this area an impenetrable denseness presents itself which does not allow awareness to progress further, a visualization may be useful. It should be noted that the visualization of an area though remarkably powerful is not the area itself, it is an idea, a mental picture. Visualization can allow one to approach and make contact at levels not previously available. But because it is one step removed from the direct experience of the area itself, its power to delve into the center of healing may be somewhat limited. The healing meditation and pain meditation are based on the direct experience of the thing itself, a mindful participation in the area. Those who find some hindrance and sense the power of visualization to open contact with an area may "see" a holding around pain or illness that reminds them of a fist cramped closed. It is a fist of resistance that holds on so, that squeezes down on our pain. As this holding becomes evident, one can visualize this fist beginning to open, finger by finger, gently, at one's own pace. Seeing the grasping so long reinforced as the large knuckled fist of our holding and resistance clamps down on our discomfort and magnifies it into inaccessible pain.

To begin to visualize this resistance, this tense-fist loosening, opening, releasing its holding around pain may give a sense of spaciousness which allows access to that area, and allows the healing in. Just as a single moment of insight can change our whole perspective, so let that fist awaken to the suffering it is causing and allow it to soften all around the sensations. Visualize it remembering to let go, reestablishing its natural openness at last. Let it sigh, let its tension be released as a new warmth and mercy flood the soft flesh of kindness and care. Discovering within the cramped fist of our holding the open-handed offering of healing. See the fist opening as though discovering a remarkable gift that lies gently in its palm. See it as the sacred hand of service. In this visualization there can be a deep softening of the ligaments, the flesh, the musculature around the place of suffering or discomfort to allow sensation to just be as it is. To float in something greater than old mind's insistent clinging.

If visualization is useful and suitable to your temperament, use it as a step on the path of healing. But don't stop there. As a visualization opens access to an area, awareness is able to enter directly into the sensations generated there. Once a conduit has been established between an area of sensation and the heart of healing, each breath can guide loving kindness and a healing awareness into the center of our needs.

Creating a mental picture of an area to be healed and the healing taking place can be quite powerful. Indeed, the fellow who could not let the healing in until he could see the radiation therapy as a golden light emitting from the palm of a divine being found it to be the key to opening deeper into the area to be healed. Visualization is also an integral part of directing medication within. So visualization, if skillfully applied, can lead to a greater spaciousness and openness that allows us to enter directly into the cosmos pulsating at the center of each sensation—each pain, each numbness, each tumor, each distrusting womb, each aching heart discovering that healing is not far behind.

There is so much more healing available to us than we ever imagined. So much healing possible that a loving visualization, though even one step removed from the body of our illness, is often sufficient to allow much balance to return to the area. Also, some people are more visually oriented. For them visualizations may be very helpful to bring light into an area of shadows in the mind/body.

The use of guided imagery meditations, of creative visualizations, has been useful to many in advanced stages of cancer and life-threatening illnesses. The work of visualizing and harnessing the immune system by selecting imageries of health and cancer resolution have helped many bodies. Indeed, visualization may bring one to relate *to* an object of pain instead of *from* it. However, the imagery chosen to increase the immune system's "resistance" is of prime concern to the heart if aggression is not to displace mercy. Indeed, the very idea of increasing "resistance" in order to overcome illness needs a deep exploration before one can skillfully take on such a practice.

One very concerned physician who has sincerely attempted to displace cancer from the body, using aggressive guided imagery, refers to those who have cultivated their resistance and overcome cancer as his "superstars." But just the other day one of the patients he had used as an example of the effectiveness of aggressively attacking cancer approached us to say that it wasn't aggression that helped. Having been cured eight years before of a cancer that was about to remove her from the body, she said, "I never really did the aggressive imagery technique. That is not what cured me. It was the love I felt from this extraordinary fellow and his wife and their deep concern for my cancer that healed me. It was not the aggression that cured my cancer, it was the love."

The encouragement to direct aggression into an area that may already be clenched tightly in the fist of resistance is a very tricky matter. One must tune very deeply and investigate the holdings in the mind and body in order to sense what technique is appropriate. For many the cultivation of aggression just creates more blockages. A patient once pointed out, "As my immune system became more ferocious and I saw it attacking the tumors, it only seemed to intensify the tightness in my gut. And my stomach cancer became more of a problem. Rather than using aggression to encourage the immune system, visualizing white alligators (lymphocytes) ravaging rotten hamburger (cancer tumors), I began instead to imagine sending love. What a relief not to stimulate hate anymore in my gut, not to fear myself there anymore." The imagery used for visualization is extremely important and must be chosen by the heart, not figured out by the mind.

Watching how love balances heavy states of mind, how fear, doubt, and anger obscure the heart of our wholeness, we get a sense of where our healing may be found. We can see how the pain of holding seems to float and dissolve in the nongrasping light of loving kindness. We can note how the touching of awareness lightens the load in heavy areas. That which so intensified our identification with our pain, with "my cancer," "my suffering," allows "the cancer," "the suffering" to melt in a universal sense of healing. "Love quiets troubled waters in my mind. Why not in my body?"

said a friend after switching from sending heavily armed soldiers into his cancer to sending a group of loving troubadors to "caress and massage and sing and tickle my tumors away." And it worked.

All visualization techniques are, of course, not based on aggressive or combative imagery. Many of the oldest forms of these meditations used by Hindus and Buddhists as well as the American Indian for thousands of years are for deepening compassion, healing others, opening energy centers, and even projecting consciousness into the heart of the divine at the moment when the body is shed. At each level of healing one might discover that seeing the area helps focus a merciful awareness on the activity received as sensation.

Because healing, like spiritual awakening, is such a creative matter, such a brailleing along individual pathways, one must sense wholly what is right for oneself. And we might reemphasize that any of the meditations offered here are still in process and seem never to speak themselves the same twice in a row, constantly changing, still on the path toward completion. So it is important that one does not take these meditations as Buddha's or Ananda Ma's or Jesus's or Mary's, or even as Stephen's or Ondrea's, but rather as one's own. Recognizing that you are the path, make each step your own, firmly, completely, mindfully.

By allowing a merciful awareness to enter "my pain," we begin to experience "the pain," the separate floating in the universal. Our little healing entering the Great Healing. Then each experience of healing is for the benefit of all sentient beings. The healing of our body into the Greater Body. The opening of our heart into the Great Heart.

A Healing Meditation

[To be read slowly to a friend or silently to oneself.]

Come to a sitting position or whatever posture the body is able to maintain for a period of time. And feel what sits here.

Allow the attention to come into the body and feel the breath as it breathes itself in soft belly.

Let the body be soft and open.

Let the awareness be gentle and allowing.

Notice any area of the body which is in discomfort. Attending to the body, notice whatever distinct sensation draws the attention.

Gently allow awareness to move toward the place that wants healing.

In this gentle approach toward discomfort, notice any resistance, any stiffness or numbness or coldness, any tension that denies entrance into this area. Notice whatever denial or fear limits access. Notice any fear or doubt that attempts to distract direct entrance into the discomfort.

Slowly, without the least force, gently allow awareness to approach the sensations generated in this area.

And begin to soften all around the sensations.

Letting the flesh soften to allow awareness within.

Softening.

Let space begin to open all about the edge of this area.

Gradually opening.

Softening all about sensation.

Softening the muscles.

Softening the tissue in which sensation arises.

Softening the muscles.

Skin soft. Flesh loosening, opening.

Allowing sensation to be as it is in soft flesh.

Feel the fibers in the muscles softening. Letting go of pain.

Tendons softening. Flesh softening. Skin softening.

Allowing sensation to float in soft flesh.

Softening.

Letting go all around sensation.

In soft body, in soft mind, just letting it be there.

Meeting the moment-to-moment sensations that arise there with moment-to-moment softening.

Softening the bone.

Softening to the very marrow.

Any tension that momentarily asserts itself allowed to float free.

Let it come. Let it go.

Moment-to-moment sensation arising in soft awareness.

Softness spreading all about sensation.

Gently, without force, gradually opening the tissue to let sensation float.

Letting go all around.

Softening to the very center of the cells.

That softening to the very center of the cells of the muscles, of the tissue in which sensation floats.

Awareness cradling sensation in soft open space.

Sensations floating in awareness.

The skin, the tissue, the muscles, the tendons soft and pliant. Spacious.

Bone soft, allowing, willing.

Sensations arising like bubbles into space.

Space floating in space.

Awareness meeting moment-to-moment sensation with merciful softness.

Moment-to-moment sensation rising, floating in awareness.

Awareness receiving the subtlest flutter, the subtlest motion of sensation.

Softly. Clearly.

Awareness entering to the very heart of sensation.

Awareness exploring sensation floating in space.

Do the sensations stay still or do they move?

Does the area of sensation have a single shape or is it constantly changing?

What is that shape?

Moment-to-moment sensation floating in soft merciful awareness that explores tenderly the moment.

Do these sensations have density?

Are they thin or thick?

Are they round? Are they flat?

Moment-to-moment sensation received in moment-to-moment awareness.

Discovering the nature of sensation.

Do these sensations have a texture?

Are they rough? Are they smooth?

Do they stay the same or are they constantly changing?

Sensations floating in awareness.

Softening all about sensation. Flesh soft, muscles relaxed and open, tissue allowing and merciful.

Notice whatever thoughts arise that might limit this softness.

Are there feelings that harden the area? Fear or doubt?

Do the sensations whisper words like tumor or cancer or pain? Do they cause tension around sensation?

Allowing levels and levels of softening to deepen all about sensation, explore the moment as it is.

And let such thoughts, such feelings, too, float in a vast boundaryless awareness.

Soft awareness meeting sensation as it is moment to moment.

Attend to even the least tension in the mind that tenses the body and soften all about it.

Deeper and deeper softening.

Noticing how even the least thought might limit softness, soften yet deeper.

Investigating the moment as sensation.

Did these sensations move, or did they stay in one area?

Are there tendrils that connect this area with other areas of sensation in the body?

Moment-to-moment awareness.

Moment-to-moment sensation.

Moment-to-moment softening, allowing, receiving.

Sensation arising and dissolving in vast space.

Are the sensations soft or hard?

Are they hot or cold? Or neither?

Is there a feeling of pressure? A vibration? A movement?

Soft awareness opening into a vast spaciousness which allows sensation to unfold moment to moment in the clear light of mercy and awareness.

Meeting sensation as it arises instant to instant.

Is there a sound there? Do these sensations have a voice?

Is the voice familiar? What does it have to say?

Noticing softly, caringly, these sensations that may have gone so long unattended to. Meet them with a soft allowing awareness.

Sensations arising and dissolving in a spacious merciful awareness.

Relating to this area, to sensation, as if it were your only child.

Meeting them with love. With kindness. With mercy.

Sensations floating in a soft open awareness met with mercy and caring.

Does some image arise there?

Is there color there?

Just noticing whatever is there, nothing to create.

Just receiving sensation in loving kindness and care.

Touching it with mercy. Touching it with forgiveness.

Is there a feeling there, an attitude that seems to surround that area?

Noticing any old-mind residue that holds even in the least to these sensations, just let them go, let them float in the new moment-to-moment spaciousness of awareness and kindness and care.

Gently allowing awareness to cradle each moment of sensation.

Each sensation received in the warmth and patience of forgiveness.

Each sensation absorbed in loving kindness and mercy.

Allow love to enter sensation, floating in the softness, in the spacious heart of being all about this area.

Floating in compassion.

Floating in mercy.

Let the healing in.

Let your heart touch sensation moment to moment.

Let this area become the heart we all share.

Let the mercy you feel for so much in the world touch your pain as well.

Each moment of sensation received so gently. Moment-to-moment sensation arising and dissolving in the vast spaciousness of a merciful awareness.

Each moment of sensation dissolving in compassion for all those in pain.

Each moment dissolving, dissolving in mercy and loving kindness.

Each moment melting into infinite compassion and kindness.

Sharing this healing with all sentient beings.

Melting the discomforts of the world in tender mercy.

Meeting these sensations with kindness, forgiveness, and compassion. Meeting the world we all share in healing awareness.

Each moment floating.

Moment-to-moment sensation arising and dissolving in the boundaryless luminescence of awareness.

Love healing the discomforts of the world.

All the despair and helplessness of all the worlds met by the loving kindness that receives sensation in the heart of awareness.

This healing healing all.

Sending mercy and loving kindness into the body we all share.

Each moment of sensation absorbed in infinite compassion and care.

Each moment dissolving into the heart of healing.

Gently allow your attention to come back to your heart. Feel the strength, the softness of mercy there. Feel the healer of this body, the healer of the world.

Let this healing be shared for the benefit of all beings everywhere.

May all beings be free of suffering.

May all beings be healed.

May all beings know the infinite compassion of their original nature.

PLEASE TAKE A FEW SOFT BREATHS
AS WE MOVE
FROM ONE LEVEL TO THE NEXT.

AS IN GROWTH, OR DYING,
WE NEED LET GO
AT THE EDGE
TO CONTINUE FURTHER.

TRUST THE PROCESS
LET GO LIGHTLY
PASS ON GENTLY.

CHAPTER 18

Entering Mindfully
the Moment

Mindfulness is the quality of awareness with which we relate to the contents of the mind, just as heartfulness is the quality of loving kindness with which we relate to the contents of the world. When mindfulness is developed the heart and mind are seen as one, are experienced, in the words of a Taos Pueblo shaman as "All same."

To enter the moment directly so that life is not experienced simply as an afterthought, as a memory of the previous instant, is to deepen presence. Presence is the quality of not being tardy for our lives.

A Gradual Awakening was written to elucidate the subject of mindfulness practice, but it might be useful to share here a few of the means by which this very instant can be wholly appreciated, ways that thinking can be seen as thought, that pain can be seen as individual sensations, and feelings can be recognized as multiple changing states of mind. A means of breaking the seeming solidity of the underdream to awaken directly into the moment which is life.

Having opened a relationship to the sensations in the body, one narrows the focus to just the sensations that accompany the breath as a means of cultivating an awareness of the precise moment. Recognizing that much of what distorts life into dream is our identification with thinking and feeling and the afterthought of self which makes it all seem so real, we focus on the breath to bring the attention to the level of flowing sensation. Sensations are not thoughts; they are the wordless hum of being constantly changing from moment to moment. They are the perfect backdrop against which to see even the slightest motion in the mind/body.

To tune to the level of sensation at which breath is always to be found is not to be lost in thinking or the reactiveness of feelings. Able to respond directly, to see thought as a bubble floating through, to see feelings like clouds in a vast summer sky, we build an appreciation for the moment. Then nothing is distraction and all becomes perfect grist for the mill of awakening.

Let the attention become present at the nostrils so as to feel the passage of each breath uniquely. Watching the multiple sensations that make up each in-breath. Noticing the space between, how nature abhors a vacuum, thoughts rushing in, images arising. Notice the complete out-breath. Its beginning, its middle, its end. Whole breath in whole awareness. Few at first can stay with even a half dozen consecutive breaths because as thoughts whisper through, and images are overlaid on the screen of consciousness the mind tends to wander off, and follow them into dream. But there are no distractions when one is awakening to life. Each moment is seen uniquely as is, perfectly presenting itself in clear and choiceless awareness. The awareness neither moving toward nor pulling back from anything. No clinging or condemning. Even judgment noticed as just another nervous tic in the long-conditioned persona, its ancient "flight or fight" syndrome, its ever-fatiguing liking and disliking of what arises on the screen of consciousness.

To be mindful means to acknowledge what is happening while it is happening. Mindfulness does not attempt to control the ever-changing weather of the mind but instead cleans the windows of our seeing to gauge whether it is a good time for a ride in the country or our time is best spent at home in the heart tidying up loose ends.

Becoming mindful of the breath, we enter into our existence at the level of sensation, noticing instantly all that is other than sensation—the least thought recognized at its inception, the heaviest state met in its fragile infancy. Everything recognizable in a blameless watching of what is as it is. Noticing the deep tendencies for control and judgment that follow in the wake of perception within a developing stillness, one watches without the least pulling back or pushing forward. As awareness explores the most noticeable activities of the mind/body, it becomes refined, able to hear the subtlest whispers of thought, feeling, and sensation. Discovering the breath inside the breath, the thought within thinking, the feeling within feelings. Breaking the illusion of someone thinking, watching our "someoneness" as just another thought bubble floating through.

Gently returning the wandering attention again and again to the breath, acknowledging all that arises, not surprised by the subtle fears and doubts that flicker across the screen. Developing courage and patience, concentration and mindfulness, openness and clarity. Just as the attention might need to be brought back to soften the belly a dozen times in an hour, so awareness is returned again and again from the passing thoughts which momentarily interpose themselves between awareness and the breath—the arising feeling, the associated memory, the fantasized future—to the coming and going of sensation at the nostrils.

To help us stay present, we employ a gentle acknowledgment, a noting of what is as it is. Recognizing that each moment fully accepted for itself has little to attract identification or suffering. Then acknowledging a moment of judgment has little to instigate further judging. Mindfulness of a moment of judgment allows it to remain unjudged, even appreciated as one would the prismatic effect of a cloud passing before the sun. To aid in staying present to the shifting contents of the moment, many use the technique of noting to acknowledge the contents of the mind as a silent whisper in the heart, as "judging" when judgment passes through the mind, and the awareness gently returns to the sensations that arise with each breath. Each breath so unique. Noticing the movement, the ever-changing quality of the state of fear with the silent noting, "Fear," as it predictably floats through. Noticing the exquisiteness of joy in all its changing qualities, equally impermanent in the flux and flow. Then "fear" does not frighten, "judgment" does not judge, "joy" does not leave us joylessly grasping for more. Each thing is as it is, and all become workable.

But here again one must watch old mind's tendencies. The purpose is not to lock into the breath but to use the breath as a means of tuning to the present. Once we have established a direct relationship to the breath, if the mind should find the momentum of fear or doubt continuing of itself, by itself, one does not struggle with the breath but allows awareness to enter wholly into the moment-to-moment unfolding of that state, just as one has attempted to gently stay with the moment-to-moment changes within the in-breath and out-breath, cultivating a choiceless awareness. Mindfulness of joy is not a quicker way to heaven than mindfulness of anger. No object of mindfulness is preferable to any other or offers any more freedom. Holding to any moment passed we exchange the living truth of *this* instant for the overscripted underdream.

We can find great awakening watching such states of mind as boredom or anger. Indeed, for many it is a relatively advanced stage in their mindfulness before the pleasant will be watched with the same acuity as the unpleasant. To be able to stay with the moment-to-moment unfolding of rapture with that same even-minded open-heartedness may take a good deal more encouragement because of its seductive nature to draw identification, to attract self into itself. So everything that arises becomes a perfect mirror for us to go beyond our ancient addiction to the contents of the mind and be able to receive the awareness reflected back from each object, to become purely conscious of awareness itself so it does not implode about any object in the mind, either ecstasy or grief. No longer mistaking the objects of awareness for awareness itself, like the sun recognizing its own light reflected from the moon, our true nature is revealed. And no grasping, no clinging to anything at all stays our healing.

For some, old mind may complain that an ongoing mindfulness of the passing show might suppress spontaneity. But much of what we call spontaneity is actually a compulsive twitch. When we are wholly present, unseen alternatives arise that increase the breadth of action rather than narrowing it. It is not hypnosis but rather "dehypnosis" as a friend long ago pointed out. Although it may sound as though one would deaden their experience, in truth one opens to yet subtler and subtler levels, recognizing that what we always experienced as the "aliveness" of thought is actually the scintillation of the awareness which receives it.

And the unconscious becomes conscious because nothing censors even the least arisal of suppressed material or the exquisiteness and gentleness and vastness of that which lies beyond all that we have for so long shoved underground. No words can describe the absolute joy and freedom and peace of an allowing mind. Which is synonymous with an open heart. Nothing to obstruct, no one to suffer. The deepest healing.

Then the questions, "Who am I?", "Who is in pain?", "Who is ill?", "Who is mindful?" become an encouragement to let everything float in awareness. Pain becomes floating sensations. Thought becomes bubbles passing through, fear becomes clouds constantly dissolving in vast awareness. Then the "who" of things is overseen instead of remaining a filter through which all is perceived. Our inherent nature, which is love and awareness directly experienced. And the natural softness of the belly, of the body, of the mind, becomes existence itself.

Many on the path have told us that saying, "Watch breath, soften belly, open heart," has become the reminder of mindfulness and mercy, which has taken them beyond the mind/body of suffering into the deep peace of their healing.

This focusing on the breath may be difficult at the beginning. We have cultivated so little concentration and so little mindfulness in the past. At first it may be difficult to stay with even a single in-breath without getting lost in the daydream of planning mind, judging mind, desiring mind. But slowly, patiently, this focus is developed equally with a willingness to receive the moment as it is. What's the rush?! Once one has one's feet on the path of healing, life takes on new meaning and time is no longer the enemy. Each step becomes every step, the healing within healing, the possibility of freedom. And life becomes exciting. This moment-to-moment awareness, encouraged and focused, allows one to meet the pleasure and pain in the mind/body and participate directly in what exists without adding the least fears or projections. It is looking oneself straight in the eyes, meeting oneself each time as if for the first time. It means entering the flow of constant change: the pulsations, the tingling, the heat, the cold, the hardness, the softness experienced as body. It is an investigation of the sensations themselves as they are generated at the point of inquiry. It is a probing of the very basis of the experience we call life, an examination of even perception itself and the filters through which all life is drawn. It means approaching life anew, without models or preconceptions. It means entering the moment with a choiceless awareness, an open-handed reception which seeks nothing except to receive life as it is.

It means approaching the moment at the ground zero of "don't know," letting go of all the attitudes, the colored lenses through which we have seen or hardly seen for so long. It means seeing and examining seeing, feeling and examining feeling, watching and examining the watcher. It is entering directly into one's life. It means unconditionally watching the conditioned. We watch the mind to see who we *aren't*.

In seeing things as they are, the grasping of old identifications to old mind diminishes. More and more, objects of consciousness are allowed to float in clear awareness. Less and less, objects of consciousness are mistaken for who we really are. Gradually, awareness itself may be directly experienced, seeing the very process out of which consciousness arises. It is going to the very root of our experience to meet anew that which has become so old.

When we see how difficult it is to "just watch the breath," we see the nature of what many call "monkey mind." The mind like a monkey swinging through the trees, propelled by its grasping from limb to limb—moved through the forest of the mind by its continual reaching out for the next object to swing from—the exquisite beauty of the forest canopy a blur of motion, indistinct, unknown.

When awareness is repeatedly encouraged to gently return to the moment, it looks straight ahead and all motion is seen as just passing show. The continual impermanence of all we had been grasping at for so long to support our confused and confusing journey at last recognized in its most minute detail. Without the least need to change our way of being, awareness changes it all by itself and a new path comes up to meet each step.

As awareness returns gently again and again to the breath as a means of opening to the contents of the moment, we experience the process in its unfolding, and the space in which it is all happening. As concentration develops, awareness receives previously unnoticed realms of being. Then the journey seems not somewhere we are going but an increasing appreciation of where we are. Awareness heals. All that we have sought is found in this very instant, being itself, the ever-healed, the ever-uninjured.

It is said, "If you can see 'just this much,' you can see everything." If we can fully open to this millisecond, this moment of existence, all will be revealed. If life is lived as just this moment, life will be lived to its fullest. But if "just this much" is not enough, life will be insufficient and old dreams of death will beckon.

Old mind is monkey mind. Old mind is thinking. Old mind is compulsive reaction to unexplored stimuli. It is the uninvited, the mechanical, the moment as dream, as a blur of confusion and suffering. New mind is "just this much." It is a new heartfulness in which the mind need not be different but is related to in a wholly different way. It is the mind sunk wholly into the heart. It is life renewed, life as healing.

There are as many ways of practicing mindfulness as there are of playing the piano. As one learns, for instance, to play the piano, one may be constantly "waiting for the time when I can really play." Or one may be enjoying the practice for itself: the daily increase in facility and the ability to express oneself. The joy of music. One may bang on the keys impatiently, waiting for the sound to get better, or one may experiment with the same note over and over again to understand the nature of "piano." Some enjoy each moment of practice; others can't wait to be virtuosos.

So too there are numerous ways in which mindfulness may be applied. Some impatiently attack the mind, insisting that it be different than it is. Others, with a deep sigh of recognition, softly smile at the joy of each moment of letting go, of clear seeing. The tendency to attack the objects of the mind and attempt to overcome them, to force clarity, can become, as one long-time meditator put it, "mercilessly attentive." This war with the mind can make one impatient and goal-oriented and create more self, more suffering. But in receiving, rather than attacking, the objects perceived, we gradually move beyond mind, beyond death, beyond even "being" to the indescribable spaciousness of beingness itself.

The tendency to try to escape our suffering instead of entering into it, to heal it, to make peace, is seen in the tendency of some meditators to "strike" the objects of the mind with an intention of making them disappear. This "hardening" of practice can make one feel uneasy with life, and quite uneasy with oneself. In "softening" practice, the objects of the mind are more appreciated for their emptiness than attacked for their solidity. Perception floats, well received. In this attitude of softening toward the mind, we approach the process gently, appreciatively, and cultivate the mercy necessary to open the pathway to the heart. When practice is as light as the breath within the breath, there is a profound element of mercy which shines within a choiceless receptivity. It does not force change but simply allows it. Indeed, it watches the tendency to force things, patiently, without alarm or condemnation.

Because of the deep tendency to attack that which we fear, one needs to apply meditation practices to the living truth of one's own moment. Much of what we read about meditation, some of it from the great teachers of the East, comes out of a monastic tradition. The application of meditation eighteen to twenty hours a day, in silence, in a controlled and supportive environment, may be somewhat different than we find in our everyday lives in the West. Thus we discover once again that we are the path and that we must apply meditation and a life of the spirit to our daily lives, not some image of ourselves as a monk or nun living in a very different way in a very different place. For our healing to be as deep as being, it must be in the living presence of our lives.

An example of how our practice can be somewhat outside our lives is the situation some years ago in an American Buddhist meditation center when two women teachers of considerable experience sitting in monasteries in Asia, having taken on a very traditional approach to practice, arrived to offer a long period of meditation to a number of awaiting meditators. Entering the meditation hall, they discovered a statue of Quan Yin, the Chinese female form of the Buddhist Bodhisattva of Compassion, placed toward the front of the raised platform from which they were accustomed to teach. Conditioned by the constricting male-dominated tradition of even such "nondiscriminating" teachings as Buddhism, they insisted that this female form, this female Buddha, be removed from the podium and be replaced by the traditional male personification of Buddhism. Perhaps too many years of "hardened" meditation had stuck them hard in old mind ideas of practice. Of Buddhism. Something within them perhaps needed yet more deeply to soften to accept their own female form, to become new in the eyes of Buddha. In refusing to teach on the same platform as a female Buddha, they refused their own Buddha nature in whatever form it might take.

Indeed, some time ago a friend with whom I had shared many years of intense practice, who had perhaps become a bit lost in fundamentalist concepts of meditation, approached Ondrea and me in some consternation after a lecture. Feeling that we were not transmitting the dharma (the teachings of Buddha, also defined as the living truth of the moment) in the traditional manner to which they had long become accustomed, they were quite uneasy. "I just don't know what I would do if I didn't have the dharma to stand behind," he said. But the dharma is not something one stands behind. It is what one lives within. So that each moment is always new. So that the moment is not forced into some concept of acceptability but is instead allowed to float in the heart of myriad possibilities.

As one teacher told me, "Don't be a Buddhist, be a Buddha. Don't be a Christian, be Christ. Don't be a meditator, meditate!" There is more to our healing than just meditation. As this teacher pointed out, "Don't leave your meditation on the meditation pillow." If sitting still for hours is all it took to liberate us, then the two dozen chickens in the hen house just outside our window would have long since been enlightened. We have watched one "Big Red" sit unmoving for days at a time and often more productively than many of the meditators hardened into practice that we have known.

When mindfulness has become balanced, a merciful awareness meets the mind not as a warrior (a mask often donned by the timid) but as a pilgrim, with fascination and respect. It does not resist or become surprised by anything. Nothing takes it unawares. It simply watches, not from some "center," some "point of view" that easily gives rise to an idea of there being "a watcher," just more self—but from within a spacious awareness that appreciates the passing process, entering from moment to moment the heart of healing.

A MINDFULNESS MEDITATION ON WATCHING THE BREATH
(with suggestions for extending the practice)

[To be read slowly to a friend or silently to oneself.]

Let the attention come into the body. Let it settle to the level of sensations generated there.

Feel the buttocks as they press against the chair or lie against the bed. Feel the hands folded in the lap or lying by one's side.

Allow awareness to experience the multiple sensations arising and disappearing in rapid succession in the body. A moment of pressure here, an instant of sensation there. Just receiving body as it is.

And gradually allow the attention to come to the sensations generated by breath in the body. Feel it in the belly, feel it in the chest, feel it in the throat. Feel it at the nostrils.

Just allowing attention to come to the level of sensation, receiving each breath arising and dissolving in the body.

As contact is established with the breath at the level of sensation, gradually allow the attention to come to the nostrils.

Noticing wherever the sensation that accompanies each breath predominates—at the upper lip, inside the rim of the nostrils, at the tip of the nose, let the attention be gently focused there.

Let awareness pervade the area where the sensations that accompany each breath are most clearly noticed.

Establishing the attention at the nostrils like a watchman stationed at the gates of a city. Let awareness inspect each sensation that accompanies the breath. With no force or leaning toward the breath, allow awareness to receive the multiple changing sensations that accompany each in-breath, each out-breath.

Noticing the space between inhalation and exhalation, recognizing thought or feelings that arise, noticing the subtle intention to exhale, allow the breath its natural tides.

Staying moment to moment with the multiple unfolding sensations in each exhalation.

Noticing the space between. Recognizing the intention to inhale once again.

Moment-to-moment mind received as words or images silhouetted against the wordless background of sensation generated with each inhalation and each exhalation.

Not thinking the breath but directly experiencing it.

Noticing as the awareness gradually deepens the subtler and subtler sensations that comprise each moment of the breath process.

Let the body breathe all by itself, no need to control or shape the breath. Just a keen gentle awareness that receives sensation as it is entering more deeply the moment with each particle of sensation received.

Noticing its motion drawn if the mind drifts off. Noting the enticing quality flashing through which has drawn awareness away from the breath simply as "pride" or "fear" or "anticipation" or "bliss." And with a gentle letting go, return fully to the breath.

No distractions. Each moment of thought or feeling or other bodily sensation simply noted as itself. And with the recognition of its occurrence a remembrance to return mercifully to the breath.

When there is thinking or feeling, notice any judgment or tension that wishes it to be otherwise. And just receive mind as it arises and dissolves in the vast spaciousness of a merciful awareness.

Returning if need be a dozen times a minute to the breath. With the lighthearted noting of "Big Surprise, thinking again, feeling again, planning again, judging again." Just noticing whatever arises as it arises and gently letting go to return to the sensations of the breath.

Letting go lightly returning to the breath.

EXTENDING THE PRACTICE

As contact with the breath is developed over some weeks of relating to the breath wholeheartedly and returning the attention to the sensations at the nostrils each time that thinking or feeling or other bodily sensations draw it away, we come to know the swing of awareness from object to object and increasingly we find ourselves in the immediate present.

Once the attention is able to let go lightly of whatever shiny object has attracted it, letting go of judgment without judging, letting go of fear without being frightened, letting go of pride without being proud, one learns the power of the healing moment of letting go.

In that instant of letting go, patience and mercy deepen with the ease of our relinquishment of our momentary holding. In the moment of letting go of thought or feeling, of doubt or rapture, to return to the sensations of the breath, we cultivate a willingness to go beyond old mind's holding, trusting the "don't know" wonderment of the next moment arising.

In each moment of letting go, we enter our birth and ease our death.

Watching closely each moment of letting go, we let things be as they are without the least force or need to be otherwise and, returning from thinking, notice thought, the bubble floating through the vast spaciousness of awareness, a fragile bubble in which is reflected our dream world and the environs of the mind.

Each moment of letting go of thinking conditions our response to the next arising of thought. Each moment of letting go of fear conditions the next moment's experience of fright. Each moment of allowing sensations to float in the body of awareness, letting them come and letting them go, conditions our response to the next moment of pain or mental discomfort.

In each moment of letting go, healing passes through the mind/body.

When the moment of letting go has been explored with the same sensitivity as the breath, as thinking, as feeling, as expectation, as disappointment, one can then develop this quality of letting go into a deeper sense of letting be, of being itself.

At this point, when thoughts turn into thinking and expectation turns into planning, imagining, as awareness notices these states, they are thoroughly investigated.

If a thought or feeling repeatedly interjects itself after having been let go of again and again to return to the breath, and continues unabated, awareness is then encouraged to wholly let go of the breath and enter directly into the state, to thoroughly explore its motion and density, its ever-changing quality, its process. Having stabilized the attention in the moment, in the sensations of the breath, one is then able to explore the shadow play of the moment. If the attention is repeatedly lured away from the breath by a memory, a feeling, a desire, a line of thought, the attention is placed wholly within that unfolding process to discover its most intimate nature and allow the familiarity which encourages letting go.

If having let go of the breath to examine a process that momentarily predominates in the mind or body, the mind begins to wander away from its new focus, sailing off through the mental catalog of old laundry lists and days gone by, the activity of this wandering is noted and, with a precious letting go, we return once again to the sensations at the nostrils to return ourselves to the present moment.

Noticing that it may be as difficult to stay with the interposing thought or feeling as it was with the illusive breath, awareness is encouraged to receive what is, as it is, with as much mindfulness as it can muster. A mindfulness of breathing becoming the foundation for our presence in the unfolding moment so that all that enters through the mind and body is received in mercy and appreciation.

Then we are not fighting with the mind, distracted, or struggling toward the breath but instead open to all that arises in the very moment of its birth. Each moment of birth and death received by that which goes beyond birth and death, awareness itself expanding from moment to moment.

Coming back again and again to the breath to enter the moment as it is, we watch the content of the mind floating in the deathless, the uninjured, the very whole. Not mistaking the objects of awareness for awareness itself. Exploring equal-mindedly, openheartedly, all that arises as it arises.

Watching the breath minutely at the nostrils, its slightest comings and goings, the whispered intentions beneath, the least movement anywhere in the mind/body is instantly recognizable. Developing a choiceless awareness, no object of exploration is preferable to any other, each is allowed fully to arise and dissolve in a noninterfering awareness.

Deepening mindfulness of the process unfolding without grasping at understanding or attempting to force healing, insight and well-being naturally arise. In the merciful softness, the willingness to be that receives the breath in clarity, that choicelessly allows the mind to manifest as it will, we are healed at levels not previously accessible.

And in the subtle whispers of the mind, intention is recognized preceding each movement of the body, each action in the world. Seeing the desire to scratch that leads to scratching allows insight into the cues from the mind that motivate each action. Intention, the middleman between desire and compulsive activity, noticed at its inception, heard clearing its throat. The tendency toward unconscious reaction broken in the clear light of letting go, of an awareness that seeks nothing but the moment.

Awaking from the mechanical quality of our life, from the constant implosion and explosion of the mind in the body, in the world, we may even get a glimpse of that to which the Zen tradition refers when it asks, "What was your face before you were born?"

In watching the ever-becoming of the mind floating in this space of constant being, we break our addiction to the mistaken identity of our suffering and receive life in the very instant of its unfolding, in the deathless nature of the underlying reality.

CHAPTER 19

Healing the Hindrances to Healing

Along the path of healing, various qualities arise that hinder and obstruct awareness and mercy from entering directly into an area of injury or illness. As the attention is directed toward our suffering, it encounters the deep tendencies to hold that maintain pain and keep it beyond the reach of healing or relief. These hindrances reinforce the unfinished business of the mind, the dead spots in the body acquired over a lifetime of compulsively pushing away the unwanted. They encourage the mistaken identity that causes us to lunge with anger or cringe in fear, the confusion of the mind that hinders the pathway to the heart and limits our healing.

But when we begin to see our hindrances as an opportunity for practice, we begin to understand what the Buddhist tradition means when it says, "The greater the hindrance, the greater the enlightenment." Then illness and injury are seen as remarkable opportunities for freedom.

Wherever there is discomfort, the hindrances will arise. And the blockages to the heart become painfully evident. Illness and discomfort have the power to uncover the long-suppressed, what in Buddhism are referred to as the *klesas* or *samskaras,* the deepest-rooted tendencies which lay latent beneath our usual shallow awareness. It is for this reason that relating directly to discomfort and illness has the power to take us to the deepest levels of healing.

Indeed, the discomfort that arises from illness can be seen metaphorically almost like a drill probing through the hard layers of armoring and denial, reaching the deep reservoirs of long-held isolations and fears. The tip of the drill is honed by our identification with feelings of helplessness and hopelessness—the inability to control the uncontrollable—which leads to apathy and depression and leaves one feeling bound by their illness, trapped in their mind/body. This exposing of suppressed and compressed subterranean materials allows a spontaneous release of long-grasped suffering—an artesian well–like fountaining. And at last the long-contracted pains and disharmonies of mind, its deep reservoirs of grief and denial, bubble to the surface. This bubbling up may sound more like an unwelcome wave than an encouragement to float. But once again we recognize that the exploration of our suffering is the path to joy.

This uncovering of the long-held clears access to deeper and deeper levels of healing. Remarkably enough, we discover that entering into the seemingly solid leaves us appreciably lighter. The pressure is released. The belly softens and opens. The edges of the breath dissolve into limitless space. No separation anywhere. Nothing to define, nothing to be. Just being itself. Just this much. Just this moment. All of it in all of it.

Just as in the vision of my children being harmed, my considerable resistance blocked a deeper seeing. It was not until I focused directly on the hindrance itself that the blockage melted in the light of an accepting awareness. Indeed, it was not the fear of this dread happening that was the obstacle but my identification with it.

The hindrances, said a friend, "are the stones rolled into the mouth of the cave against our resurrection." Our addictive focus, our inability to take our eyes off our suffering, our attachment to it is like embracing such a boulder as it is cast into the sea. To relate directly to the hindrances, we must let them go, which is to let them be, in a merciful awareness.

When we begin to look directly at the hindrances we meet along the path of healing, their qualities, their tendencies, their tone of voice, their choice of language, the way they manifest in thought, examining their characteristics and patterns in the mind/body, we begin to relate *to* the hindrances instead of *from* them. Then, relating to doubt brings confidence, relating to resistance opens acceptance, relating to fear creates a new fearlessness. It is another instance of how our old conditioning to pull back from doubt or fear, being doubtful and afraid, has stopped us cold in our tracks—blocking direct access to these hindrances which have so often disallowed reception of our natural healing. Our conditioning to avoid pain is one of the greatest causes of our suffering. We are in some ways conditioned 180 degrees off the mark. Remarkably, healing is to be found in the center of our difficulties as well as our joys, at the very heart of life. Re-entering our life beyond old tendencies of self-protection (which leave our pains unexplored and cause us always to feel vulnerable when in pain), healing, like liberation, becomes a distinct possibility.

We see that each time we let go of the hindrances we recondition the experience of their next appearance. Every time we let go of the hindrances, we increase our capacity for letting go perhaps an instant sooner the next time around. We see with an increasing easiness of mind that each time doubt or fear or resistance mechanically arise they are received in an expanding awareness which has little tendency to implode in identification and intensify suffering. Then even the hindrances are seen just as process passing through; then anger reminds us to love, fear reminds us to soften, and such as restlessness and boredom do not agitate the mind, but act as a focus for the deep calm of a steady awareness. So much that had been thought of for so long as enemies in the mind becomes reminders, allies, of the heart. Then hindrances are no longer obstacles but instead become stepping stones across the river of forgetfulness.

Rather than having these qualities take one unawares, they can be appreciated and met wholeheartedly. Doubt, for instance, may well be expected along the path of healing. But doubt is not the problem, it is our mistaken identity, our identification with doubt which limits our progress. The doubt which leads to inquiry, which demands direct experience of the truth and keeps the mind open to further possibilities, deepens healing. But the doubt that distrusts and narrows the pathways of perception does not. In the clear nonjudgmental seeing of hesitant doubt as a natural part of the process, one is able to approach directly this state of mind. In this willingness to approach doubt, though the mind may doubt it will do any good, confidence arises. When awareness recognizes doubt as simply old mind arisen uninvited, it recognizes its essentially impersonal process and no longer doubts that the hindrances can float. Trust in the process develops when we see that even doubt is empty, automatic, just more momentum playing itself out, just another of the top forty hits of the mind game. Then everything becomes workable, everything becomes another experiment in truth.

In such a healing of doubt, we have come to trust doubt enough to let it float, exploring mercifully its somewhat pessimistic nature, allowing it to be as it is instead of reinforcing it by denial or fear, the mind sinking into the healing heart. It is ironic to note that as we first approach the hindrances we may fear doubt, but as mindfulness develops we tend to doubt fear. Meeting the hindrances with softness and a moment-to-moment awareness, even the subtlest murmurs of a doubting mind can be received in the trusting heart. Then doubt becomes not the *blockage* of awareness but an *object* of awareness. It focuses the healing.

It is not unlike the story of the great Tibetan saint Milarepa, who was meditating one day when three bellicose demons appeared at the mouth of his cave. Rattling skulls and bloody swords, shrieking obscenities and exuding the smell of rotting flesh, they entered the cave howling like a hurricane. With a great smile and a grand gesture, he bid them sit by the fire and "take tea." "But aren't you terrified by our appearance?!" the demons demanded. "Not at all," whispered Milarepa, adding something like: "It is at moments like this, when the demons of fear and doubt present themselves, that I am most grateful to be on the path of healing, to be a yogi. Come, take tea. Make yourself comfortable. You are always welcome. Your hideous visage only reminds me to be aware and have mercy. Come take tea!"

Greeting with mercy and awareness the old cartoon "demons" of the mind, which have for so long blocked the pathway to the heart, one comes to know fear and doubt, judgment and anger, even in their most clever disguises. And we are no longer astonished by the ancient momentum of the mind, by the same old thing. "Of course you're here. Big Surprise! How would you like your tea?"

The closer one approaches these old mind "demons" the more detail one is capable of apprehending. When one comes to see the texture of their flesh, the hairs growing from the moles in the pores of the body of anger or fear or doubt, one is no longer overwhelmed by their empty snarls or anguished expressions. Looking the hindering "demons" straight in the eyes, one begins to see the dullness at the center of their pupils, the discoloration within the iris, the gray cataract of fear clouding their perception of the world.

When we are no longer withdrawing from these old blockages, but meeting them a bit more lightheartedly, we notice with increased enthusiasm that the sooner we greet them, noting "anger" or "fear" or whatever the catch of the day is, the less power they have to block the heart. Seldom overwhelmed by such as rage, noticing the subtleties of frustration before it flips over into anger. Noticing the subtle sooner, the greater does not overwhelm. Able to observe the momentum of desire which, unfulfilled, manifests as frustration, we are not taken unaware or surprised by anger. We just watch the process of unfolding, in a soft belly and an open heart that has room for it all.

At first, of course, it will be difficult if not impossible to open to such immensities as rage or terror. They are too big. But one can build the capacity to open to such primal holdings by working with the little angers and the everyday fears. Thus we will be able to see them sooner, before they become full-blown rage or terror. But if we started to work with the 5-pound weights and then the 10-pounders, with willingness and resoluteness we would eventually build our strength to its maximum capacity. Just as it is not skillful to try to press that 300-pound weight without long preparation, so it would not be appropriate to dive into a state as dense as rage, thinking, "I should be able to make this stuff float!" Good luck! And welcome to the world of the limping and the herniated.

We will not be able to overcome the 300-pound hobgoblins on first approach. In fact, if we are thinking in terms of overcoming anger or fear, we will just feel overcome each time they arise. But meeting them wholeheartedly, we come to know them like the backs of our hands or, more accurately, like the back of our mind. As we come to investigate the subtle processes of the hindrances, we see that such labels as "fear" or "doubt" or "anger" are just oversimplifications for a rather complex process. There is more to doubt than "doubt," more to fear than "fear," more to anger than "anger."

Exploring such hindrances as anger, for example, we come to see that it is not a single state of aversion but rather an ongoing unwinding of multiple states and changing qualities that may include a moment of frustration dissolving into a moment of greed, into a moment of fear, into a moment of doubt, into a moment of self-pity, into a moment of pride, into a moment of judgment, into a moment of unworthiness, into a moment of self-negation into a moment of resistance—moment after moment arising and dissolving one into the next, a deep momentum in old mind unfolding as it will. Fear is not just "fear," but rather a moment of trepidation dissolving into a moment of frustration, dissolving into a moment of aversion, dissolving into a moment of distrust, dissolving into a moment of attack, dissolving into a moment of self-judgment, dissolving, dissolving, one state of mind dissolving into the next. Nothing is one thing: each is composed of levels upon levels of subtleties.

Entering directly into these states of mind and body, which have so often caused us to feel separate, we discover a sense of interconnectedness. We notice the anger in fear, the fear in doubt, the doubt in anger. We experience the feeling within the feeling just as one might, at a later stage, discover the breath within the breath, the subtle expanse which inhabits the seeming solidity of all things.

There may be many states of mind that arise on the way to healing that are difficult to look at. We may push them away and deny them. This withdrawal causes us to stay shallow in our healing by denying the investigation of that which limits the mind's merging with the heart. Indeed, as one approaches an area of discomfort, many of these states of mind may be clearly seen. This deeper investigation of the feelings surrounding discomfort or illness, at some moments may lead to almost ecstatic revelations. While at other times so different is old mind from what we have hoped ourselves to be that this seeing may be quite painful. So much pain and longing to be released. So long-held is our suffering and so ancient. But in the course of healing, everything is grist for the mill. It is all just a healing discovery.

Mindful of the hindrances to healing—the doubt and fear and resistance—we come to see how difficult it may be to let go of our suffering. We are so attached to it, we are so identified with pain in our mind/body as being who we are. Our deep aversion to illness is a form of that attachment to suffering. It is a negative attachment, which means that we are busy being someone busy pushing things away. It magnifies the pain and resistance, and intensifies the sense of isolation, the helplessness and hopelessness, the feeling of being "cut off" from healing, of being removed from the very source of wholeness.

We are so identified with the mind/body that we often mistake symptoms of illness for who we are. But by investigating these doubts and fears and resistances, which surround discomfort, there is the possibility of insight into how these are involuntary processes, just old mind running off its habitual addictions and identifications. We see the difficulty of letting go of our suffering as we begin to send mercy into illness and perhaps encounter a blockage which resists such ministrations. We notice how merciless we are, how accustomed we have become to judging ourselves out of our heart. We notice mercy being hindered by thoughts such as "Sending forgiveness into my illness is just more self-indulgence!" We see how little kindness we allow ourselves, how little healing we allow in.

There is little in our daily life like illness or discomfort to tune us to the latent hindrances, the disgruntled mumbling arising in the mind and body. Indeed, the tumor, the wound, the depression, the pain can be used like a crystal ball, an extraordinary mirror for the mind's holding. For it seems wherever there is discomfort the holdings of the mind will be dredged up. Indeed, illness or stress can be used as the most exquisite biofeedback device. The least bit of tension, of resistance, of holding to our suffering can be felt as intensifying waves of sensation. This degree of feedback about our resistance to pain, to life, can become a great teacher.

When we start sending love and awareness into illness, even with the difficulties one encounters along the way, it begins to define love for us. The question arises, "What does it even mean to send love into illness?" How bizarre that it has never occurred to us before that when we hurt, instead of sending love and awareness into the pain, we send rejection, anxiety, and a desire for escape. Just when we need the energy of the heart the most, we find it least available.

To meet the hindrances with a loving awareness is the beginning of our greatest freedom. Our participation in life begins by the exploration of our deep resistance to participation.

Illness draws the hindrances into view, out of the submerged, into the light of awareness. Illness is an opportunity to become healed.

To discover the true nature of love and the wholeness, the complete spaciousness, of an unhindered awareness, to receive life directly, as it is, with no filters or unfinished business. Just things as they are, just being itself.

A pinched nerve
  at the root of the fingers—
tried to pick up
  more than it could handle—
but in the pain
  with no reserve
or wish to be otherwise—
  the Light.
Ah! there! Christ in the palm of your hand!

CHAPTER 20

Taking Tea by the Fire

Before we can speak further about developing mercy, we must acknowledge that the basis of compassion is harmlessness, noninjury. Before one thinks of "doing good," one must seriously contemplate removing oneself from doing harm. Before we can play with the angels of our compassion, we need take tea with the "demons" of our holding. To meet these hobgoblins like Milarepa, in the Halloween of the mind, not fearing desire's call of "Trick-or-treat!", we approach open-handedly, offering sweets to the tricksters, watching them regress, curled childlike by the fire, sucking at the breast of loving kindness.

Most people are basically kind and gentle but haven't yet cured themselves of the reactive, injurious quality of their anger. Few have taken tea with their outrage or confusion. Most try to push it away, causing it to explode unconsciously into a world already overflowing with violence and reactivity. Few, in order to cultivate the quality of harmlessness in their lives, have taken responsibility for their anger. To take responsibility for our anger means to relate *to* it instead of *from* it. To be responsible is to be able to respond instead of having to react. To be responsible to our anger is to bring it within the realm of the voluntary. To react to it leaves life frozen in the mechanical action of old mind. Responsibility enters the moment anew. Reactivity is the same old thing.

To react to our anger is to roll the boulders of fear and distrust into the mouth of our cave. To respond to it is to invite it in for tea, to meet it eye to eye in the light that streams through the wide entrance to our cavern. It is seldom we meet our anger so completely, usually quite unfamiliar with its presence until we become enraged. We seldom meet it in its infancy because we have a tendency to deny it and judge ourselves and anger as "bad." And so we don't notice its subtler quality on first arisal. This shadowy comprehension of our anger is a byproduct of our having pulled back so often from the unpleasant, from judging the judge, becoming angry at ourselves for becoming angry.

Everyone has anger because everyone has desires. It comes with the territory. Desire leads to anger. As desire moves toward its fulfillment, if something arises to block it, frustration occurs. That is why the deepest recognition of desire is necessary in the cultivation of noninjury in the world.

Relating directly to anger, we explore its roots. Examining the momentum of desire, one comes to understand deeply the push and pull of the mind, the nature of frustration itself, the feeling of not having, of more wanting, a denseness, a tightening, a nausea. Watching frustration closely, one explores the point where it flicks over into anger. The more often one watches this transformation, the sooner we notice anger upon its slightest arisal. The sooner we notice such potentially heavy states, the lighter they become. The more easily they are noted with the good humor of "Big Surprise, anger again!" It is very important that we explore our anger so we are not perpetually reacting to the vicissitudes of the world, leaving the debris of unfinished business in our wake. Indeed, this state of anger, as with so many other heavy states, has gone unexplored, has been shied away from so often that we hardly know it at all. Often when we are angry, we feel it is an inappropriate state and leave it uninvestigated, unhealed.

Anger unexplored breeds anger. Anger explored leads to harmony. How little mercy or attention we have for ourselves. Exploring anger, we discover how isolated we feel when angry. When we are angry, everything in the world is an "other." In anger we are already in so much pain we can hardly stand it, yet the merciless, reactive mind thinks we deserve further punishment. In fact, what would be a greater curse than if someone were to say, "May you be angry the rest of your life!" We would see and smell and taste nothing. Our life would shrivel to a fearful defense of imagined safe territory. We would not even be able to touch the world because anger acts as a film across the senses. It blocks reception. Indeed, as we watch frustration closely, we see that anger arises uninvited and has a life of its own, a momentum from all the previous moments of identifying with anger, becoming angry and separate. But meeting frustration in "don't know," nothing tightens down on the content to obscure the natural unfolding of its process as we learn to respond to it instead of reacting angrily. Reacting to anger creates the violence, the abuse, the separation which pains us so.

As mercy develops, we see how painful it is to be in anger and we are reminded to soften, to look gently on it as it arises. And we realize that we don't have to hellishly react, impulsively putting ourselves and the whole world out of our heart. Sensing the power of noninjury, we begin to respond to ourselves as we would to a frightened child, with a deeper kindness and care.

We have been taught that there were only two things we could do with our anger. One was to reactively suppress it. The other was to reactively spit it out. But both are forms of attachment to anger. One is a condemning, the other a clinging. What is ironic is that when we examine anger we notice that no matter how much we have ever emoted this feeling, we have never felt rid of it for long. We become exhausted before we can get it all out. It is more than we can handle in either manner of suppression or expulsion. The involuntary emoting of anger just creates more of the same.

Let us note here that there are, at this time, some very skillful means of working with suppressed anger that involve bringing it to the surface. For those who have difficulty making contact with their anger there are ways of stimulating it, such as beating on a mattress or screaming which such extraordinary therapists as our old friend Elizabeth Kubler-Ross have skillfully employed. Because nothing which is not accepted can be healed, some need bring up such as anger to at last have direct access to it. It is a technique that must be used in a very balanced manner so that anger brought to the surface can be investigated without being identified with as self. Like every technique, including meditation, it can become a trap if upon discovering one's hidden content one mistakes this for their true nature. In such cases of mistaken identity, one might cultivate war instead of discovering peace. It takes the most balanced of therapists to help one uncover anger without trapping one in identification with its dynamics because the expression of anger may momentarily relieve it but build its potential for the future.

Exploring its nature we discover how unskillful it can be to suppress anger. Pushing it down, it accumulates beyond the reach of our ordinary awareness. It has access to you, but you no longer have access to it. It drives you, it motivates you, it makes choices for you, but you can't see "who" has the reins in their hands because it is suppressed below the level of awareness. And just as we see that we can't get it all out, we notice that we can't suppress it quite completely either. We are always ready to explode or implode. We are hardly in the moment.

Thus we come to recognize a third alternative with anger and other heavy states. Rather than pushing them down or spitting them out, we can let them come gently into awareness. We can start to give them space, to get a sense of their texture, of their voice, of their inclination. We begin to investigate the nature of *the* anger instead of getting lost in *my* anger. Indeed, to give anger space takes courage. It takes acceptance, which, interestingly enough, is the exact opposite of anger. Anger and fear are both strong aversion reactions. Acceptance is a welcoming response. The very act of accepting anger begins to melt it and gives access to subtler and subtler levels of holding. Acceptance takes the mask off anger and lets you look it straight in the eye. It allows anger to come and allows it to go. I have seen people sitting in meditation, their clothes drenched with perspiration having come upon the deep magma of their impotent rage, just trying to stay with the moment a breath at a time. Recognizing that if that underground fire is brought to the surface, it might light our way.

When we see that anger is not a single state of mind and begin to experience it in its unfolding—frustration flipping over into intense wanting, flipping over into feelings of abandonment, into not having, into self-pity, into righteousness, into pride, into aggression, into confusion, back into self-pity and pride again—one can come to ask oneself, "Which of these states is anger?" As we relate to it instead of from it, we see that anger is a process.

We notice in our investigation of frustration a certain quality of stress that permeates the mind/body. Some react to stress with anger, others with fear. Seeing clearly each state as it momentarily predominates allows us to break old mind's automatic chain of events. We are able to reside a bit more in being itself, the space in which anger is unfolding without getting lost in its content. Not suffering from the mistaken identity that we are the anger, we instead recognize in space the tightness passing through. Anger or fear are the inevitable momentum of old mind, which, deeply observed, begins to lose its power. Recognizing the well-forged and deeply imprinted links in this chain of action and reaction, we recognize how natural it is to have anger. As natural as the underlying frustration, the underlying desire. But when we understand the naturalness of anger, when we no longer back away in shock, we see that each moment of its arisal is an opportunity for practice, for awareness and mercy. Recognizing, for instance, that we may be angry ten thousand more times, the next time anger arises, we meet it as Milarepa met the ogres at the mouth of his cave, and invite it in for closer inspection. "Take tea. Make yourself comfortable. Warm yourself by the fire." Then anger can begin to float. And instead of 10,001 more times of anger there may only be 9,999. Each moment that it is responded to mindfully instead of reacted to compulsively lightens the load and lessens the momentum of old mind. Each time we relate to anger, instead of from it, it demagnetizes. It loses its seductive quality, its mechanical, compulsive reactivity, which has so often propelled action.

I remember once looking at the "Ten Rules of Practice" on the wall of a monastery. One of the rules was "Don't be angry." And I thought, "No one is going to get enlightened in this place." For how is one going to get liberated if one excludes anything from the investigation? When someone says to you, "Don't be angry," that means don't be. To allow anger to come into being without becoming it takes a very delicate balance, but to react to anger with fear is just more of the same old thing. Until anger, like boredom or restlessness, is equally invited into the heart of mindfulness, one will always be thrown off kilter by its momentary arisal. We have been very strongly conditioned not to be angry, usually by someone who was angry at the time. We cultivate a mercilessness with ourselves, and judgment meets anger in an angry way. The hardness tightens; we become the object and subject of abuse.

Anger, like all heavy states, even pain, is workable when we ap-

proach it with a merciful awareness. In fact, anger can be quite
fascinating to watch. We begin to see anger's grade B script, its
shadowboxing and interior monologue. "They should have done
this." "They ought to be like that." "If it was up to me, I'd do this."
We watch it run out its game, and if we stay with it long enough we
notice, quite to our chagrin, that it begins the same old story line all
over again. We start to see the tape-loop quality, the impersonal
process, which repeats over and over again what it has already said
—listening mercifully to the repeating images, the all-too-familiar
insistence that we are right, the pride, the sense of rejection, the
feeling of not being loved enough, we begin to have compassion for
our anger and bring it a cup of tea. We begin to have mercy on that
poor painful state of mind, that compulsive violence to itself, that
closedness, that hard living. Then anger reminds us to soften the
belly and that no one is an object, but all are a living suchness, baby
flesh, ourselves.

The exploration of such a state becomes a very interesting endeavor. You explore it, listen to it, feel it, come to know it. What is
anger in the body? What is its voice in the mind? What is its tone of
voice? What is the script it reads out? Are there other accompanying
states of mind? What precedes it? What follows? The process unfolding in vast space.

As our anger comes within the circle of responsibility, we get a
sense of what it means to be fully alive. And that circle widens to
allow more and more of our states of mind, and the states of mind of
our loved ones, to come within the deep stillness of a choiceless
investigation, of a willingness to be. We no longer hide in the dark
forest of reactivity, constantly ambushed by our feelings, frightened
and hardened to the world. Instead, we go deep within and notice if
we add love to any situation we are angry about, the cause of anger
dissolves. Staying with the changing qualities of anger in the mind/
body, the words in the mind, the images, the denseness in the body,
we discover under all this anger a deep sadness. Omitting nothing,
the investigation continues into the sadness, all the moments of not
having, all the frustrated griefs of a lifetime, and beneath that sadness we discover an ocean of love beyond our wildest dreams.

So the investigation of anger becomes an end of injury in the
world and leads us directly to the love beneath, to our underlying

nature. Having taken anger into the area where we can respond to it, where we can investigate it, where we can embrace it, it emerges into the light of our wholeness. Then even anger does not close our heart. Then anger is no longer a hindrance but a profound teacher, a reminder to go deeper, to discover what is real.

In the Tibetan Buddhist tradition, they speak of taking anger and turning it around to motivate practice because in anger are qualities like straightforwardness and resoluteness which can be turned into commitment. It can be the anger of "I am not going to let my heart be closed a moment longer—enough is enough!" It is not a destructive anger, it is the creative urge to get on with our work. In anger's tendency toward reaction can be discovered an energy which can be redirected toward entering the moment wholeheartedly. Anger too has the quality of an unwillingness to allow things to remain as they are. Separated from its aggression, that quality of discontent can motivate us to take the path of healing. It is alchemy. You take the dross and turn it to gold. Then we see that anger has not been the problem but our manner of relating to it.

Having taken tea so many times with our anger, we are no longer frustrated or surprised by its deep tendency to draw identification, but mercifully acknowledge that the nature of the mind is to grasp, to think about itself, and instead of tightening in just more identification, more repulsion toward mind, toward the seat of pain, we learn to have mercy. We learn to let the mind be in the heart. We learn to love ourselves.

Then we see how the nature of anger is resentment, an integral part of the armoring about the heart. And we see that anger is a form of grief. It is a response to loss. It is a response to not getting what we want. We recognize that anything we are angry about we are actually grieving over. And so our relating to anger becomes the grief work that calls on our heart for mercy and healing. To see what closes us and to stay awake a millisecond longer the next time.

In making this much room in our heart for anger, we acknowledge that at times our anger is so great that we have very little room for it. The thoughts are so seductive that identification automatically adheres and pride nurses it into flame. But that is only the beginning. We see that the mind, in its long personal history, feels every right to be angry, and we do not block that either, for we know that without permission to be angry we don't have consent to be alive. So we allow anger to come wholeheartedly into the mind, instead of getting lost in the old way of trying to squeeze it into some manageable shape.

When anger becomes so intense, its nature so identified with that there is no space in the mind in which to investigate, we learn to come into the body and start to examine anger as sensation. Because often you can stay mindful of anger longer as sensation than you can as thought. It may be very difficult to examine fear in the frightened mind, but it is always accessible to exploration in the body—its denseness, its rapidity of change, its tension quite noticeable in the gut, the throat, the lower back. Every state of mind has an accompanying, a concomitant state of body. The thoughts won't float, but the sensations will. It may be in the early investigation of such as anger that one directs awareness into the body again and again to rediscover the body pattern of anger so the mind does not get sucked into reinforcing it. So that you can start to see some of its empty quality, so that some aspect of it at least can be touched with mercy and awareness. Theoretically, if we had no mind to be angry, still anger would be recognizable by the contractions and patterns it left in the body. Indeed, one could tell whether one was joyous or frightened, doubtful or expectant, by the bodily echo of these states. When we can't stay with the mind of anger, we always have access to the body of investigation. And there we can stay with it at least one more millisecond of not being angry but being with anger. One more opportunity for freedom from the old. One more way of moving toward life instead of backing away from it.

It is when we relate so wholeheartedly to these heavy states, to these emotions, that we can let go of attempts to be rational about emotion. To be rational about emotions is to try to fit a square peg in a round hole. Emotions have their own nature, just as thoughts have theirs. They are not the same. They are two separate levels of the mind. To try to be rational about emotions is to go crazy. The back wards are filled with people who are trying to think their feelings rather than experience them as they are, trying to control the world by limiting the wide range of emotion into the narrow confines of thought.

A useful example of how we attempt to be rational about emotions can be found in our relationship to the state of mind called guilt. For instance, we go out one day and say to someone, "Life!" and he or she says, "Ahhh, how wonderful, that's just what I needed to hear." We feel just fine about ourselves. Then we say "Life!" to the next person, and this person says, "That's terrible—how could you say that to me?" And we feel awful. We said the same thing, did the same thing; our motivation was exactly the same, but one action was followed by the feeling of pride and the other by feelings of guilt according to the response. You are reacting to their world, not responding to yours. Indeed, their reactions have nothing to do with you. Emotions are not rational, nor need they be. To attempt to make them rational is to cause great conflict within. But to simply watch how the mind emotes, how it smiles and frowns in reaction to the world, can give some insight into its natural unfoldings. When the world is allowed within the heart, we deeply understand there is nothing to judge and all our healings are based on intention. The intention "Life!" was the same for all. Only the reaction was different and, therefore, the mind's reaction to reaction. One might say that guilt is just the friction released as two conflicting desire systems pass each other. The mind suggests, "Why don't you have an ice cream cone?" And five minutes after having finished the ice cream cone, the mind turns to you and says, "I wouldn't have done that if I were you." No wonder we're all crazy. So we see that guilt may be present, even though we have done nothing to be guilty for.

This was the case in an East Coast hospice when a nun visited the ward for the first time. Moving from room to room, she was introduced to various terminal patients. Coming to the bedside of a fifty-five-year-old woman, whose mental pain played like shadow work across her face, and left temporarily alone with her, the nun sat down next to this very unhappy patient and took her hand. Not knowing what to do, but obeying her heart, she sat quietly with the patient for a moment, then said, "I have this hand and God has your other." At that moment the woman died. The nun was immediately overcome with feelings of guilt and confusion. She had done exactly the right thing at exactly the right moment, but nonetheless the irrationality of guilt played itself strongly across her mind.

So we come to meet guilt as an exploration, as a deepening of life, as an opening of the passageway into the heart. Guilt is just another of the top forty doing its thing. Nothing to be rational about, nothing to be left unappreciated.

Exploring the hindrances deeply, developing the precept of noninjury, we attempt to make nothing other than it is. Just to see its nature as it plays itself out. No longer angry at anger or guilty that guilt at times arises. When there is anger, there is just anger. When there is fear, there is just fear. And when there is joy, there is just joy. We have room for it all. We take life as a blessing instead of a curse.

Introduction to
A Mindful Exploration of Heavy
Emotional States

Healing follows awareness. Our healing is as deep as our investigation. By cultivating a deeper mercy and awareness, healing enters levels of the mind/body previously unexperienced.

If one should feel "overwhelmed" by fear, anger, guilt, doubt, confusion, greed, shame, lust, mercilessness, or any of the great high-density clouds that pass through the mind, such an exploration as here suggested might prove quite useful.

Such intense emotional states have a certain hallucinogenic quality about them and insistence on being more real than anything which has passed through lately. A quality of agitation and disquiet that states unequivocally that this discomfort shall continue forever, or get worse. That it will burn us to the ground. But in truth we have never experienced a single emotion which has ever stayed. All is in process. Neither the worst feelings we have ever had, nor the best, could be maintained indefinitely. To tune to the flow of change in which these feelings float is to break identification with the seeming solidity of "the suffering" as well as "the sufferer."

It may take a while before you can meet the age-old pains of the mind with the acceptance and lightness of "Big Surprise, you again!" And invite them in for a healing. But it is meditations such as these that establish that familiarity and comfort with the workability of even such heavy feelings.

Indeed, the word "feelings" has a double meaning. One is of emotion. The other of sensation. But this is no casual happenstance of language, it is an insight into the correlation between the mental experience and its bodily expression. Each state of mind has a corresponding body pattern. Often thoughts of fear, doubt, etc., are too seductive, their content too identified with as *"my* fear" or *"my* doubt,"* to see the process of *"the* fear,"* *"the* doubt."* We just can't get any space around these feelings, so quickly does the old mind of conditioning and preconceptions implode about their imagery.

But by focusing awareness on the bodily expression of these states we may discover a way through. We may not be able to stay mindful of the thoughts in anger for even a minute before identification seduces us into becoming angry. But letting the content of thought unfold as it will and directing the attention toward the body, rather than thought, pattern of this feeling—the clenched teeth, the hardened belly, the tightened sphincter—we can stay quite present for some time.

This meditation allows us to lighten the load of heavy emotion, dissolving the threatening solidity of these states by examining one by one their incremental composition in the mind/body.

The quality of exploration cultivated in this meditation allows us to relate *to* these states instead of *from* them. This examining ever more deeply, layer after layer, of the seeming solidity of these heavy states could be likened to looking through a microscope at a piece of polished stone. At first we discover the considerable porousness of its seemingly smooth surface. Then, focusing deeper, its crystalline structure comes into view. Going yet deeper into the seemingly solid, we see the vast space between molecules, an enormous empty sky in which their scattered constellations glitter. And yet deeper, the cosmic spaciousness of the atom. So much space in so little solidity. So much room for awareness to infiltrate and experience its own spacious nature even in the midst of the seemingly solid.

A MINDFUL EXPLORATION OF HEAVY EMOTIONAL STATES

[To be read slowly to a friend or silently to oneself.]

When identification with dense mental states such as fear, doubt, anger, or pride contract the mind and narrow access to the heart, find a comfortable place to sit and take a few smooth, deep breaths into the body.

Although the mind has many voices, let its words just float. Notice the intense momentum rapidly unfolding.

Just let thoughts think themselves in the mind as the even flow of breath begins to soften the body.

Let the belly begin to soften to receive the moment.

Allow awareness to settle into the level of sensation in the body.

Allow awareness to roam free in the body, exploring.

Notice any areas of tension or denseness.

Notice areas of pressure or movement.

Of heat or cold.

The tinglings, the vibratory quality.

Slowly allow awareness to receive the body.

Feel the sensations that accompany this state of mind as they arise in the muscles, bone, and flesh. Feel the physical imprint of this mental state.

Explore the sensations in the stomach and belly. Is there tension? holding? resistance?

Let the attention move gently into the chest. Is the breath constricted? Is there some desire for control which attempts to shape and hold the breath?

Let awareness move slowly through the spine noticing any tingling or heat or coldness.

Letting the attention be drawn to whatever sensations predomi-nate, explore the body pattern of this state of mind.

What has mind labeled these feelings?

How has it described this experience to itself?

Does it call it fear?

Does it call it anger?

Does it call it joy?

Each state of mind has its own particular qualities. What are the qualities of this state of mind?

Let awareness explore the moment to moment process of this feeling in the body.

Are these sensations changing?

Do they move from one area to another?

Is the body pattern of this state enunciated more in one area than another?

In the back or the neck?

In the gut?

What are the sensations in the tongue? Is it pushing against the teeth? Pressed against the roof of the mouth? What holding is exhibited there?

What is occurring at the top of the head?

Noticing, area by area, the mind's expression in the body.

Examining the wordless presence at the center of sensation, ex-amine the constant unfolding of thought silhouetted against this silent backdrop.

What are the voices in the mind/body?

Simply listen. Nothing to answer back.

Just receiving.

Noting the intonation of these voices, their intensity.

Allow the awareness to settle a bit more deeply into its listening.

Is it an angry voice?

A frightened voice?

A confused voice?

Listen to the tone.

Feel its texture.

Is there a noticeable *intention* in the voice?

What is the intention of this state of mind/body, of this emotion, of this aspect of the personality?

Does it make you feel better or worse about yourself?

Does it wish you well? Does it take you closer to your true nature? Does it accept you as is?

What might be the effect of bringing forgiveness or love into this mind/body? Would it resist letting go of its suffering?

Is this a voice we wish to take counsel from? Does it lead us to wholeness or defeat?

Is there wisdom or love in that voice?

Or is there judgment or pity or doubt?

Just listening.

Just receiving the moment as it is.

Do these feelings have a point of view, a direction they insist you travel?

Where is the love?

Where is the mercy and kindness?

Where is the healing in their offering?

Now allow the attention to sink into the deep movement within this state.

Is it a single emotion or is it made up of many different feelings? Does it display a single mood or is it constantly changing expressions?

Perhaps many feelings are noticed.

A moment of pride dissolving perhaps into a moment of anger.

A moment of aggression dissolving into a moment of self-pity.

A moment of judgment dissolving into a moment of hopelessness.

Each feeling melting, dissolving constantly from one state into the next.

Begin to focus on the process, not simply the content.

Notice the quality of change within this seemingly solid state.

Focus on the movement within.

Like a microscope which fine-tunes through levels of seeming solidity, entering beneath the multiple tiny fractures and blemishes of the surface to explore its deep molecular structure, let awareness open into a moment-to-moment examination of the discrete elements which constitute the flow of this experience. See the multiple tiny thoughts and sensations which form the molecular framework of this experience.

Notice the impersonal nature of these states we took so personally.

Notice how they plead their case.

Notice how they insist they are real and insist they will go on forever, even though they are constantly changing.

Notice the repetitive quality within.

Notice how each voice, each sensation, each feeling, melts automatically, one into the next.

Watch how naturally each thought ends.

Watch how spontaneously each next thought arises.

Observe the next voice, the next feeling entering.

Watch how each state of mind/body is in process, arising and dissolving into the next.

Notice how the "script" is constantly unfolding.

Let it all float in awareness. Let it unfold moment to moment.

Watch how each state arises uninvited.

Constantly coming and constantly going.

Watch the incessant birth and death of thought.

Watch how life is constantly unfolding all by itself.

Observe how thoughts think themselves.

Notice how feelings feel themselves.

Give these constantly changing sensations and thoughts a little more space, a little more room to unfold in a soft body and an open heart.

Let the belly breathe all by itself.

The chest clear.

The throat open.

The tongue soft and gentle in the mouth.

Just receiving the moment as it arises without the least clinging or condemning.

Nothing to change.

No one to be.

Just the merciful space of exploration in which the moment-to-moment process unfolds.

All which seemed so solid before is seen as constantly dissolving into change.

Not creating the moment, just receiving it.

Watching it all as process unfolding, observing wholeheartedly what is.

Letting each moment of experience arise as it will in spacious awareness. Floating, constantly unfolding in vast space.

Watching thought come and go in spacious mind.

Letting sensations arise and dissolve in soft body.

Allowing.

Soft belly noticing even the slightest holding.

Soft breath opening around even the least tension.

Receiving.

Observing.

Letting come.

Letting be.

Letting go.

Space for it all.

This moment an opportunity for healing.

This unfolding, life itself, so precious, so fully lived.

CHAPTER 21

Qualities of Healing

All mind is old mind a moment after its perception. Therefore, inquiry into its present nature is the way to live in new mind. To live in the moment is to live anew. All thought is old by the time the following recognition has arisen. To hold even to insights of the past is hindrance. When we don't carry the past as "me," but instead see it as the mind, we live at the center of being, of healing itself. Then we live with no unfinished business, "leaving no traces," as one teacher put it. All that hinders healing falls aside in the moment of clear awareness, seeing that the hindrances too are impermanent, a momentary arising and dissolving in the vastness. Nothing pulls us back to the past or trips us headlong into the future. In this moment all we seek is found.

We watch how our resistance, our denial, our longing for things to be otherwise cause us to filter every moment, every perception, every taste, every touch, every hearing, every smelling, through a kind of psychic sieve. It is the semipermeable membrane of perception, of our way of seeing the world, of attempting to control and shape the uncontrollable that haltingly meets the world at every juncture with trepidation and a limited willingness to be. Our whole perception is dragged through this reduction valve, which only admits those particles small enough not to threaten it, to allow it to feel safe and deal with life on old mind's terms. This means to make reality fit the dream, distorting it and reforming it in our own self-image and likeness.

Examining perception, we focus on the filter, this resistance to life, this insistence on having things our own imagined way. And we come to notice how we have always pulled back from the direct perception of our edge, from the unexplored wilderness of our lives, from the crucible of growth. And we come to see how much has limited our healing and caused us to live feeling as though our backs are pressed against a wall. We have pulled way back from life to get "a perspective on things," which means to make things seem so far away, so "off in the distance" as to appear small and unthreatening. We notice how seldom we approach closely enough to see the pores and blemishes on the face of life that peers back at us from afar. We have pulled back from perception itself and exchanged the suchness of this moment, the pulsating quickness of life, for an afterthought. We have traded direct experience for the underdream. Our healing, like some watery mirage, shimmering in the far-stretching deserts of our fears and denials. Healing is to press our nose against the lens of perception, to enter our life directly with our eyes and ears and body and mind wide open, discovering the unimagined spaciousness and clarity in which all distortion floats and heals back into its original nature.

In the meditation experience of seeing my children's dying, I came to recognize that any holding at all, even the least clinging to the slightest passing thought, was unendurable agony. I recognized not just something about the nature of "my mind," but the nature of mind itself. Any holding to the past, to even an instant's previous content, whether pleasant or painful, was suffocation in comparison to the openness of a single moment's tranceless entrance into the present.

So we see that it is not simply a matter of "converting the hindrances," of the demons "getting religion," but rather of profoundly entering into the space in which they float. For instance, though the investigation of doubt breeds confidence, one need not hold even to confidence but enter the process of which it is all a part. It is an entering into the undefinable, though definitions may be seen floating within the experience.

Grasping is our suffering. There has never been a pain in our lives, in our minds, that has not been the result of holding to things being otherwise, either more of the same or less of the same. Any holding whatsoever, even to the idea of "nonholding," is painful denseness next to the sense of unlimited completeness arising when one participates directly in the unfolding moment.

This depth of letting go, which actually means *a choiceless letting be,* is easier said than done. On the way to deepening our letting go, not only do the hindrances need to be clearly recognized and allowed to dissolve, but certain qualities of healing can be skillfully cultivated to clear the path more fully for a greater entrance into the uncramped moment.

As we let go into the investigation, the openness of the heart receives it all as it is, and we enter the body as an avid student enters a classroom, to take the lessons and do the homework suggested. We get a sense of being a visitor in the body come to the earthly plane of conflict and joy, of suffering and elation, to this realm of impermanence and grief, to saints' school, to receive the healing we have so longed for.

As this becomes clearer, we see that healing corresponds in many ways to how the heart relates to experience. Investigating our old ways of seeing, we go beyond clinging to the content of old mind and enter directly the energy which effortlessly continues the unfolding, recognizing that what moves thought through the mind moves the stars across the sky. Then it is no longer "I am the body," or even "I am the process," it is just "am-ness" itself, the vastness through which all content and process float. And we go beyond old or new, beyond birth or death, to the timeless, formless, boundaryless nature of awareness itself. We experience the light which produces consciousness on the screen and discover creation itself, our true nature.

Then, all which arises is grist for the mill. And we do not lean toward or pull back from any aspect of the mind. Nothing is hindrance. We are learning to keep our heart open in hell. And everything takes care of itself. Opening past all hellish resistance, we enter the heart of the moment, experiencing the depth of our extraordinary compassion and sympathetic joy. To open the heart in hell is to enter the love that goes beyond conditions. It is an entering into the underlying reality, the essential connectedness that exists beyond liking and disliking, beyond pleasure and pain.

Many do not begin this work until they receive a terminal prognosis. Don't wait to live until you have been told that death is only six months away. This is not work to be done at some later date when a frightening diagnosis or prognosis is received. This is the healing available to us this very instant. Entering our heart is a process of letting go of our suffering.

This process of going beyond our suffering is a bit like the story of the eight Hasidic scholars translating an ancient Hebraic text when they came across the line "Suffering is grace." They stopped short, sharing with each other in great candor that although they had heard this text many times, they didn't really comprehend it. "How can suffering really be grace?" Each, feeling uncomfortable with any casual translation of such a remarkable concept, felt that they could go no further without some deeper understanding. "How can it be so?" each asked the other. Then, one of the rabbis suggested, "Just outside of town lives crippled Jonathan. Jonathan has known great travail and many illnesses in his life. His son was killed by the great floods that ruined his land and covered his home with mud. But as he was burying his son and cleaning up the soil that ruined his house, he began to sing to God. Some years later his wife became quite ill because he could hardly grow enough food to support them. But that did not stop his song. Later, when he broke his leg and couldn't afford a physician so that it never healed quite properly and left him with a rather painful limp, Jonathan seemed still unruffled. Jonathan, even in those sparse fields, even during drought, constantly spoke and sang to God. If anyone knows how suffering may be grace, Jonathan would be the person to ask. He is so poor and has had such misfortune, yet he seems to be at peace." So the eight rabbis set out to the impoverished farm of Jonathan and his wife. Meeting Jonathan at the porch, they were invited to share in the meager supper. Of course the rabbis demurred, noting that he had so little and was so generous to share, which brought them to the reason for their visit. They told Jonathan of their difficulty in honestly translating, "Suffering is grace." They felt that he of all the people they knew, might be able to elucidate its meaning because somehow all his misfortunes seemed not to have diminished his heartfulness. "How Jonathan, with the loss of your child and farm, and you and your wife's poor health, can you still sing to God? How have you found that suffering can be grace?" To which Jonathan sheepishly replied, "I am very sorry you made this long trip and that I cannot help you. You have come to the wrong man to ask this question. I am not suffering."

Those we have known who have entered healing the most deeply spoke of beginning to experience love in the area of illness. They were no longer simply sending love into that area but began to receive love whenever awareness touched their illness. Illness became a mirror for their heart. Having looked deeply into their own discomfort and fear, they discovered the ocean of love that lies just beyond doubt and trepidation, just beyond the mind. Though at first they had to cultivate a deeper awareness to get by the hindrances and send love into illness, somehow that love had burned through even the need to be loved, and only love remained. Their illness had become a repository for their loving kindness. Their relationship to illness became a reflection of their mercy with themselves. They approached the essence which goes beyond either body or mind and plays joyously in the boundaryless mystery. Their healing became an entering into that which goes beyond pain and illness, mind and body, life and death. They went beyond someone experiencing healing or someone experiencing meditation, to just experience itself, the spacious ease in which there was no one meditating, only meditation meditating itself. They entered the equanimous spaciousness which in Zen may be referred to as "no mind," the formless awareness which choicelessly observes the creation of creation. "Am-ness" expanding everywhere at once, edgeless, just being itself, the essential nature all share. And once again they were reminded that "no mind" is all heart.

A Meditation on Letting Go
(from *Who Dies?*)

[To be read slowly to a friend or silently to oneself.]

Let your attention come to the breath.

Not the thought of the breath, but the direct sensation of the breath, as it comes and goes by itself.

Let the awareness come right to the edge of sensation as the breath enters and leaves the nostrils.

Let the awareness be soft and open, making contact with each breath without the least interference.

Experience the natural tides of the breath, as it comes and goes. Don't attempt to control or change it. Just observe it.

Open to receive each changing sensation that accompanies the breath, moment to moment.

Let the breath breathe itself. Without comment. Without any attempt to control it in any way. Allow the breath to be as it is. If it is slow, let it be slow. If it is deep, let it be deep. If it is shallow, let it be shallow. Allow awareness and sensation to meet, moment to moment, with each inhalation, with each exhalation.

Let the breath be completely natural and free. In no way held by the mind. Just the breath breathing itself. Sensation arising, instant to instant, in the vast spaciousness of awareness.

If you notice the mind attempting to shape the breath, to control it in even the least way, just watch that tendency and let the breath float free. No holding. No control.

Completely let go of control of the breath. Let the body breathe by itself. Don't interfere with the subtle flow.

Just awareness. Vast as the sky. Spacious.

The sensations of the breath, arising and passing away within this openness. Nothing to hold to. Nothing to do. Just the breath as it is.

Each breath unique. Sensations changing, moment to moment.

From the body, other sensations arise and pass away within boundless awareness. The hands folded in the lap. Buttocks touching the pillow. Each moment of sensation floating free. Each moment of experience just as it is. No need to label. No need to interrupt anything.

Not naming experience, just contacting it directly. Just being. Experienced in the vastness of awareness.

Sensations of the breath. Sensations of the body. Floating free. Not holding to the breath. Not creating the body. Just moments of experience, appearing and disappearing, within the vastness.

Notice how thoughts arise. Commenting, remembering, thinking. Each thought a bubble passing through the vast spaciousness of mind. Existing for an instant. Dissolving back into the flow. No need for control. Just the vast open flow of change. Just process unfolding, moment to moment.

Thoughts think themselves. Nothing to condemn. Nothing to add. Let go of control in even the least way. Just let things be as they are, approaching and receding within the vastness of being.

Let go of the body. Let sensation float in vast space. Let go of the mind. Thoughts. Feeling. Arising and melting away. Nothing to hold to.

Nothing to do but be. Soft. Open into the vast edgelessness of awareness.

Thoughts that you "own," or are "responsible" for, the mind seen as just more thought bubbles, floating through. Thoughts of "me" and "mine," arising and passing away. Instant to instant. Let them come. Let them go.

No one to be. Nothing to do. Nowhere to go. Just now. Just this much.

Let go of the body. Let go of the mind. Experience being unfolding all by itself. Without the least need of help or control. No judging. No interfering. Just being. Just flow and change.

Be silent and know.

Once and for all, completely relinquish control. Let go of fear and doubt. Let each thing float in its own nature.

Dissolve into the vast spaciousness of awareness. No body. No mind. Just thought. Just feelings. Just sensations. Bubbles. Floating in vast space.

An instant of thought. Of hearing. Of remembering. Of fearing. Like waves, rising for an instant and dissolving back into the ocean of being. Into the vastness of your true nature.

No one to be. Nothing to do.

Let each instant unfold as it will.

No resistance anywhere. Let the wind blow right through you.

No one to be—just this much. This instant is enough.

Nowhere to go—just now. Just here.

Nothing to do—just be.

Holding nowhere, we are everywhere at once.

CHAPTER 22

Relationships as Healing

When Ondrea and I met in the late seventies at a workshop I was leading, she had already had two operations for cancer. She had come as a participant to broaden her understanding of death and to prepare. We have been together ever since. In the first operation, her cervix and uterus were removed. In the second, work was done on the bladder. Both times malignant tumors were excised.

Though we came together with the promise I would do all I could to be bedside with her when she died, our relationship expanded so rapidly that we very soon went beyond death. There was something too precious here not to offer all our energies into: a healing relationship.

It is no coincidence that during Ondrea's healing work on the lower abdominal area, where her cancer had originated, we were inspired to create the womb meditation. Indeed, when originally she sat with the womb meditation, she ovulated for the first time in nine years.

We sensed in each other's energy the possibility of wholeness. In each was a perfect mirror for the other's holdings and the potential of our letting go into love, into life.

Our marriage vows were:

I offer you my fear, ignorance, and old clinging to share in emptiness and love.

I offer you my mind's ever-changing tides—to grow together, uncovering the living truth in each moment we can open to.

I offer you my heart's love and commitment to help guide us to the other shore.

My life comes full circle with this vow, to work this lifetime together to go to God, to come to the love that goes beyond form.

During the first few years, healing was a primary investigation. Old ideas about being healed peeled back one after another. Healing was no longer simply something that was done to you as in going to a physician or healer. It was no longer "being healed" but instead followed a path of deepening awareness so as to experience "healed being." In a sense she, we were no longer healing for ourselves but rather for the union of beings. One might say that the selfishness went out of it and with each level of deepening awareness and healing the possibility of such union became more distinct in the increasingly experienced, undefined, interconnectedness of the gut. And the committed in-breathing of the other's suffering into the shared heart.

In those first years there was, of course, the play of minds introducing themselves to each other and themselves, but again and again the healing was allowed deeper as old ways were auditioned and dismissed. Even in the times when the mind was clouded, beyond such confusion was the ever-present, palpable interconnectedness and commitment that reminded us always to go beyond the mind of separation to the heart of healing. At times it was hard to tell if we were pilgrims on the path or clowns in a circus, but always the next step was the same, to let go into love, to deepen mercy and awareness, to put down the load as we were able, a moment at a time, lightening the burden, healing.

The power of a healing relationship can be seen as analogous to the practice of triangulation in the world of radio electronics. When there is difficulty in finding the unknown source of a radio transmission, one receiver is sufficient to calculate its distance, but it takes two to determine its precise location. It is necessary to focus on the source from two different angles in order to uncover its position. In a sense, Ondrea and I were using relationship as a means of triangulating on the mystery, on the unknown, on the process out of which all originates and the space into which all dissolves. Indeed, much of this book about healing is a process of our learning out loud as we braille our way toward the light. Much of this material is the work our minds and bodies called out for along the way. These are the techniques used to work with Ondrea's cancer and my congenital spinal disorder.

About two years after we met, a much-trusted friend, a highly respected oriental medicine person, told Ondrea there was a distinct possibility that she might die within the next six months. He is an expert acupuncturist, someone we certainly would have visited had we not lived a thousand miles away. However, he showed me with a pen on her body the different acupuncture points that he felt must be regularly stimulated for her body to reorient and heal itself. Although I had never done acupuncture before, he gave me a set of needles and said, "This isn't how I would have chosen to do it, but considering the seriousness of the situation, you really have nothing to lose. Just be sensitive and trust your inner touch."

For the next year, at least three times a week, I inserted needles into extremely sensitive areas of Ondrea's back, knees, and abdomen in hopes that this would bring energy to areas that needed healing. Sometimes the sessions went very smoothly and she felt instantly revivified. But at other times Ondrea winced with pain and cried because my inexperience and ineptitude with the needles caused a searing flash to pass through her body. It was one of the most extraordinary situations I had ever found myself in—I was causing pain to the person I wanted most in the world to be without pain. It was an incredible teaching in helplessness that deepened our "don't know" trust and commitment. I was causing suffering in the course of relieving suffering. We trusted what one teacher calls "the pain that ends pain"—willing to experience on the physical level what, in the often painful exploration of the mind, is a willingness to enter long-held suffering in order to bring the merciful light of a healing awareness. It wasn't the "no pain, no gain" principle, but a gentle application in the physical realm of the teachings we had found so often healing in the dissolution of pain in the worlds of the mind. Recognizing that we usually are entangled with the "pain that continues pain," we made a conscious decision to relate directly to the hindrances that maintain suffering. Uncovering layer upon layer of old holding, we experienced the painfulness of releasing the long-cramped fist back into its natural openness. Uncovering the pain in the mind/body to heal it into the heart of wisdom, to heal it into the heart of mercy and awareness. Quietly listening for what the next skillful step might be.

Sometimes we would both be crying as I turned a needle or placed another deeper. Sometimes the children would come into the bedroom and discover Ondrea lying on her stomach, a dozen needles protruding like porcupine quills from her back and, with a wince, quickly retreat. But even with their aversion to pain, at times they would just sit in the room and chat—something deep within them trusting the love which permeated.

The need for our absolute surrender and trust in the process to bring us through became a powerful part of the yoga of our healing. Constantly triangulating on the source—the deathless. It was an extraordinary time.

Now some years after that period of "heaven/hell," Ondrea's body is devoid of cancer and the toxins which so threatened its existence. Looking back at that time, we are unsure whether it was the accupuncture or the enormity of the love we shared that allowed the healing in. Or perhaps it was both, combined with an ever-deepening capacity to give to herself what she had so long offered to others since she was a teenager serving those in pain in local hospitals and nursing homes.

If you were to ask either of us, now ten years after her last cancer diagnosis, how Ondrea dispelled cancer from the body, we would each have to answer, "Don't know." But it seemed to be a combination of love and appropriate techniques for deeply focusing a merciful awareness on the area to be healed—not fighting against death but entering into the preciousness offered—which restored balance to the mind/body.

There is now a school of thought, widening daily, that is exploring the profound potential of the family and relationships to heal the body. As one might send love into their own illness and pain, think how much more powerfully magnified that process might become when others too are directing their attention and mercy into that area which wishes healing. Imagine how powerful it might be when several minds and hearts focus on an illness in a loved one's body. Each triangulating toward the source. There is in the family, large or small, as well as in one-on-one relationships, a considerable potential for healing. The two discovering the One as one.

Dyad Healing Meditation

[To be recorded or read slowly by a third party.]

Taking a comfortable position, sit across from your partner so that your eyes can meet softly.

Now let your eyes close for a moment.

See all the light in that darkness behind closed lids.

Let your eyes soften as they open to naturally meet the other person.

Let your eyes meet.

Those who are extenders of healing, allow your heart to be expressed in your eyes.

Whatever love is felt, whatever caring is there, let it come into the eyes.

Don't be "cow-eyed." Don't make your eyes seem loving; just let love begin to see through these eyes.

Knowing that you are looking into the eyes of one who at moments has suffered unbearably, who at times just couldn't stand it, let the heart make contact with this loved one's pain through soft eyes.

Looking directly into the eyes of someone who wants to be loved too, send this loving kindness into their mind.

Touch every rising mind state of fear or self-consciousness or doubt with your deep kindness and mercy. See each mind state as a passing show playing across their eyes.

Send forgiveness into each changing thought and feeling, one by one meeting them with love and a healing awareness.

A moment of their fear floating in your wish for their well-being.

And for the person who is opening to receive this healing, just let that love in. Let go of your unworthiness. Let go of your fear of being loved.

Soften and receive this healing. Let go of the barriers to love, to healing, and let it in.

Let this love be shared "just this much."

Two hearts sitting in a healing circle. One sending love, allowing love to be transmitted. The other receiving it, allowing it to enter deeply into any area of holding or pain in the mind/body.

One person directing healing into another. Letting the heart make contact through soft eyes, hearts are joined in a healing contract. Each healing in the process.

One directing love. Another drawing this love into the unhealed. Both healing.

Watch for any quality of eye strain. Not trying to keep the eyes unblinking—no imposters—just eyes meeting eyes in this shared healing.

Soften . . .

Not trying to appear loving, just allow love to appear.

Not being "someone" sending love or someone being healed, we go beyond the separations of our imagined self to enter the heart of healing.

Allow yourself to love. Allow yourself to be loved.

Notice how a single thought can create an opacity, a veil across the eyes.

Notice what separates, notice what allows connection to be reestablished.

Soften . . .

Allow love to be sent.

Allow love to be received gently.

Feel the whole body drinking at the eyes of love.

Feel the body fed by the love of another.

Let their eyes, their love touch that place inside that wants healing.

Feel the light in your partner's eyes filling the spaces in the mind/body that thirsts for wholeness.

Let their love dissolve your heart's armoring. Breathe their love into your open heart.

Let the love be like a poultice that draws the disquiet from the mind and body. Feel the tingling spread in the healing area.

Let their light in. Fill the area to be healed with their loving kindness and forgiveness. A humming, a vibrating at the center.

Feel their eyes drawing the holding out of the mind/body.

For those extending healing there is no reaching out to take away another's pain, but just a sending of love that dissolves doubt and tension and offers completion.

Let love do the healing. Let your awareness enter into the areas of discomfort in another with the loving touch by which you might relate to your only child.

Feel that love drawing out the discomfort, let it go.

Feel the scintillation that replaces the forgotten numbness or long-held pain.

Now let your eyes close.

Just feel the energy focused in the body. For those with illness, look into that area, see it clearing, lightening, opening.

For those sending this energy, look into this loved one's body with clarity and loving kindness, opening, softening areas of discomfort or pain.

Allow yourself to feel the fullness, the emptiness, the fear, the lack of fear, all of it.

The connectedness. The fear of connectedness. All of it. Feel all of it.

And now reverse roles continuing to share the healing so that those who were before receiving love in an area of injury are now sending, allowing the expression of that love in their eyes, with their heart.

And for those who were before an extender now become the receptor, the allowing openness which receives healing.

Receiving love into the mind and body. All separation dissolved in the heart.

Without force. Not a staring but a looking, a seeing.

Allow yourself to be loved. Letting go of the unworthiness. Letting go of all the confusion, allowing the depth of that love into the mind of separation as it sinks into the heart of healing.

Even though at times each has been confused, angry, or frightened, still there is so much love. So much love there for you to just receive, to just love, to just be.

Across the chasm of separate identities, love is the bridge.

Breathe that love through your eyes into the body of healing.

Breathe it in to the center of discomfort.

Soften . . .

A moment of caring so powerful, entering through the door of the eyes into another's heart bringing a merciful awareness and loving kindness that illuminates even the darkest corners of the mind/body.

Gently and with kindness deepening the mercy you both share.

Healing the world, within.

Notice how this love is directed and received.

See what blocks it. One moment it's there, another moment we are thinking.

Knowing that you are looking into the eyes of God, of the Goddess, of all the holy men and holy women who have ever lived, receiving you in their heart, soft eyes reflecting back to you your pain. It is the pain we all share.

As our eyes meet, we see there is not one who is healer and another who is to be healed but just a healing of the pain we all share in the heart we all have access to.

Soften . . .

Breathe the heart's AHHHH into your pain. Breathe AHHHH into the healing.

And here we all are, "all same," healing that which separates us into the universal heart we all share.

See how love can fill the body, the world, with healing.

Let your eyes close. Let them rest now.

Soften . . .

Feel this body and mind of giving and receiving. Feel this one body we all share healing.

Now open your eyes and look into the eyes of the other person without either the effort of sending or receiving. Just let love be.

Not being loving, just being which is love itself.

Just being. Just the being we all share.

Now reach out and take the hand of the person sitting across from you and close your eyes. Just feel them there.

Just let that shared healing deepen beyond who we seem to be visually. Beyond the mask, the pain, the separateness.

Just feel being shared as it presents itself moment to moment.

Just allowing. Just two as one.

All as one.

Notice what allows this healing to be shared. Notice too what limits or conditions it. Nothing to create, just feeling now what is. Just being.

Soften . . .

Draw through your hands their healing. Feel it as a tingling, a presence that moves up into your arms and into your heart.

Let it radiate out from your heart to fill the whole body/world.

Feel it gather into the area of holding or illness and let it be healed.

Let the healing in. Feel it fill the area like clear water a mountain pool.

Feel the coolness of the cleansing.

Feel the warmth of active healing—the vibrating waves of kindness and mercy that wash away the holding and discomfort.

Let their heart sink into your body and mind. Feel their AHHHH at the center of your discomfort.

Feel your heart cleansed and cleared by this sending.

Moment to moment deeper levels of love exposed and sent on to another.

Soften . . .

As it feels appropriate, allow your eyes to open.

Just feel this shared body of healing that sits there.

Looking again into the eyes of your partner in healing, take a few moments to share what some of the levels of experience might have been. Share in truth, not what you would have liked it to be, but how it really was. What opened you to giving and receiving love? What limited it?

Just seeing together the truth in a conspiracy toward healing.

CHAPTER 23

Living in the Laboratory

Although we have been speaking about working with the great imbalances and hindrances in the mind and body, it is in the application of these techniques to the little pains and blockages that confidence is cultivated. Many may have come to this book seeking a means of healing great illness in the body such as cancer or heart disease as well as the great hindrances in the mind of fear or self-doubt. But it is when we meet the lesser pains, our ordinary grief, our common disappointments, that we recognize the power of mercy and awareness, of softness and acceptance. Slowly accumulating a deeper intention to move beyond the apparent, we enter difficulty directly, as an invitation to awareness, to participate in our life more fully.

Some of these techniques are thousands of years old. Others have developed within the last few years' investigation. As our understanding about healing deepened, Ondrea and I began using our bodies as a kind of laboratory to test these insights. Living in a large adobe house heated by wood stoves, our arms might occasionally come in contact with the hot metal when adjusting the coals or adding fuel. Sending love into that area after the initial reaction to pull away, the initial tightening was noticed and softened around and opened into with love and care and a willingness to receive at the center of the heart the area which was burned. We noticed that burns healed very rapidly when forgiveness and loving kindness were sent into the multiple tingling arising there. Often in an hour or two only a red mark remained, rarely a blister. And usually within a few days the affected area was completely without injury. To test this process of embracing that which had always been pushed away, we noticed that if we burned ourselves and allowed the mind's insistent reaction of withdrawal and fear to remain without the application of these techniques, that the burn might last for a week or more after blistering and generating considerable sensation in that area. Living in the laboratory, it became something of a game to send love to one area of injury but not to another. To see for ourselves just what this process entailed. As Kabir said, "It is only true if we have experienced it for ourselves."

We saw the effectiveness of this process in working with a kidney stone, the second in ten years, which began to develop and then disintegrated to a fine powder easily discharged when we both focused on the area of growing discomfort. We discovered the healing power of a merciful awareness once again when this energy was sent into an abscessed tooth, a strep throat, a pinched nerve. At first we felt their dissolution was just a bit too good to be true, that perhaps, somehow, we were doing magic. But as we continued to apply these techniques, we discovered the magic of a deeply focused awareness and the wonderment of mercy and forgiveness to enter that which had been closed off by a conditioning to withdraw, and allowed this deeper, gentler access. We realized a deeper power to heal the mind/body of self-inflicted injury as well as the "happenstances" of life that occasionally arise in the form of physical and mental pain. It reminded us again and again of the saying of Zen Master Suzuki Roshi, "Nothing happens outside yourself." All is within the realm of awareness and the possibility of a deeper mercy.

But burns on the arm or an abrasion or a toothache are the lesser of the pains one might experience in the course of living in a body. We have mentioned in the "Relationships as Healing" chapter how Ondrea shed cancer by combining these insights with appropriate techniques. But this was not the only opportunity we had to experiment with these methods in the living laboratory. When I was nineteen, it was discovered that I had a "congenitally weak spine." Disks in the fourth and fifth lumbar region had ruptured when I was in college, causing me to return home for surgery. For years after the operation, aspirin and limited function were used to deal with the occasional discomfort in my lower back. Some years later, in my forties, the disks in my neck began to disintegrate, releasing considerable pain and yet more limited function. At first my reaction was the old mind's conditioning of taking medication and hoping it would go no further. But this didn't seem to work. The pain intensified, sending waves of discomfort down my right arm. My arm started to become numb, intermittently tingling, pain in the neck and head radiating into my right eye. Having by this time begun the investigation of this healing work, I had to ask myself, "Should I be writing a book about healing when I am not myself healed?" This was at an early stage when I still imagined healing as the body. But as I continued to send forgiveness into the pain instead of fear, as I began to respond with compassion instead of reacting with anger, a new confidence in the ability to heal arose. Instead of doubt and a sense of personal weakness, I noticed a deeper trust in the process as the pain began to diminish. I noticed the ability to turn my neck increasing. X-rays of the area met with a doctor's frown, and his suggestion that surgery would be necessary once again was left behind in a new "don't know" at the possibility of going beyond what others insisted was unhealable. Now, some years later, what was becoming incapacitating is at times only discomforting. The progression of the spinal disintegration seems to have diminished, and I am without symptoms or loss of flexibility for very long periods. Now when pain occasionally arises, it reminds me to refocus my attention on the area and spend some time meditating on softening and opening into the healing that always awaits.

Now any increasing sensation in that area teaches me compassion and harmlessness, a sense of universal participation in incarnation. It allows me to hum in the laboratory as the mind heals in the doing. Clearly the writing of this book is a case of teaching what we need to learn.

One reads of the "wounded healer," the person who learns from pain the end of pain and a connectedness with all others in similar discomfort. Spinal discomfort has taught me something of the reintegration of the heart which seems constantly to be reflected in the body, a softening around pain, an investigation of the incessant resistance and despair manifest in the desire to escape. In the first year of the spinal pain, bargaining with my discomfort, seeking healing techniques that might relieve me, like throwing meat to a rabid dog in order to keep him at bay a moment longer, hardly investigating that which intensified the disagreeableness of the experience, I went to one of my teachers to ask how I might get rid of the pain. But instead of buying into my escape mechanisms, he said, "Don't look for relief, look for the truth!" This sentence has done more to propel our investigation than any other that comes to mind at this moment.

We are all wounded healers on the way to completion, entering our wholeness just beneath the surface of our superficial holdings. The investigation of discomfort leading us to a sense of satisfaction and wholeness we never imagined possible. Living in the lab, life becomes an experiment in truth.

CHAPTER 24

Wholehearted Holism

Of the hundreds we have seen become whole in the course of healing the body, as well as healing into death, most trusted something of their own unique genius for sensing a way through their particular predicament. Among the most successful healings—mentally, physically, and spiritually—we have witnessed, there seems to be a certain self-reliance that went beyond dependence on the methods and techniques prescribed. Each seemed to share a common attitude that discomforts were not a curse or punishment but rather a teaching, almost an initiation.

As perception cleared, they let go of analyzing their illness, asking the whys and wherefores that keep us superficial in the mind and entered directly into the thing itself. They saw beyond the current platitudes about the cause of illness, sensing that such oversimplifications often missed the point. They did not take their healing secondhand but participated in it directly for themselves, recognizing the creativity necessary to apply their chosen treatments to their particular necessities.

Though deeply indoctrinated, like us all, by the origination myths of illness—ranging from illness being a punishment from God through the nervous karmic explanations of action and reaction, or the often misused "holisms" that express genesis in terms of old psychological holding—they did not mistake the finger pointing to the moon for the moon itself. They saw that the uncovering of old holding was not a cause for judgment but an opportunity to heal.

They no longer *analyzed* illness. Noticing old holding, they did not anguish about it as cause but just continued to let go of whatever might be uncovered. They penetrated what one patient called "the

calcified outer ring of thought" that formed around illness to discover for themselves the teaching within. They stopped thinking
their lives and entered directly into healing. Seeing how deeply
healing might enter into the mind and body when one no longer
tarried with "Why am I angry?" and instead entered into "What is
anger?", they discovered the root of the problem. They no longer
asked, "Why am I ill?" but "What is illness?" Not "Why am I in
pain?" but "What is pain?" They went beyond such current "holistic" platitudes as "You are responsible for your illness," refining
that statement to a deeper truth that we are not so much responsible
for our illness as we are responsible *to* our illness.

They understood that to be responsible for your illness impuned
blame and stimulated the judging mind. But to be responsible *to* our
pain, *to* our injuries means we are able to directly relate to them,
able to respond rather than forced to react. To think we are responsible for illness can keep us shallowly in old mind, blocking healing
by cultivating shame and grief. To be responsible to illness is to let
the healing in, to respond from the heart instead of reacting from
the mind.

I have seen many people thinking themselves responsible for
their illness die in considerable pain, feeling they were a failure for
not being able to heal. Feeling such disgust for themselves and all
else that they could hardly say goodbye or touch with love anything
around them. They had actually cultivated the stress that blocks
healing and intensifies discomfort while encouraging the hindrances to the heart to act as a navigator through the realms that
awaited. On the other hand, we have seen several people sensing
themselves responsible to their illness die with their heart wide
open markedly able to meet the moment as it was. Sensing the
power of the practice of harmlessness, they embraced themselves
gently and took another merciful step forward. They did not meet
their discomforts with judgment but with a noninjurious awareness
that received in appreciation all that life produced.

Judgment breeds a tightness that stresses healing. Mercy and
awareness breed a wisdom capable of finding its own way through.

Told by some that their cancer was anger stored in their liver or "a
lesson from a previous life," or that it was the outcome of unresolved holdings turned to stone (as tumors, for instance), they did

not stop there. Approaching illness with great "don't know," they took its teaching and moved closer to the mark. They saw that half-truths were particularly dangerous when swallowed whole. They did not try to keep illness reasonable and neat so as to control it or superficially "understand" it. They recognized that to even imagine we know the origin of disease, considering all the lessons we took birth for, may well be a sign of what one patient called "the arrogance of our knowing." Recognizing the many examples of those who had lived exemplary lives without holding and stress, who nonetheless experienced illness in their body, they allowed their "don't know" to deepen.

A doctor friend, whose card read "Holistic Practitioner" until he got cancer, called many of his colleagues who offered such partial truths "half-holes." He felt all such concepts about the causation of illness had to be removed so direct contact with the cancer could be made. He said he cured his cancer "by going beyond the half-truths of others into the heart of the matter." He trusted his own genius for healing.

If I may paraphrase some of what this fellow said some years later, "I used to call myself a holistic practitioner, but I was not particularly whole myself. I separated so much, my life was in so many little compartments. I was a doctor in the office, but I seemed to need so much doctoring when I got home. I was sort of trying to force myself to be whole with diets and workshops and stuff like that. But I was doing it all in my head. I kept thinking about myself doing all this stuff instead of just doing it. Then, when I got cancer, this idea that I created my illness, that I had stressed myself into it, which I had previously taught so many clients, made me feel so helpless it almost killed me. I really felt responsible and thought very badly about myself for not being able to cure me. I was doing everything I knew to get rid of it, but nothing worked. I was in both private and group therapy. I did assertiveness and anger-release workshops. I was on a special diet. And all of these treatments seemed to help a little—I mean, I wasn't quite as underground as I had been, but I was still dying. Then I saw the war. All these concepts were making me hate myself and my cancer more. I felt like such a hypocrite and a failure. But I saw all these ideas about being responsible for my sickness were just making me sick with anger and self-hatred. I felt so helpless; I was my own worst enemy and couldn't trust myself to heal. I felt I was wrong-minded and wrong-hearted because I had caused it but couldn't cure it. My life was filled with tension and "doing it right"; I was only half-alive. But then I saw the awfulness of how I was treating me, and I began sending love and forgiveness into my tumors, and after a few months they just seemed to dissolve. It was the first time I was wholeheartedly in my healing. I was simply learning to pay attention, to love and forgive. I stopped thinking me and started being me. This cancer taught me what ten years of practice had never touched. It is hard to believe I was so superficial, so righteous, as to tell patients they had a choice to live or die and it was solely up to them. I see that to choose to die would pretty much block my ability to heal, but I also see quite clearly that though choosing to live might have an effect on the outcome, it certainly wouldn't wholly determine it. I asked the forgiveness of those I had misled by not testing so many theories within myself. But that cancer turned things all around. It made my holism so much more whole. It has been seven years now since they told me I was going to die, but I am more alive now than I ever was. In fact, I think if it weren't for my cancer I wouldn't be alive today."

Even such currently popular ideas as "We choose to live or choose to die" can be taken a good deal deeper so as not to reinforce the "half holism" that the mind so quickly settles for, compromising the truth to a bumper-sticker-like slogan.

This originally well-intended truism has disconcerted many, leading to a certain condemnation that those who have died may purposefully have abandoned us, having "chosen to die," a sense that they have failed their life spark. And along with this comes the righteousness that those who have gotten physically well have simply "chosen to live," but it is a good deal more complex than that. I have seen too many die who have wholeheartedly attempted to live to concur with such statements that their death was a pushing away of life. I have seen their heart heal into life along the way and their death pass healing along to all who came near. I have seen such statements injure those who have arduously attempted to cure themselves of cancer, of AIDS, of heart disease, of genetic abnormalities whose bodies did not reflect physical healing, die angry at life and at themselves for not having the "right stuff."

I have seen such comments as "you are responsible for your illness" or "you choose to live or you choose to die" block healing and cause the passageway to the heart to wither in fright or self-judgment. I have seen too many ninety-year-old widows strapped into wheelchairs in convalescent hospitals, whose husbands had died ten years before, praying each day for death, as they gradually lost confidence in a merciful God because death was not forthcoming, to believe that choosing death is all it takes to die.

Just as each moment is a crossroad in which we choose new mind or drowsily drop back into the old, so it is evident that the choice to live or die *affects* the course of illness but does not *determine* its outcome. A choice to live is the cultivation of the qualities of willingness and investigation. "Should I live or should I die?" is old mind's question, forgetful of its essential wholeness in or out of a body.

The mind grasps too quickly at answers. It is like trying to understand the essential nature of fruit by playing the child's game of bobbing for apples. Wide-mouthed, face drenched, grasping at whatever floats to the surface, we collect a pile of tooth-marked, hardly tasted fruits, which molder in a mound behind us. Mouth agape, fishing for more. So different from sitting down with an apple in hand, experiencing the feel, the smell, the sight of the apple for ourselves, the sweet crunch of the fruit in the teeth of inquiry—tasting for oneself—the direct experience of apple. Recognizing that a ton of apples randomly collected will not give us the same insight as a single apple wholly eaten. All apples within each apple. It is the difference between investigation, the what of things, and analyzing, the why of things (which leads so quickly to old mind's sense of "poor me!")

So we see that choice affects *how* we are ill, not always *that* we are ill. We can choose this very moment to be fully alive. We do not have to wait as many seem to for a terminal diagnosis before we give ourselves permission to be alive. We can choose right now, in "just this much," to investigate the old mind and discard the half-truths that litter the paths toward wholeness. We can choose right now investigating mercifully the lesser pains to discover for ourselves how stress affects discomfort, how resistance magnifies pain. We can choose right now to explore the pain and to receive the teaching it imparts. We can choose right now to be alive right now, investigating fear so that terror may dissolve that much more quickly. We can choose now to be alive without denigrating the possibility of healing into death.

Recently in a workshop, a woman with terminal cancer was berating herself because of her belief that she created her own reality. "If I create my own reality, I created this cancer. But I can't create the cure. I'm not the person I thought I was. No wonder I am sick." Her superficial understanding, her self-judgment, seemed to limit her healing. When I asked her, "Are you the *sole* creator of your reality?", her mouth hung agape with confusion and helplessness, and then gradually a smile came across her face, and she said, "No, I guess not after all. But I sure am a major contributor." In an odd way misunderstood theories that she had created her reality robbed her of faith and trust in herself instead of instilling the confidence that may have originally been intended. Opening in "don't know" trust to deeper and deeper levels of herself, she went beyond her old knowing to a profound investigation of "What does 'I' mean?"; "What does 'create' mean?"; "What is reality?" Sometime later, she said to me, "You know, maybe this idea that I am the creator of my reality is not so much a falsehood as it is a riddle to discover what that 'I' refers to. The deeper I go, the more this 'I' becomes the whole universe which creates itself out of itself. Maybe I was just taking that statement from too personal a location." Now, instead of trying to fend off illness with the idea "I created my own reality," she works with the investigation of "Who creates?" and "Who dies?" Whatever the future may hold she is more prepared.

A few years ago we were told by a physician a story about one of his patients who had "tried her damnedest to get rid of her cancer but couldn't." Though she had applied the latest techniques as best she could, the cancer spread to a point where it seemed that she was about to die. Deciding to take "a last vacation," she went to the West Coast to spend some time on the beaches of Southern California. During the course of her visit, she met a well-known healer who in two sessions of laying hands on her body apparently completely removed the pain and cancer. Two weeks later, she killed herself.

After the healing she told a friend that if it was that easy to heal she really must be a failure as a person. "I really do deserve to die." All the ideas she had absorbed about being responsible *for* her illness and having not previously "chosen to live" left her feeling great despair and distrust in her own personal strength.

Because of her belief system, being healed in this manner disempowered her. Someone forgot to tell her that all the work she had done up until that time had worked to open her to allow the healing in. The healer, thinking he was responsible *for* her healing instead of *to* her healing, perhaps kept too much credit for himself instead of sharing with her that she was already so prepared that all it took was a little extra energy in the system to shift the tides.

The greatest healers I know generally say that they do nothing, "that God does it all." They re-empower the individual who is healing. They do not encourage them to be a "victim of healing," any more than they would encourage them to be a victim of illness. They encourage them to recognize that healing is their birthright, that it occurs when we get out of our own way and let the separation between the mind and heart dissolve.

Ramakrishna, the great Indian saint, said there were two things that made God laugh: when a healer says, "I healed them," and when bickering lovers say, "We have nothing in common!"

As our doctor friend said, "Don't be a half-hole." There is nothing we know that we can't know at a deeper level. The healing never stops.

Our half-hearted holism is a bit like the story of the fellow who finds himself sitting in his easy chair one afternoon and notices that the river has overflowed its banks and is beginning to fill his home. Standing on the chair, he watches the waters rise. Along comes two neighbors in a canoe, inviting him to safety. "No, I won't take your canoe. God will save me!" he says with a sweep of his hand. Continuing to watch the waters rise, he climbs to the second story of his home. His furniture is floating all about him when along comes a rubber dinghy manned by the local sheriff's department.

"Climb aboard!" they implore him.

But with a shake of his head he turns away, saying, "No, I don't need your help. God will save me!"

An hour later, sitting on the very peak of the roof, the water midchest, a helicopter hovers above and drops down a ladder insisting that he climb aboard.

"No, I don't need your help," he replies. "God will save me!"

The waters continue to rise, and he drowns . . . Finding himself in the heaven realms, he approaches God rather brusquely and inquires, "Where were you when I needed you?!"

And God gently bends her head toward him and says, "Well, first I came as a canoe, and then I came as a rubber dinghy, and then I came as a helicopter."

To see God in everything, to recognize that everything is process, lets us go beyond ideas of "God" or "process" and to enter the suchness which these terms feebly represent. It allows our healing to cut through "the calcified outer ring of thought" and be experienced as a sense of pure being.

CHAPTER 25

Entering the Fire

There is a saying, "This is not a world of my making or even of my choosing, but this is the world into which I am born to find God."

Few perhaps would have chosen this realm of impermanence and holding as a rest stop, but many have discovered its value as a classroom. Birth is our painful initiation into the awkward realm of duality. Sliding sideways into whatever opening is available in the family matrix, we attempt to fit our whole ghost into an ever-shifting world of people and things, of liking and disliking, of gain and loss. Born into a realm where most have traded happiness for momentary enjoyment, we often wander haplessly between pleasure and pain, at times unable to distinguish between the two.

But here we all are in the midst of the passing show, exploring our pleasure and our pain, searching for the light within the fire. Learning to keep our heart open in hell, we go beyond heaven and duality.

The remarkable Sufi poet Rumi speaks of God's presence, our original nature, as "always being there in front of us":

"A fire on the left, a lovely stream on the right.
One group walks toward the fire into the fire, another
toward the sweet flowing water.
No one knows which are blessed and which are not.
Whoever walks into the fire appears suddenly
in the stream.
A head goes under on the water's surface,
That head pokes out of the fire.
Most people guard against going into the fire,
And so end up in it.
Those who love the water of pleasure and make

it their devotion
Are cheated with this reversal.

He suggests from the very heart of a life turned toward the spirit
that moving toward the fire we enter the pain that ends pain, cultivating the profound joy of an unobstructed awareness. But, that in
what appears to be the waters of pleasure, we enter the pain that
perpetuates pain and cultivates the thirsts of our ordinary grief,
protecting old mind's denial and grasping, leaving us waterlogged,
wrinkled, and swollen, unloved and unlovely, bereft of life and
living.

He affirms that the truth is always available but seldom regarded.

> The trickery goes further
> The voice in the fire tells the truth,
> saying I am not fire
> I am fountainhead. Come into me and don't
>   mind the sparks.

He urges us to explore the painful hindrances to the heart which
arise in the mind. He reminds us to open to the discomfort that may
be experienced when approaching that which has always discom-
fited us. Peeling back finger by finger the long-cramped fist of our
holding to reveal the open palm, the very spaciousness of our true
nature.

> If you are a friend of God, fire is your water.
> You should wish to have a hundred thousand sets
>   of moth wings
> So you could burn them away, one set a night.
> The moth sees light and goes into the fire. You
>   should see fire
> And go toward light. Fire is what of God is world-
>   consuming.
> Water, world-protecting.
> Somehow each gives the appearance of the other.
> To these eyes you have now
> What looks like water burns. What looks like
> fire is a great relief to be inside.

Entering into the grief that demands pleasure as distraction, the spacious heart opens like Milarepa to warm itself by the fire. Fire gets the heart's attention and calls for healing. Water often lulls us into the recurring dream of separation that like a duelist demands satisfaction. Fire consumes what is. Water thirsts for more.

A friend dying from Hodgkins disease commented, "I know there is no way out but through, but it is hell in here." A few weeks later, after exploration of his grief at not healing in the way he wished, and a deeper saying of goodbye to the past, he turned to me one day and said, "You know, acceptance is magic." His face beaming, the fire having burned him clean. His death a single breath expelled. A single tear rolling from the corner of his eye as he let go of life, entering life completely, healing into death.

When we finally acknowledge the depth of the potential for suffering as well as joy, we start to become fully born. Becoming fully born, death is not excluded. As one teacher said, "A life that does not include death can be very confusing." Becoming born, we begin to take life as it is, wholeheartedly.

And at last we stop trying to be someone else. We stop trying to grieve correctly, or die someone else's death, we stop being "model prisoners." We live our life and die our death. Entering fully the fires of our discomfort, we discover, in a new confidence and strength, the cool waters of our healing. Taking things as they are in a gentle recognition that though the heart may not always be open and the mind not always clear, still, we have a merciful awareness which has room for even our closedness. Again and again we remind ourselves to soften the belly and make room for peace.

We have always been led to believe that healing, like grace, will make us feel better, but first entering the fires of our healing may not always be pleasant. One may experience a profound desire to pull away from the fire and try to force the pain out of the mind/body, trying to discover some oasis of pleasure in which to submerge oneself. This struggling away from the fires of the moment, driven by an urgency not to see, leaves us not with a sense of floating but of one which resembles drowning.

It takes a slow approach to the fire to recognize that the tow-haired boy going by on the bicycle is not your son killed three months before by a hit-and-run driver. That the woman with the gray hair and the flowered shawl in the checkout line just ahead is not your mother who died a year ago. The mind sees itself everywhere. The mind looks everywhere for water and is burned. The heart enters the fire and is cooled. The denial of our pain, our unwillingness to enter wholly into the moment, leaves us like someone trying to pick fruit in the midst of a burning orchard.

Although all this looks good on paper—entering into the pain, letting the mind sink into the heart, taking healing in the midst of suffering—it is not always easy.

Recognizing that only we can sense the timing appropriate to our own process, not dashing into the fire, we take one mindful step at a time closer. To take a step, sit a moment, then take another step. To gradually accustom oneself to the heat, to enter gently through the molten armoring of the heart. Unburned by grief or separateness, meeting the pains of the world in the absolute love of universal healing.

CHAPTER 26

Healing into Death

To let go of the last moment and enter wholeheartedly the next is to die into life, is to heal into death. To enter completely each moment, not distorting the past or hiding from the future is to be fully alive, not excluding our death from our healing. To heal into death, into life, is to open our heart in each transition—to make room for the new without holding to the past—to find the divine in "just this much," to receive grace, our real nature.

Our dying has a quality of healing when all about us are touched by the recognition of the preciousness of each moment. Our dying is a healing when all that has been unsaid is touched with forgiveness and love, when all imagined unpaid obligations of the past are resolved in mercy and loving kindness. To heal into death is to awake within the dream. To bless the life just past and the shared moment so precious. To heal into death is to let go of all that blocks the heart—to let the hindrances float. To enter life completely, excluding nothing, open to evolution and change. To heal into death is to let go of attachment to content and enter wholeheartedly the process. To see death as an event during the process, a doorway into the continuum of endless being.

Healing into death, the separate self dissolves into universal being, seeing that any separation from life is a separation from healing. That denying death or trying to hammer it into some reflected image of our imagined self, denies healing. To heal into death is to use that aspect of our living, which we call our dying, as an opportunity to dissolve into the heart of healing. It is the experience of our "someoneness" as it melts into the unity of all things, the tension of the separate dissolving, participating in the essential spaciousness of the unfolding.

As the processes which produce the thought "me" are seen clearly floating in the spaciousness of our letting go, we break the mistaken identity that it is "me" who creates these processes instead of the other way around. We take the experience of these processes as they intertwine and alternately predominate as something personal. The ever-changing underdream we call "I." But observing how these qualities form our experience and create some sense of an imagined separate self, we come to realize that even this separate "I," which we feel we will lose upon dying, is but a reflection of the awareness by which these processes are seen.

HEALING INTO DEATH MEDITATION

[To be read slowly to a friend or silently to onself.]

Find a comfortable position and allow the attention to come to the breath.

Let the mind and body begin to still.

Let the body soften. Let the breath come all by itself.

If the in-breath is longer than the out-breath, let it be so.

If the out-breath exceeds the in-breath, so be it.

Nothing to change, nowhere to go, just this much.

Moment to moment softening the body, opening around the sense of the solid.

Feeling the pull of gravity on this earthen body. Feel its denseness, its solidity beginning to soften and melt at the edges.

Let your arms and legs lie loose by your sides. You have relied on these hands, these arms, your whole life to pull the world closer or to push it away. Now let go of the strength in your arms and allow it to converge in your heart. Let the tension in the hands and arms melt into the spaciousness in which each sensation floats.

Sensations from the legs, from the torso, from the shoulders, from the head received in soft belly, in spacious heart.

Like an ice cube melting, let this body soften from its hard solidity into the soft open flowing of its essential fluidity. The body no longer frozen in form, but melting into the sweet waters of a sense of greater spaciousness and fluidity.

Pain disappears, the body of awareness, the light body within, beginning to float free of its dense earthen vessel.

As the sense of solid body dissolves into the quality of liquidity, the senses turn within. Receiving life moment to moment as it gradually leaves the body behind, floating free.

The edges melting, the solidity softening like a crystalline ball of ice melting away to water, evaporating into air, distributed equally throughout the spaciousness.

Letting the heart melt each holding as it arises—letting go of name, letting go of reputation, letting go of family, letting go of form—mercy pervading each moment of existence.

Each thought received, melting in the boundaryless patience and kindness of our essential nature.

Each sensation dissolving one into the next, the process unfolding in awareness. Awareness slowly floating free of the body.

Each moment of mind, of body, absorbed in the vast spaciousness of the light body of undying awareness.

Melting, softly melting into space.

Gently letting go of all that pulls toward the body.

Thanking the body, blessing it and with gratitude saying goodbye to it as this sense of fluidity predominates.

Floating, gently floating, the light body free as the fluidity dissolves into space. Evaporating into a sense of edgeless being and perfect safety.

Consciousness as light as air, floating in gratitude and appreciation of the classroom/body just left behind.

Letting go. Space merging with space.

Light merging with light.

Each perception, each thought, each sensation, each feeling floating gently, dissolving, dissolving into vast boundaryless space.

Visions of the life just past dissolving one after the other, the images so fresh as to almost seem "real." (Unable for a moment to decipher on which side of the dream we have awakened.)

Each image dissolving into the breath as the breath dissolves into thin air.

Letting the last breath come.

Letting the last breath go.

Dissolving, dissolving into vast space, the light body released from its heavier form. A sense of connectedness with all that is, all sense of separation dissolved in the vastness of being.

Each breath melting into space as though it were the last.

Each inhalation drawing in awareness and mercy. Each out-breath sending forgiveness and blessing into the world.

Each breath dissolving into space.

Each breath the last. The connection dissolved between the heavy body and the body of light, the body of awareness within. Each breath disappears. Each thought dissolving in space.

Gently floating free.

Going beyond now. Floating free. Altogether beyond, altogether free.

Moving gently into the light of awareness, free from this dense body. Free from this incarnation now.

Let go into the Light. Into the pure open luminosity of your original nature.

Just space. Space floating in space.

Letting go completely, entering gently the Light.

Just Light floating in vast space, floating free in edgeless awareness.

Just awareness dissolving into Light. Light experiencing itself within itself.

Space within space. The sense of separation dissolving into pure "am-ness."

Just being floating free in the vastness.

Open endless space. Vast edgeless space.

Today, the day you died, more than two hundred and fifty thousand others died as well. Sensing the wonder that awaits them, wish them well.

May all beings be free of suffering. May all beings take a healing from their death.

May all beings trust their process enough to trust death, to dissolve mercifully into the unknown.

May all beings trust the heart of healing to take them through death alive and well. Entering wholeheartedly "just this much," we expand into the miracle of unending awareness. Of infinite mercy.

CHAPTER 27

Stopping the War

"No one deserves to be in pain. No one deserves to suffer."

How does the mind relate to that statement? Who deserves to suffer? Does Hitler deserve to be in pain? the rapist? the abuser? the unforgiving? Who deserves to suffer? It is an important question because it defines those parts of ourselves that we condemn to hell, to the unexplored darkness of the long-suppressed painfulness of mind. How much of our life remains unlived, how much are we still in conflict with? Can the heart still stay open when the cruel, the insensitive, the self-serving, the merciless, the unforgiving arises in the mind? Or do we meet these emotions, these feelings, these drives, this denseness with yet less forgiveness, less awareness and mercy. Are we at war with ourselves when the unkind aspect of mind presents itself? Do we just add more unkindness to an often insensitive world? Or do we remember that we can stop the war by meeting the mind in the heart, by tapping into "our natural goodness"? How do we end the struggle within ourselves that makes us fear the mind instead of seeing it as an exquisite tool capable of meeting these heavy feelings with a greater light? At what moment do mercy and awareness manifest to meet the ancient wars within? At what point does "just this much" become the heart of the matter? At what point do we see our pains not as punishments but as a remarkable opportunity to make peace?

Once again the ancient question arises: How do I make peace where there has always been war? How do I find love in the midst of the struggle?

How do we come to the clear-headed acceptance and lighthearted recognition that allows the poet Wendell Berry to write in his poem "Confession":

> I wish I was easy in my mind, but I ain't
> If it wasn't for anger, lust and pride, I'd be a saint.

These are questions that do not require an answer. These are the questions life asks itself. This is the strategy of our awakening. The particular path each must tread to go beyond the particular and the individual, to end the separation that is war. To relinquish the role of hero in our own melodrama, to discover something heroic and of great merit beyond. It is the wisdom of the heart, the great peace-maker, the resolver of opposites that senses the next step to be taken, that crosses the abyss and approaches the mind with bless-ings instead of fear and cursing. The mind, like the disquieted body of illness, taken within the heart as is, to heal and manifest its own innate perfection.

Some years ago during the Korean War, Paul Reps, the long-time meditator and writer, was trying to gain entrance into Japan so that he might spend some time studying and practicing at a Zen monas-tery in Kyoto. But at this time Japan was being used as a military staging ground for the air battle and troop movement to the Korean War. Nonmilitary Westerners were not given visas. Filing the neces-sary documents with the Asian immigration officer, he was told it would not be possible for him to visit Japan as he was not "militarily allied." Sitting opposite the immigration officer, he turned his visa request over and on the back wrote, "Making a cup of green tea, I stop the war," and handed it back to the official across the desk. The immigration officer took a long look at the poem, reading it silently to himself, "Making a cup of green tea, I stop the war." Turning the paper over, he initialed approval for Reps' entry into Japan. Look-ing up, he said, "We need more people like you in our country right now."

But what does it mean to make a cup of green tea that stops the war? Reps wasn't being clever, he was being real. He was speaking of meeting the incessant struggle for control, our long-conditioned inner conflicts, with something other than old mind's old ways of violence and "victory," of mercilessness and inner strife. To make a cup of tea that doesn't continue the war, that doesn't deepen the conflict, the impatience, the waiting, the desires for things to be otherwise, one simply lets the water boil. Have we ever simply let the water boil? Have we ever simply been there standing in the body with nowhere else to go, open to just this much? Or are we thinking the water boiling? Expecting it to boil? Imagining it boiling? Impatient if it is not boiling? Have you ever boiled a cup of water without goals, without needing the water to be different? Without waiting? Waiting is war. Impatience is war. The moment is unsatisfactory, and there is no peace to be found. The war continues in the mind, the urgency that the moment is not enough, and "where is my tea?!!!" Making a cup of tea, I feed the war. More conflict. More of an idea of how things should be and less space for how things are.

Not leaning into the next moment, not struggling to create a satisfactory present, we sense how in "just this much" is all we'll ever need. Sitting at the table, noticing, "Would I like a cup of tea!" Noticing how the mind/body thinks a cup of tea would taste so good right now. Watching the motivation to create tea, not "I have to have a cup of tea right now." That is war, the frozen waters of demanded pleasure, that is more tension, more conflict, the same old stuff. Noticing standing up from the table, noticing walking to the cabinet, noticing expectation. Expectation is war. Expectation is suffering. Expectation is disappointment. But instead just being there. No conflict. Not rummaging through the various parcels of tea to discover that which would most stimulate the palate, but instead letting the tea choose you. Allowing the tea to come into your hand instead of grasping at it.

Making a cup of green tea, I stop the war. Watching, noticing, tasting the desire for tea as the hand extends to the teapot. Feeling the cold metal of the teapot handle in the warm flesh of the hand. Feeling the texture of the handle. Nothing else to do, nowhere else to be. Just this moment forever. Just this suchness. Feeling the floor beneath your feet as you walk to the sink. The arm extending, feeling the weight of the teapot as the hand reaches toward the faucet. Feeling the coldness of the faucet, receiving the cold. Nothing else need be otherwise. The sound of water as it splashes into the pot. Noticing how the sound changes as the pot fills. Watching the expectation of the full pot. Noticing the subtle fear that the water might overflow. Reaching up to turn off the cold water, feeling the condensation on the handle, hearing the creak of the washer as the handle closes off the water flow. The hand moving to the handle, feeling the musculature of the fingers as it curls around, the extended arm now carrying greater weight than a moment before as the full pot is moved to the stove. Hearing the pop of gas as it ignites beneath the teapot, perhaps feeling the heat as it curls around the pot and reaches the hand. Noticing the hand withdraw. Noticing, too, any subtle fear of being burned. Staying fully in the moment. Nothing extra. Nothing of the past dragged into the present to filter this moment. Just the moment as it is. Just standing. Just the sound of the air bubbles released from the cold water as it heats. Feeling the legs lifting and moving as they walk across the room toward the tea cannister. The eyes touching the cannister. Noticing recognition. Noticing desire. The cannister in hand. The glass bottle cold. Tea and I are here. Nothing else. Feeling the muscles as they lift the bottle of tea from the kitchen counter. Hearing the clink of the glass as it is removed from the tile. Just this much. Turning, turning the top on the cannister of tea. Feeling the muscles, the extensors and flexors in the arm, feeling the fingers, feeling the different textures between the glass and the metal lid. Opening. The aroma of green tea in the nostrils. Just sniffing the tea. Just appreciation. Spoon in dark tea, shiny, the present moment received as it is, no war, no being elsewhere. All of it right now. Putting tea in cup. Clink of spoon. Hand retracting.

Moving back to the kitchen chair, feeling the knees bend. Feeling the weight of gravity on the body. Feeling the cushions come up to support this heavy body. Hearing the water boiling. Nothing else to do but be. Then steam. The mind's intention to stand, to take the water to the tea. Just water boiling. Just standing. Just a handle felt now warm in the hand. Just the muscles pulled on by the weight of the full pot. Just the feet against the floor walking to the table. Just the pot put down safely where nothing will burn or be scorched. Noticing the intention, feeling the changes in the musculature of the arms as the pot is tilted toward the cup. Just the feeling of the pot getting lighter as the water mixes with the tea. Just steam rising, just tea. Nothing to be otherwise. Just the feel of the cold spoon in the hand. Just the sound of the spoon as it whisks the tea through the water. Just the fragrance of tea steeping. Each moment received as it is, sufficient. Not drinking tea that is not yet made, not more war, just this much. Just the extraordinary spaciousness of nothing having to be any other way than it is. Standing there, you can't wait patiently. You are either waiting or you are patient. Patience is peace. Waiting is war.

Not waiting for tea, not waiting for anything, not even waiting for this story to be over. Reading this story, do you stop the war or do you continue it? Is this moment not quite enough or is it all of it? How much of this moment are you experiencing? Just recognizing that tea is done. Not "cup of tea at last!" Just a cup of tea. Just another opportunity for healing. Just the hand reaching out to receive the handle of the cup. Just noticing hot. Noticing texture and fragrance. Just a cup of tea. Just this moment in newness. Just the hand touching the cup. Just the arm retracting. The fragrance increasing as the cup nears the lips. So present. Noticing the bottom lip receiving heat from the cup, the top lip arched to receive the fluid within. Noticing the first taste of tea before the tea even touches the lips. The fragrance and heat rising into the mouth. The first noticing of flavor. The touch of warm tea on willing tongue. The tongue moving the tea about in the mouth. The intention to swallow. The warmth that extends down into the stomach. What a wonderful cup of tea. The tea of peace, of satisfaction. Drinking a cup of tea, I stop the war.

This is an image we have shared with many groups at various times. Recently, after sharing this process of just a cup of tea, during a break as I walked down the center aisle of the auditorium, slowly from the other end of the aisle, a fellow moved gradually toward me supported by a walker. Obviously he had been ill for some time. His body thinned to a near skeletal form. Meeting at the center of the aisle, he looked up with sparkling eyes and said, "Dying of cancer, I stop the war." Standing there in the middle of the aisle, surrounded by a pool of silence as people streamed noisily by on either side, our eyes met in just this much. Layers and layers of personality and old history peeling back as incarnations of holding and someoneness dissolved into a shimmering presence of being meeting being in being itself. It was quite extraordinary. In his eyes was the answer to that first question, "Should I give up healing and just let myself die?" He had gone beyond life and death, beyond thinking himself a body or some separate entity inhabiting it, he was healing itself. He was who we are when we stop becoming who we think we are. To say he was enlightened would not be proper. The term "enlightenment" has caused as much suffering and confusion as any concept I can think of. But to say he was "lightened" would be completely appropriate. He wasn't backing away from cancer or anything else in his life. He was so fully in the present that the struggles of a lifetime had come to resolution, allowing a great spaciousness for life, for cancer, for pain, for death. He told me how pain had taught him that any escape just increased the war. He had a deep trust in the peace of essential being. He had discovered the miracle in a cup of tea. He had discovered the marvel of a day fully lived. He had discovered healing from his cancer.

He was no longer at war with himself or with anything else. He was just dying of cancer. When he was sad, he was just sad. When there was fear, there was just fear. When he was happy, he was just happy. Not forcing change but allowing the moment to change as it would, he was emanating a softness from his heart which soothed the conflicts of the minds all about him. No longer at battle with life, he passed the healing on to his loved ones standing quietly by, learning themselves how to die with grace, how to live in the present moment. Years of jockeying for position in the academic world, of struggling with cancer, of bed-ridden pain, of fighting *with* life in the guise of fighting *for* life, had burned through his long-conditioned desire to stay safe and hidden, and had caused him to come out of the closet of his life into a world of just being. "Dying of cancer, I stop the war."

How often does our healing stop the war? How often even do our spiritual practices stop the war? Or is it just another holy war, another battle in the name of healing the mind or body? How often do we take our healing as an opportunity to be fully alive?

Is the healing a healing or is it just another holding on? When we begin to ask these questions, healing touches every level and we start to hear the song of peace, the subtle whispers of our heart. It is one sensitive to such whispers who puts out his hand to pacify his friends and says, "It's okay. My heart is only singing." Having a heart attack, I stop the war.

A woman in a recent retreat almost explosively confessed that when her children were still quite young there were moments when she felt like throwing them out the window. And she had never forgiven herself for these feelings. She hated herself for the "heartless way my mind can be at times." As she was speaking, her whole body was shaking with the long-held fear and resentment she had for herself. Enraged at her anger, she continued the war. But when we asked the group how many of the parents there had felt these same feelings, dozens of hands were raised, and someone in the back of the room yelled, "Big Surprise!" and the group rolled with laughter. It was clear to everyone how often we send hatred into the mind for its vagaries and self-interest. There was a great sigh in the room as many took themselves into their heart, recognizing once again the self-cruelty we so continually manifest in relationship to the natural swings and twists of the ever-changing mind. It was in that moment of the recognition of our mercilessness that it became clearest how precious it was to bring compassion and mercy into our world. The more we see the mercilessness and fear in the mind, the less we add to the mercilessness in the body we all share, in the universe each of us inhabits. Seeing how unloving the mind can be, I stop the war.

Taking a step at a time, I stop the war. Appraising that step, judging it, analyzing it, I continue the war. When all is seen as "just this much," nothing hinders the open heart, nothing is detriment or distraction. And we come to see that though letting go of our suffering may be the hardest work we have ever done, it is also the most fruitful. All is seen as passing show with a lightness that simply recognizes the unfolding of the long-conditioned mind. There are few surprises on the path of healing when healing is seen as our birthright and the heart meets each moment in wholeness.

As a friend said, "We are all God, but none of us are saints." We have each taken birth to discover what took birth. We have each come here to finish the curriculum, to learn to keep our heart open in heaven/hell, to meet joy and delight as well as confusion and pain with awareness and mercy. We are each in the process of completing our birth, of becoming wholly present. It is as Kabir said:

We are all struggling, none of us has gone far.
Let your arrogance go, and look around inside.

The blue sky opens out farther and farther,
The daily sense of failure goes away,
The damage I have done to myself fades,
A million suns come forward with light,
When I sit firmly in this world.

I hear bells ringing that no one has shaken,
Inside "love" there is more joy than we know of,
Rain pours down although the sky is clear of clouds,
There are whole rivers of light.
The universe is shot through in all its parts
by a single sort of love.
How hard it is to feel that joy in all our bodies!

Those who hope to be reasonable about it fail.
The arrogance of reason has separated us from that love.
With the word "reason" you already feel miles away.
How lucky we are that surrounded by all this joy
We sing inside our own little boat.
These poems amount to being meeting itself.
These songs are about forgetting dying and loss.
They rise above both coming in and going out.

Entering healing beyond ideas of life and death, we become who
we have always been, that which preceded birth and survives death.
Recognizing that healing never ends, our life becomes whole, each
step so precious, each moment approaching the grace of the ever-
healed, the always uninjured, the deathless.

Sipping at the nectar of existence, I stop the war.

PLEASE TAKE A FEW SOFT BREATHS
AS WE MOVE
FROM ONE LEVEL TO THE NEXT.

AS IN GROWTH, OR DYING,
WE NEED LET GO
AT THE EDGE
TO CONTINUE FURTHER.

TRUST THE PROCESS
LET GO LIGHTLY
PASS ON GENTLY.

Book List

Rather than repeat the book list at the end of *Who Dies?* we would like to simply add a few books published in the four years since that compilation.

Only Don't Know, Sueng Sahn.

A Still Forest Pool, Aachan Cha, edited by Jack Kornfield.

Open Secret—Versions of Rumi, trans. John Moyne and Coleman Barks.

The Miracle of Mindfulness, Being Peace, Thich Nhat Hanh.

How Can I Help? Ram Dass and Paul Gorman.

Love Is Letting Go of Fear, Teach Only Love, Goodbye to Guilt, Gerald Jampolsky.

Seeking the Heart of Wisdom, Jack Kornfield and Joseph Goldstein.

The Ruins of the Heart—The Lyric Poetry of Rumi, trans. Edmund Helminski.

In the mid-1970s, while working with Ram Dass (*Grist for the Mill,* 1976) and teaching meditation in the California prison system, STEPHEN LEVINE met Elisabeth Kübler-Ross. For the next few years he led workshops with her and learned from the terminally ill the need for deeper levels of healing and the profound joy of service (*A Gradual Awakening,* 1979). In 1980 he began teaching workshops with his wife, Ondrea, as they continued to serve the terminally ill and those deeply affected by loss as Co-Directors of the Hanuman Foundation Dying Project (*Who Dies?,* 1982). For three years Ondrea and Stephen maintained a free-consultation telephone line for those confronting serious illness or the possible death of a loved one (*Meetings at the Edge,* 1984). As the Levines continued to gain insight from those who overcame illness and surpassed death, their explorations deepened while further meditative techniques were developed to "let the healing in." Their guided meditations for the healing of illness, grief holdings, heavy emotional states, and sexual abuse and subtler forms of life/death preparation brought them international recognition (*Healing into Life and Death,* 1987), having aided thousands of people worldwide. Presently Stephen and Ondrea Levine are living in the high mountains of the Southwest, "attempting to practice what we preach" in the silence of the deep woods. They are seeking the "healing we took birth for," working on a new book, feeding the animals and the trees, and "examining the weatherbeaten outcroppings and the sun-dappled forests of the mind, sipping at the clear wellsprings of the heart."